An Index to Spirituals

An Index to Spirituals

KATHLEEN A. ABROMEIT

Published by State University of New York Press, Albany

EU GPSR Authorised Representative:
Logos Europe, 9 rue Nicolas Poussin, 17000, La Rochelle, France
contact@logoseurope.eu

For information, contact State University of New York Press, Albany, NY
www.sunypress.edu

Library of Congress Cataloging-in-Publication Data

Name: Abromeit, Kathleen A., author.
Title: An index to spirituals / Kathleen A. Abromeit.
Description: Albany : State University of New York Press, [2026].
Identifiers: LCCN 2025045512 | ISBN 9798855807233 (hardcover : alk. paper) |
    ISBN 9798855807240 (epub) | ISBN 9798855807257 (PDF)
Subjects: LCSH: Spirituals (Songs)—Indexes. | African Americans—Music—
    Indexes. | LCGFT: Indexes.
Classification: LCC ML128.S4 A27 2026 | DDC 016.78225/3—dc23/eng/20251212
LC record available at https://lccn.loc.gov/2025045512

*This book is dedicated to those enslaved people
who turned suffering into beauty
by creating this important body of music.*

Contents

Acknowledgments

I am indebted to those at the Sterling Branch of the Cleveland Public Library who, with the federal government's support, created the first index to African American spirituals in 1937, and to those who have kept spirituals alive by continuing to study and perform them.

I first began working with and on the topic of spirituals as a librarian some thirty years ago. My thinking has evolved over three decades, resulting in many improvements in this book compared to my 1999 book, *An Index to African-American Spirituals for the Solo Voice* (Greenwood Press). I would first like to thank the anti-racism book group of which I am a member. It has been a frank but safely held and honored space where my understanding of American history and the birth of this body of repertoire has deepened. From this new learning, I developed a deeper engagement with these songs, their lyrics, topics, scriptural references, and melodic content. As a result, my researching and sleuthing out new anthologies to index hit an all-time high. In addition to my personal foraging, I am grateful to the many friends, performers, and scholars who have sent me suggestions for anthologies to index.

Research for this book was done primarily at the Oberlin College Conservatory Library. I have been strongly supported not only by the Oberlin Libraries but also by the Oberlin Conservatory. I extend a deep and heartfelt thank you to Valerie Hotchkiss; Azariah S. Root, director of Oberlin College Libraries; and William Quillen, dean of the Oberlin Conservatory. For creative support and encouragement, I thank my colleague, friend, and mentor, Deborah Campana, head of Oberlin Conservatory Library (retired). For technical support, I wish to offer a HUGE thank you to Sandy Austin, master script writer and FileMaker Pro guru from Oberlin's Center for Information Technology.

Thank you for obtaining many items through ILL, Diane Lee and Jennifer Schreiner; for ordering the many scores I have requested for purchase, Justin Long; for quickly cataloging or allowing me to sneak a peek at new acquisitions, Rebecca Belford, Kimberly Fixx, and Faith Hoffman; for being fabulous music librarians who cheered for me and offered insights into the systematic management of such a large body of material, Kyler Decker, Krista Mitchell, Emerson Morgan, and Gwen Oeseburg. You have made me a better librarian. I am especially indebted to the following "reffies" (Oberlin students working at the reference desk) for their many hours of computer work and their uncanny ability to find inconsistencies in the data: Eliza Balmuth, Jake Balmuth, Wren Chan, Ryan Dearon, Gwen Gemmell, Lynn Giam, Ricardo Guerra, Julia Harbutt, Alexis Merane Hart, Abigail Heyrich, Julia Klein, Rachel Liss, Katharina Mueller, AJ Neubert, Melvin Nimtz, Karisma Palmore, Jesse Parham, Liesl Quigley, Michelle Ravitsky, Paul Schubert, Emily Springer, Philip Swigon, and Felix Veser.

Many people have supported me with editorial expertise. It was a pleasure to work with SUNY Press staff members Richard Carlin, who offered valuable advice and feedback at all stages of the project and didn't shame me at my two missed submission deadlines, and Jenn Bennett, who can speak casually about the capitalization of phrasal verbs in song titles. She is an editing ninja! I am grateful to Kay Norton, Limmie Pulliam, and Holling Smith-Borne for their review assistance. Special thanks to my sisters, Terrie Collins and Mary Churchill, for their assistance with textual analysis and to my dharma sister, Marta Laskowski, for our weekly updates on our book projects. She certainly kept me on task! Many thanks to my tremendously valued research colleague, Randye Jones.

I would also like to extend a special and second thank you to Limmie Pulliam for his deep understanding of these spirituals and willingness to help me better understand them. I am a better researcher, scholar, and person because of him. My Circle Family walking friends offered help in a thousand different ways without ever knowing they were doing so. I thank them. John Sabin, my forever life partner and best friend, went above and beyond in editing dialect for hours and hours. I am grateful. Most importantly, I thank him for the ordinary days we shared, and continue to share, and how he helps bring clarity out of the tangle. Finally, I dedicate my efforts to my loving children, Dyani, David, Brook, and Dorian: May you all continue embracing the awareness that respecting the dignity of all is the basis for moving society forward in love and justice.

Preface

My interest in spirituals started in 1993 when I received a question while working at the Oberlin Conservatory Library reference desk, where I worked as a reference librarian. A student was looking for the printed music for "Hear the Angels Singing" and "Chatter with the Angels." She was about to do an audition for an a capella group on campus, and she wanted to use one of those spirituals. I began looking for an index to these songs in our library. To my delight, I found that in the late 1930s, a WPA project under President Roosevelt at the Cleveland Public Library involved indexing anthologies of spirituals. From the volume's preface, "The work was reproduced from a type-written copy and was initiated at the Sterling Branch Library." (*Index to Negro Spirituals*. Cleveland: Cleveland Public Library, 1937.) The Center for Black Music Research reproduced it with a foreword by Samuel A. Floyd in 1991. The Cleveland Public Library aided in locating "Hear the Angels Singing," but locating the other required a great deal of time, flipping through many scores.

Because of that frustration, I started a database project indexing the anthologies of spirituals in the Oberlin Conservatory Library. Eventually, researchers around the country began hearing about my indexing project and contacting me with questions. One such researcher was a Yale graduate student in American studies who was examining American novels. She had created a list of all the musical references in one novel and wanted to determine which were for hymns and which were for spirituals.

The researcher arrived in Oberlin, Ohio, for a week, and she spent the mornings with the late hymn scholar Mary Louise Van Dyke. They would compare songs in the book with items indexed in the *Dictionary of American Hymnology*, which at that time was located on Oberlin's campus and is now available online (https://hymnary.org/dnah). She spent the afternoons with me using my database and the Oberlin Conservatory

Library collection. That database was later published as *An Index to African-American Spirituals for the Solo Voice*, Greenwood Press, 1999.

The reference interaction with that researcher piqued my curiosity about where spirituals intersected with other disciplines, cultural experiences, and usage in all forms of music. I undertook a new project and compiled *Spirituals: A Multidisciplinary Bibliography for Research and Performance*. Middleton, WI: co-published by Music Library Association and A-R Editions, Inc., 2015. This 1000-item annotated bibliography contains articles, books, and dissertations published between 1902 and 2014 and examines the intersectionality of spirituals with art, music, literature and poetry, American history, religion, and African American studies.

Since publishing *An Index to African-American Spirituals for the Solo Voice* in 1999, many new anthologies of spirituals have been published. It is a good time to return to the indexing of those anthologies and refocus my efforts on my first encounter with spirituals.

Scope and Contents

According to *Grove Dictionary of Music*, spirituals are "a type of sacred song created by and for African Americans." These songs were created between the late 1700s and the end of the American Civil War in 1865.

> Spirituals grew out of an American culture of slavery that was distinguished in significant ways from slave cultures in other parts of the Atlantic world. The lyrics of spirituals retold stories of the Old and New Testaments, and African Americans took special delight in stories that related the triumph of ordinary men over powerful foes, such as Daniel in the lion's den, Jonah in the whale, and David fighting Goliath. Other popular figures included Jacob, the angel Gabriel, John the Baptist, Mary and Martha, and Jesus. Moses delivering his people from Pharaoh was an especially potent story for the slaves, who identified with the captive Israelites. Satan was frequently a comical figure, who likely represented white masters. African Americans were selective in their approach to Christianity, avoiding stories about masters and obedience.[1]

This is a closed body of repertoire that constitutes one of the largest and most significant forms of American folk song. If I was unable to verify that the song came from that time period, I have not included it in this book. It can be confusing to determine what exactly is a spiritual, a hymn, or gospel. That became even more evident when the Yale graduate student came to Oberlin to split her time between the *Dictionary of American Hymnology* and my spirituals database. For example, we often think of "Amazing Grace" as a spiritual, but it is a hymn published in 1779 and written in 1772 by English clergyman and poet John Newton.[2] Despite being written in the time period discussed as spirituals, this song was written by a former slave trader who became an abolitionist, not by enslaved African people.

It is also worth noting that many composers who lived after 1865 have written compositions based on spirituals, most notably Harry T. Burleigh. In addition to Burleigh, many composers have used the melodic and textual content of spirituals, and those works have been included in this index along with the earliest published versions of these songs.

The first collection of slave songs, including spirituals, work songs, and community leisure songs, appeared in 1843, without musical notation, in a series of three articles by a Methodist Church missionary known only as "c." Collections that included musical notation began appearing in the 1850s and proliferated following the Civil War. The earliest book-length collection of spirituals containing lyrics and music was published jointly in 1867 by William Francis Allen, Charles Pickard Ware, and Lucy McKim Garrison. Their effort, *Slave Songs of the United States*, with a 38-page introduction, contains 136 songs, including seven in Louisiana French and African Creole. This was to become one of the most important collections of spirituals of its time. And so began the extensive publishing of and about spirituals.

An Index to African-American Spirituals for the Solo Voice (Greenwood Press, 1999) systematically indexed some sixty collections scored for solo voice. There has been a widespread resurgence in the popularity of spirituals since 1999, and this current book indexes 233 anthologies. Most of the anthologies are scores for solo voice and piano, but some variations are indicated in the bibliography and the scoring notes included in the title index of this book.

Methodology

Items included in this index were located using *Worldcat*, a database of library collections that allows users to search for materials across thousands of libraries worldwide (http://www.worldcat.org/); Theodore Front Musical Literature, a sheet music and music book dealer, particularly known for serving university music libraries, (https://www.tfront.com/); Harrassowitz, a leading supplier of scholarly resources and library services to academic and research libraries worldwide, (https://www.harrassowitz.de/); eBay, an online marketplace where many older and lesser-known anthologies were purchased, (https://www.ebay.com/); and general word of mouth and networking with American music scholars and singers who perform spirituals. This book follows the stylistic conventions of the *Chicago Manual of Style*, eighteenth edition.

Organization

Explanation of Sample Entry

[1] Uniform Title: Because of the various spellings and titles used for a given spiritual, the title index is searchable on the "uniform" title. If a spiritual is known by more than one title, a "— see —" reference will suggest other entries to consult. In addition, some spirituals are known by one title with multiple versions of the text. Such spirituals include a text excerpt for easy identification.

[2] First line of text. This may be a representative first line. For example, if one source repeats the opening phrase multiple times, to save space, the opening phrase is only listed once.

[3] Classification of the primary topic of the spiritual. See the song classification index for a complete list of this book's topics.

[4] Scriptural Biblical Reference/s. Note that each reference is followed by a symbol that indicates where the reader may look at the original reference.

> ^ *African American Heritage Hymnal.* Chicago: GIA Publications, 2001.

> + Collins, T. L. compiler, published in *Spirituals: A Multidisciplinary Bibliography for Research and Performance.* Middleton, WI: co-published by Music Library Association and A-R Editions, 2015.

> # *Dictionary of American Hymnology* (https://hymnary.org/dnah).

> * Sandilands, Alexander. *A Hundred and Twenty Negro Spirituals.* 2nd ed. Basutoland: Morija Sesuto Book Depot, 1964.

[5] Source code for each score anthology listed in the bibliography.

[6] Page number within the source — note that if a "d" follows the page number, that indicates that the song includes dialect.

[7] Information regarding that spiritual within a source. Note that each listing in this book receives a notation about the specifics available in that source. Notations include:

- Instrumental Ensemble accompaniment

- Solo voice with piano accompaniment

- Solo voice with cello accompaniment

- Solo voice with piano accompaniment and chord symbols

- Solo voice with piano accompaniment and additional historical information

- Melody only

- Melody and chord symbols

- Melody, chord symbols, and additional historical information

- Melody, chord symbols, and piano accompaniment

- Melody and instrumental ensemble accompaniment

- Melody and additional historical information

- Choral arrangement

- Choral with piano accompaniment

- Choral with piano accompaniment and additional historical information

- Choral unaccompanied with additional historical information

- Text only

- Text only; Source includes additional historical information

- Text and chord symbols

- Uses Tonic Sol-fa notation

Uniform Title Index

The main body is an alphabetical list of the spirituals indexed.

Sample Entry:

Ain't That Good News (1)
 Ain't that good news ain't that good news
 Heaven
 Proverbs 25:25^
  HERB, 3, d, Text only
  MCIB, 59, d, Melody and additional historical information
  PETL, 20, d, Text only

Ain't That Good News (2)
 Got a crown up in de Kingdom ain't dat good news
 Proverbs 25:25^
  AAH, 592, d, Choral with piano accompaniment and additional historical information
  BOAT, 7, d, Solo voice with piano accompaniment
  CALA, 1, d, Melody only
  CHET, 231, d, Text only
  CLES, 114, d, Choral with piano accompaniment and additional historical information on the spiritual
  CREO, 20, d, Solo voice with piano accompaniment
  HERB, 2, d, Text only
  LIF, 180, d, Choral with piano accompaniment and additional historical information
  LOYS, 6, d, Solo voice with piano accompaniment
  PAYN, 7, d, Solo voice with piano accompaniment
  PETL, 20, d, Text only
  WHII, 4, 14, d, Solo voice with piano accompaniment

Dialect Title Index

Any titles listed in dialect can be found in the dialect title index with a "see" reference to the appropriate title in the uniform title index.

Sample Entry:

A Great Camp Meetin' in de Promised Land — see — Walk Together Children

Note that some titles in the dialect title index refer to a uniform title that is also in dialect. For example, we know "Come by Here" as "Kum ba Yah," so the uniform title is "Kum ba Yah" rather than the standardized English title. At the same time, you will notice "see" references for other variations of that title

Sample Entry:

Come by Yuh — see — Kum ba Yah

In some cases, the "see" reference directs the reader to a standard English spelling although the uniform title is also in dialect.

Sample Entry:

Trubble Dun Bore Me Down — see — Trouble Done Bore Me Down

Fisk University[3] opened in Nashville in 1866. The school was named in honor of General Clinton B. Fisk of the Tennessee Freedmen's Bureau. He provided the new institution with facilities in former Union Army barracks. The first students ranged in age from seven to seventy but shared common experiences of slavery and poverty. Fisk was only open for a couple of years before they started having financial trouble, so they offered a series of local concerts to raise money.

George L. White, Fisk treasurer and then music professor, created a nine-member choral ensemble of students and took it on tour to earn money for the university. The group left campus on October 6, 1871, but the singers modified their performance by eliminating the singing of spirituals. Instead, they sang a repertory of patriotic tunes, hymns, and popular songs of the day, assisted by student Ella Sheppard (1851–1914), who served as soprano and pianist. The singers' tour initially followed the route of the Underground Railroad in Ohio, with the aim of finding sympathetic audiences.

On November 16, 1871, the Fisk Jubilee Singers arrived at Oberlin College in Ohio to perform before a national convention of ministers. That performance took place at First Church, and White told them that if the situation needed some energizing, they were to sing a spiritual. After a few standard ballads and a somewhat flat audience, the chorus broke into the spiritual "Steal Away." "Steal Away" is one of the songs that is said to have been used on the Underground Railroad.

> *"Steal away, steal away, steal away to Jesus!*
> *Steal away, steal away home, I ain't got long to stay here"*

The singing of the spiritual was met with such enthusiasm that the Fisk Jubilee Singers stopped singing ballads and other art music and from that day forward only sang spirituals. George L. White's arrangements of the spirituals were influenced by tune books, hymnals, parlor songs, and the performers (particularly the Hutchinson Family Singers) on whom he modeled his troupe. The Hutchinson Family Singers was an American singing group of the mid-nineteenth century and a significant figure in the development of American popular music traditions. The Hutchinson Family Singers "appealed to 'respectable' middle-class audiences who believed in the importance of family life, Protestantism, liberalism and improved well-being through the power of education."[4] George White used this as a model.

There was criticism of adopting the performance practice of a white popular group rather than embracing the folk practices of the Black community. Sandra Jean Graham outlines these differences in her article on spirituals in *Grove Dictionary of Music*, "The arranged spirituals of the Jubilee Singers of Fisk University came to define the genre in the second half of the century. Replacing the heterophony of folk practice with synchronized homophonic (SATB) textures; dialect with standard English; ambiguous pitches with exact intonation; raw timbres with cultivated vocals; moving, percussive bodies with still posture; and an undifferentiated dynamic with a range of expressive devices (for example, crescendos, ritards, holds), they created a presentational style of performance intended to interpret Black American folk practice within the conventions of European composed concert music.[5] The preface to *Jubilee Songs*[6] defends the decision:

> The manner and style of singing in the South depends entirely upon the degree of culture in the congregation. There is a very great difference between the lowest and the highest, in this respect. . . . The Jubilee Singers, no doubt, represent the highest average of culture among the colored people, but the singing of these songs is all their own, and the quickness with which they have received impressions and adopted improvements from the cultivated music they have heard, only affords an additional illustration of the high capabilities of the race.

Interestingly, White's decision not to sing in dialect was the beginning of what developed as a historic dialog, and Fisk University itself changed its stand on this. Fisk Jubilee Singers started touring in 1871 without any dialect, and by 1909 in their historic recording of "Swing Low Sweet Chariot," they were using dialect. That recording was made under the direction of John W. Work II.[7]

The discussion continues today: Should spirituals be sung in dialect or not? One thing is for sure: This dynamic, linguistic issue is thoroughly intertwined with African American history and linked in many ways with African American literature, education, music, politics, and social life. African American dialect is one of the most extensively studied and discussed varieties of American English and it will probably continue to be so for many years to come. To honor the early practice of using dialect for these songs, all dialect in individual anthologies is included, but uniform titles are used to collocate the variants for ease of use in this book.

First Line Index

As one might expect when working with songs that originate from an oral tradition, there are considerable inconsistencies in identifying some spirituals. For example, "Down by the Riverside" frequently has the first line of text "We'll wait till Jesus comes . . ." but is also known by the text "When Christ the Lord was here below . . ." As a result, the user of this index may need to consult multiple listings to complete a comprehensive search for the desired title. The text issue is complicated in the oral tradition; please note that the texts come from different sources and may have variations, especially if the score text is in dialect.

The first line of each spiritual is listed in alphabetical order followed by a "— see —" reference to the appropriate spiritual. All dialect has been included in the first line index.

Sample Entry:

A little talk with Jesus makes it all right all right — see — A Little Talk with Jesus Makes It Right

A wheel in a wheel a wheel in a wheel — see — Wheel in a Wheel

Adam in de garden Eve she disobeyed — see — Good Lord Done Been Here

While this book follows the stylistic conventions of the *Chicago Manual of Style,* eighteenth edition, I have chosen to deviate from its conventions when capitalizing deity pronouns. CMOS seems to give the author some latitude around this topic, "Pronouns referring to God or Jesus are not capitalized unless a particular author or publisher prefers otherwise. (Note that they are lowercased in most English translations of the Bible.)"

> Example: They crucified my Lord and he never said a mumbling word

I discussed the capitalization with many potential users of this book, and I received three general responses: first, with some conviction, that I should follow the CMOS guideline and not capitalize the pronouns; second, that out of respect for readers, I should capitalize the pronouns, and third, with the most conviction, and a healthy dose of "I can't believe you're considering NOT capitalizing the pronouns," that I should capitalize them. Years ago, a wise friend once said that when someone responds with a visceral response, the response is "old" from a deeper part of our belief system or experience. For those who felt strongly that all deity pronouns should be capitalized, it was evident that these were visceral responses. I want to honor those deeply held beliefs, so deity pronouns are capitalized in this book. This also supports the second body of responses, which stated that I should capitalize the pronouns out of respect for readers. Respect is one of those choices that brings up a visceral response for me!

> Example: They crucified my Lord and He never said a mumbling word

SONG CLASSIFICATION INDEX

The spirituals have been separated into the following eighteen topical subjects. Naturally, many could fit several categories, but each spiritual has been assigned only one topic for this index.

- Admonition/Judgment
- Aspiration
- Christmas
- Church

- Death

- Deliverance

- Easter

- Faith/Assurance

- Heaven

- Jesus

- Praise

- Prayer

- Rituals of Preparation for Renewal/Regeneration

- Satan

- Songs of Spiritual Journey

- Suffering

- Women

- Work Songs

Scriptural References Index

While the title index does indicate which scriptural references are included in the text of a given spiritual, the reader may want to reverse that process and, for example, identify spirituals that use a particular book in the Bible or specific chapter and verse.

Sample Entry:

Deuteronomy
    Deuteronomy 9:1'Tis Jordan's River
    Deuteronomy 9:1Wasn't That a Wide River
    Deuteronomy 11:31Deep River
    Deuteronomy 26:7Going to Write to Master Jesus
    Deuteronomy 34:1–5Brother Moses Gone
Ephesians
    Ephesians 1:11–23Peter Go Ring Them Bells
    Ephesians 4:29–31Does You Call That Religion

The need for this index became evident when a scholar reached out and asked if I was able to tell them which spirituals were based on Psalms texts. One of the issues with an oral tradition is that snippets or sections of scripture may be included but not enough to say with certainty that a given spiritual is based on a particular scripture. As such, while most spirituals at least hint at a scriptural reference or biblical teaching, there can be debate and discussion about whether a particular scripture is fully embraced in a given song. To document with a greater degree of certainty, I have identified the source of the scriptural citation. In the uniform title index, please note that each reference is followed by a symbol that indicates where the reader may look at the original citation.

^ *African American Heritage Hymnal.* Chicago: GIA Publications, 2001.

+ Collins, T. L. compiler, published in *Spirituals: A Multidisciplinary Bibliography for Research and Performance.* Middleton, WI: co-published by Music Library Association and A-R Editions, 2015.

Dictionary of American Hymnology (https://hymnary.org/dnah).

* Sandilands, Alexander. *A Hundred and Twenty Negro Spirituals.* 2nd ed. Basutoland: Morija Sesuto Book Depot, 1964.

I have been asked and was interested to see that the top ten books of the Bible quoted in spirituals are, in order of frequency:

1. Revelation
2. John
3. Luke
4. Matthew
5. Genesis
6. Daniel
7. Exodus
8. Mark
9. Psalms
10. Isaiah

Bibliography of Sources Index

The bibliography of sources indexed includes 233 items. Source codes are in **bold**. Items that have been reprinted numerous times have been combined into a single citation, such as the **ALLS** example. The code for each item is usually four letters (first three letters of the last name + first letter of the title of the anthology). Some anthologies have been printed in both low and high voices. In that case, each anthology has its entry in the bibliography, such as **ALBGL.**

Sample:

ALBGL Albritton, Andy M. *Great Spirituals: An Anthology or Program for Solo Voice and Piano for Concert and Worship (low voice)*. Alfred Publ., 2007.

ALLS Allen, William Francis, Charles Pickard Ware, and Lucy McKim Garrison. *Slave Songs of the United States*. A. Simpson, 1867. Reprints, John Ross, 1871; Peter Smith, 1929, 1951, 1965; Oak Publications, 1965; Books for Libraries, 1971; Clearfield, 1992, 1997; Ayer, 1992; Applewood Books, 1995; Dover, 1995; Genealogical Pub., 1997, 2004; Pelican, 1998; Hal Leonard, 2005, 2007; Kessinger, 2008, 2010; Lightning Source, 2009.

Librarians are "culture keepers" who preserve and promote cultural heritage through collections, services, and advocacy for access to information. It is said that reference works are among the most enduring of scholarly publications. Creating a bibliography like this one is essentially a preservation project. These songs cannot be lost when there is a material record of where they were published and what was included in that source.

Not only have these songs influenced every aspect of American music and culture, but they are also the most powerful music we are likely ever to encounter. I doubt that we can fully understand the depth of these songs, nor should we expect to take the atrocious events from which they were born and make them look tidy and easy to understand. We are left with questions and heartache and an intimate view of the time of enslavement from the inside. We are asked to witness the enslaved individuals' creativity and resistance. These songs speak universally about human suffering and the human condition, and this is relevant today as we are still grappling with the systemic racism that has been part of United States history for four hundred years.

Notes

1. Graham, Sandra Jean. "Spiritual." *Grove Music Online.* 2001. Accessed 21 Mar. 2025. https://www.oxfordmusiconline.com/grovemusic/view/10.1093/gmo/9781561592630.001.0001/omo-9781561592630-e-1002225625.

2. The *Olney Hymns* were first published in February 1779 and are the combined work of John Newton (1725–1807) and poet William Cowper (1731–1800). A digitized version of the hymnal is available at the Internet Archive https://archive.org/details/olneyhymnsinth00newt/olneyhymnsinth00newt.

3. For information on Fisk University history and the Jubilee Singers, please consult https://www.fisk.edu/about/history/.

4. Cockrell, Dale. "Hutchinson." *Grove Music Online.* 2001. Accessed 31 Mar. 2025. https://www-oxfordmusiconline-com.ezproxy.oberlin.edu/grovemusic/view/10.1093/gmo/9781561592630.001.0001/omo-9781561592630-e-0000013618.

5. Graham, Sandra Jean. "Spiritual." *Grove Music Online.* 2001. Accessed 21 Mar. 2025. https://www.oxfordmusiconline.com/grovemusic/view/10.1093/gmo/9781561592630.001.0001/omo-9781561592630-e-1002225625.

6. Seward, Theodore Frelinghuysen, and American Missionary Association. *Jubilee Songs as Sung by the Jubilee Singers, of Fisk University, (Nashville, Tenn.) Under the Auspices of the American Missionary Association.* Biglow & Main, 1872.

7. Fisk Jubilee Singers, "Swing Low Sweet Chariot" (1909). Accessed 21 Mar. 2025. https://www.youtube.com/watch?v=GUvBGZnL9rE.

Bibliography

Abromeit, Kathleen A. *An Index to African-American Spirituals for the Solo Voice.* Foreword by Francois Clemmons. Greenwood, 1999.

Abromeit, Kathleen A. *Spirituals: A Multidisciplinary Bibliography for Research and Performance.* Co-published by Music Library Association and A-R Editions, 2015.

Cleveland Public Library. *Index to Negro Spirituals.* Cleveland Public Library, 1937.

Uniform Title Index

A Change Has Got to Come
    In the time of change I'm-a pressin' on
        Faith/Assurance
            HAIS, 1, d, Solo voice with piano accompaniment

A Little More Faith in Jesus
    All I want is a little more faith in Jesus
        Faith/Assurance
        Mark 9:24, 11:23*
            CHAT, 11, Solo voice with piano accompaniment
            MARS, 178, Choral unaccompanied with additional historical information
            PIKJ, 218, Choral unaccompanied with additional historical information
            SANH, 19, Uses Tonic Sol-fa notation
            SEWJC, 63, Choral unaccompanied with additional historical information
            WORJF, 61, d, Text only; Source includes additional historical information

A Little Talk with Jesus Makes It Right
    A little talk with Jesus makes it all right all right
         Faith/Assurance
            HERB, 3, d, Text only

According to My Lord's Command
  Jonah was a lad he was Amittai son
    Aspiration
    Jonah 1:1–17+
      KENMM, 47, d, Text only; Source includes additional historical
        information

Adam in the Garden Pinning Leaves
  First time God called Adam
    Admonition/Judgment
    Genesis 3:7–10+
      CHET, 231, Text only
      LOMJO, 4, Melody only
      LOMJO2, 4, Melody only
      MCIB, 37, d, Melody and additional historical information
      PETL, 3, d, Text only

**Adam's in the Garden Pinning Leaves — see — Adam in the Garden
Pinning Leaves**

After a While
  World is full of forms and changes
    Admonition/Judgment
      ODUN, 133, d, Text only; Source includes additional historical
        information
      PETL, 156, d, Text only

Ain't Going to Tarry Here
  Sweep it clean ain't goin er tarry here
    Faith/Assurance
      CHET, 232, d, Text only
      MCIB, 47, d, Melody and additional historical information
      PETL, 112, d, Text only

Ain't Gonna Let Nobody Turn Me Round
  Ain't gonna let nobody turn me 'round
    Faith/Assurance
      CHET, 232, d, Text only

Ain't Gonna Worry My Lord No More
   I'se a gwine tuhleab yuh en' it won' be long
      Faith/Assurance
         GUL, 1, d, Text only

Ain't Got Long to Stay Here
   Heab'm I'm Heab'm bound
      Songs of Spiritual Journey
         JESM, 34, d, Solo voice with piano accompaniment and additional historical information

Ain't Got Time to Die
   Lord I keep so busy praising my Jesus
      Praise
         CHET, 232, Text only
         HERB, 2, d, Text only
         PETL, 112, d, Text only
         WARE, 18, d, Solo voice with piano accompaniment and additional historical information

Ain't I Glad — see — I Ain't Going to Die No More

Ain't I Glad I've Got Out the Wilderness
   Ain't I glad I've got out the wilderness
      Deliverance
      Revelations 21:4*
         PETL, 342, d, Text only
         WORF, 18, d, Choral unaccompanied with additional historical information

Ain't That Good News (1)
   Ain't dat good news oh Lord
      Heaven
      Proverbs 25:25^
         HERB, 3, d, Text only
         MCIB, 59, d, Melody and additional historical information
         PETL, 205, d, Text only

Ain't That Good News (2)

Got a crown up in de Kingdom ain't dat good news
Heaven
Proverbs 25:25^
AAH, 592, d, Choral with piano accompaniment and additional historical information
BOAT, 7, d, Solo voice with piano accompaniment
CALA, 1, d, Melody only
CHET, 231, d, Text only
CLES, 114, d, Choral with piano accompaniment and additional historical information
CREO, 20, d, Solo voice with piano accompaniment
HERB, 2, d, Text only
LIF, 180, Choral with piano accompaniment and additional historical information
LOYS, 6, d, Solo voice with piano accompaniment
PAYN, 7, d, Solo voice with piano accompaniment
PETL, 205, d, Text only
WHII, 4, d, Solo voice with piano accompaniment

Ain't You Glad

Ain't you glad you got a hiding space
Heaven
BOAS, 66, Solo voice with piano accompaniment

Ain't You Glad You Got Good Religion

Ain't you glad ain't you glad you got good religion
Faith/Assurance
PETL, 205, d, Text only

All God's Children Got a Song

I got a song you got a song
Praise
CHET, 233, d, Text only

All I Do the Church Keep Grumbling

All I do the church keep a-grumbling
Suffering
BALS, 70, d, Choral unaccompanied with additional historical information

HERB, 4, d, Text only
JOHJB, ii, 130, d, Solo voice with piano accompaniment and additional historical information
PETL, 3, d, Text only

All I Do the People Keep Grumbling
All I do the people keep a-grumbling
Suffering
DITT, 29, d, Choral arrangement
PETL, 3, d, Text only

All I Want — see — A Little More Faith in Jesus

All I Want Is a Little More Faith — see — A Little More Faith in Jesus

All My Sins Been Taken Away
I'm going to Heaven and I don't want to stop
Deliverance
Isaiah 6:7; Revelation 1:5*
BALS, 11, d, Choral unaccompanied with additional historical information
COLS, 76, d, Solo voice with piano accompaniment
HAWD, 105, d, Text only
MCIB, 67, d, Melody and additional historical information
ODUN, 60, Text only; Source includes additional historical information
PETL, 206, d, Text only
SANH, 90, Uses Tonic Sol-fa notation

All My Trials
Hush little baby don't you cry you know your mama was born to die
Death
LIES, 12, Solo voice with piano accompaniment

All Night All Day — see — Angels Watching Over Me

All Night All Day — see — He's Got the Whole World in His Hands

All Night Long
Paul and Silas bound in jail

Deliverance
Acts 16:23–26+
    LOMAF, 486, Melody, chord symbols, and additional historical information
    ODUN, 126, Text only; Source includes additional historical information

All of My Sins

All of my sins been taken away glory hallelujah to His name
Deliverance
    BOAS, 24, d, Solo voice with piano accompaniment

All Over This World (1)

All-a-my troubles will soon be over with
Death
    WORJF, 57, d, Text only; Source includes additional historical information

All Over This World (2)

It was all ober dis worl'
Death
    MCIB, 51, d, Melody and additional historical information
    PETL, 264, d, Text only

All the Way to Calvary

I had so many many sins
Easter
    HALC, 64, Choral with piano accompaniment and additional historical information
    PETL, 306, d, Text only

All Through the Night

Sleep my love and peace attend thee all through the night
Faith/Assurance
    HAWD, 164, Text only
    WAL25H, 4, Solo voice with piano accompaniment
    WAL25L, 4, Solo voice with piano accompaniment

Almost Done Toiling Here

Most done toiling here oh bretheren

   Death

      JOHJB, ii, 140, d, Solo voice with piano accompaniment and additional historical information

      PETL, 236, d, Text only

Almost Done Traveling

My mudder's in de road most done trabelling

   Songs of Spiritual Journey

      ARM, 215, d, Choral unaccompanied with additional historical information

      FENC, 43, d, Choral unaccompanied with additional historical information

      FENR, 43, d, Choral unaccompanied with additional historical information

      PETL, 29, d, Text only

Almost Over

Some seek the Lord and they don't seek Him right

   Admonition/Judgment

      ALLS, 74, Melody only

      PETL, 156, d, Text only

Am I a Soldier

Am I a soldier

   Aspiration

      NAA, 30, Melody and chord symbols

Am I a Soldier of the Cross — see — Soldier of the Cross

Am I Born to Die

Dark was de night an' col' de groun'

   Death

      HALC, 31, d, Choral with piano accompaniment and additional historical information

      PETL, 4, d, Text only

Amen
　　Amen amen amen oh Lawdy
　　　　Faith/Assurance
　　　　　　CLES, 147, d, Choral with piano accompaniment and additional historical information
　　　　　　LIF, 233, d, Choral with piano accompaniment and additional historical information
　　　　　　WARE, 27, d, Solo voice with piano accompaniment and additional historical information

Amen
　　Amen amen see the baby lying in the manger
　　　　Jesus
　　　　Psalm 89:52+
　　　　　　AAH, 649, Choral with piano accompaniment and additional historical information
　　　　　　ANDW, 7, Choral arrangement
　　　　　　CALA, 2, Melody only
　　　　　　CHET, 233, Text only
　　　　　　JACL, 28, Choral with piano accompaniment and additional historical information
　　　　　　LIES, 18, Solo voice with piano accompaniment
　　　　　　LUE, 8, Melody, chord symbols, and piano accompaniment

Amen
　　Amen halelujah praise Jehovah
　　　　Praise
　　　　　　NEW, 502, Choral with piano accompaniment and additional historical information

An Ante-Bellum Sermon — see — Joshua Fought the Battle of Jericho

Anchor Believer Anchor — see — Anchor in the Lord

Anchor in the Lord
　　Anchor believer anchor anchor in the Lord
　　　　Faith/Assurance
　　　　Hebrews 6:19; John 5:8, 9:7, 14:3*
　　　　　　DANF, 49, Melody only

Angel's Waiting at the Door
My sister's took her flight
Death
MARS, 189, Choral unaccompanied with additional historical information
PETL, 157, d, Text only
WORJF, 58, d, Text only; Source includes additional historical information

Angel's Waiting at the Tomb
Doubtin' Thomas doubt no mo'
Death
KENMM, 20, d, Melody only

Angels Are Watching Over Me
All night all day angels watchin' over me my Lord
Faith/Assurance
Psalm 91:11^
HERB, 5, d, Text only
NORS, 22, Melody and instrumental ensemble accompaniment

Angels Done Bowed Down
Angels done bowed down
Jesus
CHET, 278, Text only
HERB, 81, Text only
MCLS, 59, d, Solo voice with piano accompaniment
PETL, 4, d, Text only

Angels Done Changed My Name (1)
I went to de hillside I went to pray
Rituals of Preparation for Renewal/Regeneration
KENM, 36, d, Melody only
MARS, 227, Choral unaccompanied with additional historical information
MAR3, 261, Choral unaccompanied with additional historical information

Angels Done Changed My Name (2)
    I know I've been changed
        Rituals of Preparation for Renewal/Regeneration
            SIX, 24, Solo voice with piano accompaniment

Angels in Heaven Going to Write My Name
    Write my name de angels in de Heab'n
        Heaven
            BALS, 37, d, Choral unaccompanied with additional historical information
            JOHJB, ii, 118, d, Solo voice with piano accompaniment and additional historical information
            PETL, 382, d, Text only

Angels Watching Over Me
    All night all day angels watching over me
        Faith/Assurance
        Psalm 91:11^
            AAH, 130, d, Choral with piano accompaniment and additional historical information
            ANDW, 25, Choral arrangement
            BALS, 23, d, Melody only
            BRYA, 8, Melody, chord symbols, and additional historical information
            PETL, 52, d, Text only
            SNES, 1, Solo voice with piano accompaniment

Animals a Coming
    Animals a-comin'
        Aspiration
        Genesis 7:2–3, 8–9+
            PETL, 206, d, Text only

Anybody Here — see — Is There Anybody Here

Anyhow My Lord
    Anyhow anyhow anyhow my Lord

Deliverance
    PETL, 382, d, Text only

Anyhow My Lord
Ennyhow ennyhow ennyhow muh Lawd
Deliverance
    BALS, 57, d, Melody only
    GUL, 39, d, Text only
    HERB, 5, d, Text only
    SPI, 1, Melody and additional historical information

Apollyon and the Pilgrim
Just behold how many dangers
Faith/Assurance
    DETD3, 11, Choral unaccompanied with additional historical
        information

Archangel
Who is de ruler arkangel
Faith/Assurance
    MCIB, 49, d, Melody and additional historical information
    PETL, 52, d, Text only

Archangel Open the Door
I ask all them brothers around
Heaven
    ALLS, 32, Melody only
    PETL, 343, d, Text only

Are You Ready
Are you ready fer de judgment day
Admonition/Judgment
    MCIB, 53, Melody and additional historical information
    PETL, 264, d, Text only

Around About the Mountain
Roun' about de mountain
Praise
    HAYMF, 85, d, Solo voice with piano accompaniment and addi-
        tional historical information

HAYMS, 85, d, Solo voice with piano accompaniment and additional historical information

As I Went down in the Valley to Pray — see — Down in the Valley to Pray

At the Bar of God
Mourner
Admonition/Judgment
PETL, 264, d, Text only

At the Judgment Bar
At the judgment bar
Admonition/Judgment
BALS, 51, d, Choral unaccompanied with additional historical information
PETL, 265, d, Text only

Auction Block — see — Many Thousand Gone

Away Down in Sunbury
Massa take dat new bran coat
Suffering
ALLS, 99, Melody only

Away in the Kingdom
There's plenty-uh room
Heaven
GRIN, 18, d, Melody only
PETL, 336, d, Text only

Away in the Middle of the Air
Some o' dese mornin's bright an' fair
Heaven
ODUN, 105, d, Text only; Source includes additional historical information

Aye Lord Don't Leave Me
Crying aye Lord don't leave me
Songs of Spiritual Journey

>BALS, 13, d, Choral unaccompanied with additional historical information
>PETL, 157, d, Text only

Aye Lord Time Is Drawin' Nigh — see — Lord Time Is Drawing Nigh

Baby Bethlehem — see — New Born Baby

Baby Mine
If I had it you could get it
Work Songs
>ODUN, 261, Text only; Source includes additional historical information

Baby's in Memphis
Baby's in Memphis layin' around
Work Songs
>ODUN, 248, Text only; Source includes additional historical information

Babylon's Falling
Pure city Babylon's falling to rise no more
Deliverance
>ARM, 248, d, Choral unaccompanied with additional historical information
>DETR, 2, d, Choral unaccompanied with additional historical information
>FENC, 76, d, Choral unaccompanied with additional historical information
>FENR, 76, d, Choral unaccompanied with additional historical information
>PETL, 265, d, Text only
>SIX, 30, d, Solo voice with piano accompaniment

Balm in Gilead
There is balm in Gilead to make the wounded whole
Faith/Assurance
Jeremiah 8:22#
>AAH, 524, Choral with piano accompaniment and additional historical information

RAGS, 3, Solo voice with piano accompaniment

SEV, 475, Choral with piano accompaniment and additional historical information

SILSP, 62, Solo voice with piano accompaniment

SIMA, 22, Solo voice with piano accompaniment

SKEG, 14, d, Solo voice with piano accompaniment and chord symbols

SNES, 1, Solo voice with piano accompaniment

SPAG, 6, d, Solo voice with piano accompaniment and chord symbols

UNI, 375, Melody only

WAL14H, 9, Solo voice with piano accompaniment

WAL14H, 20, Solo voice with piano accompaniment

WAL14L, 20, Solo voice with piano accompaniment

WAL15H, 9, Solo voice with piano accompaniment

WAL15L, 9, Solo voice with piano accompaniment

WALSH, 140, d, Solo voice with piano accompaniment

WALSL, 140, Solo voice with piano accompaniment

WARE, 93, d, Solo voice with piano accompaniment and additional historical information

WORJF, 43, d, Text only; Source includes additional historical information

WORJT, 6, Choral unaccompanied with additional historical information

Band of Angels

There was one there was two there was three little angels

Heaven

DITT, 30, Choral arrangement

HAG3, 184, Solo voice with piano accompaniment

ODUN, 104, Text only; Source includes additional historical information

PETL, 208, d, Text only

TRAH, 77, Melody, chord symbols, and piano accompaniment

Band of Angels

My latest sun is sinking fast my race is nearly run

Heaven

SHEH, 8, Melody and chord symbols

Baptizing Hymn
Freely go marching along
Rituals of Preparation for Renewal/Regeneration
PETL, 208, d, Text only

Be Still and Listen
Sometimes I feel so lonely sometimes I feel so blue
Rituals of Preparation for Renewal/Regeneration
CHAT, 89, Solo voice with piano accompaniment

Be with Me
Be with me Lord be with me
Faith/Assurance
PETL, 5, d, Text only

Bear Your Burden (1)
Lord is listening all day long
Admonition/Judgment
ODUN, 82, d, Text only; Source includes additional historical
information

Bear Your Burden (2)
I'se gwine to bear Lord
Admonition/Judgment
WHIF, 24, d, Solo voice with piano accompaniment

Bear Your Burden (3)
Bear your burden bear your burden
Admonition/Judgment
BALS, 16, d, Choral unaccompanied with additional historical
information
PETL, 113, d, Text only

Been A-Listening — see — I've Been Listening All Night Long

Been Down into the Sea
Hallelujah Lord I've been down into the sea
Songs of Spiritual Journey
BARO, 44, d, Melody only

Been Washed in the Blood
  Redeem redeem been wash in de blood ob de Lamb
    Rituals of Preparation for Renewal/Regeneration
      MCIB, 61, d, Melody and additional historical information
      PETL, 307, d, Text only

Before I'd Be a Slave
  Before I'd be a slave I'd be buried in my grave
    Suffering
      BARO, 25, d, Melody only

Before This Time Another Year
  Before this time another year I may be gone
    Death
      CHET, 234, Text only
      LOMJA, 586, d, Melody only
      PETL, 5, d, Text only
      WORF, 31, Choral unaccompanied with additional historical
        information
      WORJF, 52, d, Text only; Source includes additional historical
        information

Behold That Star
  Behold that star up yonder
    Christmas
    Matthew 2:10–11^
      AAH, 216, Choral with piano accompaniment and additional
        historical information
      BURS, 123, d, Solo voice with piano accompaniment
      BRYA, 17, Melody, chord symbols, and additional historical
        information
      CALA, 1, Text only
      HAY1L, 34, Solo voice with piano accompaniment

Believer I Know
  I know I know Lord believer I know
    Faith/Assurance
      PARS, 131, Melody only

Bell Done Ring
I know that the bell done rung
Faith/Assurance
MCIB, 85, d, Melody and additional historical information
PETL, 382, d, Text only

Bell Done Ring
Live humble humble humble your soul
Faith/Assurance
PARS, 164, Text only; Source includes additional historical information

Bell Done Rung
I know member know Lord
Faith/Assurance
ALLS, 34, d, Melody only
PETL, 158, d, Text only

Belshazzah Had a Feast
Belshazza' had a feas' 'n' dazza han'writin' on de wall
Admonition/Judgment
JOHHT, 24, d, Solo voice with piano accompaniment

Benediction
Lord bless Thee and keep Thee
Praise
MAR3, 299, Choral unaccompanied with additional historical information
MARS, 265, Choral unaccompanied with additional historical information

Better Walk Steady
Better walk steady Jesus a-listenin'
Admonition/Judgment
KENMM, 89, d, Melody only

Big Camp Meeting in the Promised Land
Dis union oh dis union band
Songs of Spiritual Journey
BARO, 29, d, Melody only

Big Fish
Lord the big fish swallow ole Jonah whole
Faith/Assurance
ODUN, 141, Text only; Source includes additional historical information

Black Bird and the Crow
Ay said de blackbird to de crow
Songs of Spiritual Journey
BURP, 10, d, Solo voice with piano accompaniment

Black Sheep Where You Left Your Lamb
Black sheep black sheep
Faith/Assurance
FISS, 4, d, Solo voice with piano accompaniment and additional historical information

Bless My Soul and Gone
My good Lawd done been heah
Deliverance
JESM, 20, d, Solo voice with piano accompaniment and additional historical information
JOHRS, 20, Solo voice with piano accompaniment

Blessed Are the Poor in Spirit
Come Thou fount of every tune my heart to sing Thy grace
Deliverance
BOAS, 81, Solo voice with piano accompaniment

Blessed Hope
Blessed hope that in Jesus is given
Faith/Assurance
ODUN, 146, Text only; Source includes additional historical information

Blessed Quietness
Joys are flowing like a river
Faith/Assurance
CLES, 206, Choral with piano accompaniment and additional historical information on the spiritual

Blind Man Lying at the Pool
Blin' man lying at de pool
Suffering
CHET, 234, Text only
HALC, 62, d, Choral with piano accompaniment and additional historical information on the spiritual
PETL, 6, d, Text only

Blind Man Stood on the Road and Cried
Blind man stood on the road and cried
Suffering
BALF, 7, d, Solo voice with cello accompaniment
BURA, 14, d, Solo voice with piano accompaniment
BURS, 99, d, Solo voice with piano accompaniment
CALA, 4, d, Text only
CHET, 278, Text only
HALC, 29, d, Choral with piano accompaniment and additional historical information
HAWD, 21, d, Text only
JOHHG, 36, d, Solo voice with piano accompaniment
JOHHH, 43, d, Solo voice with piano accompaniment
JOHJB, i, 108, d, Solo voice with piano accompaniment and additional historical information
KENM, 100, Solo voice with piano accompaniment and additional historical information
KENM, 106, d, Solo voice with piano accompaniment and additional historical information
LOMAF, 473, Melody, chord symbols, and additional historical information
LOMJA, 596, d, Melody only
ODUN, 136, Text only; Source includes additional historical information
PETL, 6, d, Text only
PETL, 158, d, Text only
WHIF, 92, d, Solo voice with piano accompaniment

Blood Done Sign My Name
Blood o the blood
Admonition/Judgment
BALS, 65, d, Choral unaccompanied with additional historical information

DITT, 20, Choral arrangement

ODUN, 122, d, Text only; Source includes additional historical information

PETL, 383, d, Text only

Blood Done Sign My Name

In the wilderness (een duh wilduhness)

Admonition/Judgment

HUTS, 3, Melody and additional historical information

Blood Will Never Lose Its Power

Blood that Jesus shed for me

Jesus

CLES, 184, Choral with piano accompaniment and additional historical information on the spiritual

Blood-Strained Banders

If you want to go to Heaven

Songs of Spiritual Journey

LOMJO2, 24, Melody only

Blow Gabriel

Blow Gable at the judgment

Admonition/Judgment

LOGR, 8, d, Melody only

ODUN, 86, d, Text only; Source includes additional historical information

WHIF, 107, d, Solo voice with piano accompaniment

Blow Trumpets Blow

Blow mighty trumpets blow

Jesus

MCKF, 16, Solo voice with piano accompaniment

Blow Your Gospel Trumpet

Blow your gospel trumpet

Admonition/Judgment

BALS, 43, d, Choral unaccompanied with additional historical information

PETL, 209, d, Text only

Blow Your Trumpet Gabriel
The tallest tree in paradise the Christian calls the tree of life
Admonition/Judgment
ALLS, 3, Melody only
APPA, 158, Solo voice with piano accompaniment
CHEA, 7, Solo voice with piano accompaniment
CHET, 234, Text only
FISS, 8, d, Solo voice with piano accompaniment and additional historical information
PETL, 159, d, Text only

Book of Life
Brother Joe you ought to know my name
Rituals of Preparation for Renewal/Regeneration
PETL, 307, d, Text only

Bound for Canaan Land
Where you boun' boun' fer Canaan land
Songs of Spiritual Journey
CHET, 234, Text only
MCIB, 42, d, Melody and additional historical information
PETL, 343, d, Text only

Bound for the Promised Land
On Jordan's stormy banks I stand
Songs of Spiritual Journey
HAWD, 151, Text only
LOMJF, 442, d, Solo voice with piano accompaniment and additional historical information

Bound to Go
I build my house upon the rock
Songs of Spiritual Journey
ALLS, 22, Melody only
LLOA, 136, Solo voice with piano accompaniment
PETL, 343, d, Text only

Bow Low Elder
Bow low elder Jesus is a-list'nin'

Prayer
>KENMM, 89, d, Solo voice with piano accompaniment and additional historical information
>WORJF, 74, d, Text only; Source includes additional historical information

Branded in the Forehead
See dat ship Maria bran' een duh fo'head
>Suffering
>>GUL, 3, d, Text only
>>HUTS, 5, d, Melody and additional historical information

Brethren Rise and Shine — see — Rise and Shine

Bright Sparkles in the Churchyard
May the Lord He will be glad of me
>Heaven
>>ARM, 200, d, Choral unaccompanied with additional historical information
>>DETR, 174, d, Choral unaccompanied with additional historical information
>>FENC, 28, d, Choral unaccompanied with additional historical information
>>FENR, 28, Choral unaccompanied with additional historical information
>>MAR3, 262, Choral unaccompanied with additional historical information
>>MARS, 228, Choral unaccompanied with additional historical information
>>PETL, 53, d, Text only

Brother Guide Me Home
Brother guide me home and I am glad
>Heaven
>>ALLS, 86, Melody only
>>PETL, 209, d, Text only

Brother Have You Come
Brother have you come to show me the way

Songs of Spiritual Journey
Acts 9:10–17; Matthew 26:41*
    SANH, 26, Uses Tonic Sol-fa notation

Brother Moses Gone
Brother Moses gone
    Heaven
    Deuteronomy 34:1–5+
        ALLS, 49, Melody only

Brother You'd Better Be a Praying
Brother you'd better be a prayin'
    Prayer
        ODUN, 80, d, Text only; Source includes additional historical information

Brothers Are You Getting Ready
Brothers are you getting ready
    Praise
        MARS, 254, Choral unaccompanied with additional historical information
        MAR3, 288, Choral unaccompanied with additional historical information

Brothers Don't Get Weary
Brothers don't get weary
    Admonition/Judgment
        ALLS, 95, Melody only
        ARM, 180, Choral unaccompanied with additional historical information
        FENC, 8, Choral unaccompanied with additional historical information
        HERB, 59, Text only
        PETL, 84, d, Text only
        PETL, 88, d, Text only

Brothers Don't Get Weary
Feasting on milk and honey and wine
    Admonition/Judgment
        DANF, 18, Melody only

Brothers Don't Stay Away
Brothers don't stay away
Heaven
Luke 14:17, 22, 23*
HAWD, 139, Text only
SANH, 92, Uses Tonic Sol-fa notation

Built a House in Paradise
My brother build a house in Paradise
Aspiration
ALLS, 29, Melody only
PETL, 209, d, Text only

Burden Down
Burden down Lord burden down Lord since I lay my burding down
Death
ANDW, 5, d, Choral arrangement
GUL, 4, d, Text only

But He Ain't Coming Here to Die No More
But He ain't comin' here t' die no mo'
Jesus
CHET, 234, d, Text only
DETR, 103, d, Choral unaccompanied with additional historical
information

By and By (1)
By and by I'm going to lay down my heavy load
Death
Matthew 11: 28–30; Mark 7:37#
BAP, 506, Choral with piano accompaniment and additional
historical information
BAYF, 16, d, Solo voice with piano accompaniment and chord
symbols
BELT, 16, Uses Tonic Sol-fa notation
BOAT, 17, d, Solo voice with piano accompaniment
BRYI, 29, d, Melody only
BUR2H, 5, d, Solo voice with piano accompaniment
BUR2L, 5, d, Solo voice with piano accompaniment
BURA, 23, d, Solo voice with piano accompaniment

BURS, 103, d, Solo voice with piano accompaniment
CALA, 1, Text only
CHAT, 16, d, Solo voice with piano accompaniment
CHET, 235, Text only
CLES, 164, Choral with piano accompaniment and additional historical information
DANF, 29, Melody only
DETD4, 9, Choral unaccompanied with additional historical information
DETR, 124, Choral unaccompanied with additional historical information
FISS, 12, d, Solo voice with piano accompaniment and additional historical information
GREF, 4, d, Solo voice with piano accompaniment
GUIU, 24, d, Solo voice with piano accompaniment
HAWD, 85, Text only
HERB, 6, d, Text only
JOHJB, i, 98, d, Solo voice with piano accompaniment and additional historical information
LLOA, 149, Solo voice with piano accompaniment
LUE, 76, Melody, chord symbols, and piano accompaniment
MIL3, 15, Solo voice with piano accompaniment
ODUN, 144, d, Text only; Source includes additional historical information
PETL, 6, d, Text only
SANH, 93, Uses Tonic Sol-fa notation
SNYS, 24, d, Solo voice with piano accompaniment
SPAG, 7, d, Solo voice with piano accompaniment and chord symbols
WALSH, 144, d, Solo voice with piano accompaniment
WALSL, 144, d, Solo voice with piano accompaniment
WHIF, 12, d, Solo voice with piano accompaniment
WORF, 45, Choral unaccompanied with additional historical information
WORJF, 70, d, Text only; Source includes additional historical information

By and By (2)
By and by we all shall meet again

Death
Matthew 11:28–30; Mark 7:37#
   PETL, 7, d, Text only
   WORJA, 228, Choral unaccompanied with additional historical information

By and By (3)
Oh by an' by by an' by I'm goin' to lay down dis heavy load
Death
   BURC1, 4, d, Solo voice with piano accompaniment

Bye and Bye
Lord I wonder by an' by
Death
   HALC, 60, d, Text only
   PETL, 114, d, Text only

Calinda
Michie preval li donin gran bal
Faith/Assurance
   ALLS, 111, Melody only

Calvary (1)
Calvary calvary calvary calvary calvary surely He died on calvary
Easter
Luke 23:1–49#
   AAH, 239, Choral with piano accompaniment and additional historical information
   BOAS, 6, Solo voice with piano accompaniment
   BOAS, 69, Solo voice with piano accompaniment
   CALA, 4, Melody only
   CHET, 235, Text only
   CLES, 87, Choral with piano accompaniment and additional historical information
   FRAS, 12, Solo voice with piano accompaniment
   HERB, 7, Text only
   LIF, 32, Choral with piano accompaniment and additional historical information
   OWEN, 12, Solo voice with piano accompaniment

    PATN, 12, d, Solo voice with piano accompaniment
    RAGS, 6, Solo voice with piano accompaniment
    TAYA, 2, d, Solo voice with piano accompaniment
    WHAG, 7, Solo voice with piano accompaniment

Calvary (2)

Ev'ry time I think about Jesus
  Easter
  Luke 23:1–49#
    HALC, 35, Choral with piano accompaniment and additional historical information
    JOHJB, i, 112, d, Solo voice with piano accompaniment and additional historical information
    PETL, 265, d, Text only
    WHIF, 96, d, Solo voice with piano accompaniment

Calvary's Mountain

Calvary is a mountain high
  Easter
    DETD3, 26, Choral unaccompanied with additional historical information

Can't Help from Crying Sometimes

Lawd uh cya(n)' he'p f'um cryin' sometime
  Suffering
    GUL, 11, d, Text only
    HUTS, 15, d, Melody and additional historical information

Can't Hide Sinner

You may run to the rock
  Admonition/Judgment
    BALS, 35, d, Choral unaccompanied with additional historical information
    PARS, 142, Melody only
    PETL, 265, d, Text only

Can't You Live Humble

Can't you live humble praise King Jesus

Admonition/Judgment
    DANF, 32, Melody only
    HERB, 7, Text only
    JOHJB, ii, 138, d, Solo voice with piano accompaniment and additional historical information
    PETL, 159, d, Text only
    WORF, 25, Choral unaccompanied with additional historical information

Carry Me Home
Swing low sweet chariot comin' for to carry me home
    Death
        ALBGH, 18, Solo voice with piano accompaniment

Carry the Key Gone Home
Maussah Jedus lock duh do'
    Rituals of Preparation for Renewal/Regeneration
        HUTS, 13, d, Melody and additional historical information

Certainly Lord (1)
Have you got good religion
    Faith/Assurance
    Psalm 107:2; Mark 16:16#
        AAH, 678, Choral with piano accompaniment and additional historical information
        ANDW, 6, Choral arrangement
        BRUS, 10, d, Solo voice with piano accompaniment
        CALA, 5, Melody only
        CLES, 161, Choral with piano accompaniment and additional historical information
        DETD3, 15, Choral unaccompanied with additional historical information
        GUIU, 28, Solo voice with piano accompaniment
        HAWD, 64, Text only
        HERB, 8, d, Text only
        JOHHG, 5, d, Solo voice with piano accompaniment
        JOHHH, 13, d, Solo voice with piano accompaniment
        JOHHH, 194, d, Solo voice with piano accompaniment

LIF, 132, d, Choral with piano accompaniment and additional historical information

Certainly Lord (2)
Well have you been to jail
Faith/Assurance
Psalm 107:2; Mark 16:16#
SILS, 12, d, Solo voice with piano accompaniment

Changed My Name
Tol' Jesus it would be all right if He changed
Deliverance
CHET, 235, d, Text only
CLES, 118, d, Choral with piano accompaniment and additional historical information

Chatter with the Angels
Chatter with the angels soon in the mornin'
Heaven
BRYA, 9, Melody, chord symbols, and additional historical information

Cheer the Weary Traveler — see — Let Us Cheer the Weary Traveler

Children Did You Hear When Jesus Rose — see — Did You Hear When Jesus Rose

Children Do Linger
Member will you linger
Faith/Assurance
ALLS, 51, Melody only
PETL, 344, d, Text only

Children Don't Get Weary
Children don't get weary
Admonition/Judgment
BOAS, 80, Solo voice with piano accompaniment
HAWD, 148, Text only

Children Go Where I Send Thee
> Children go where I send thee
>> Christmas
>>> ANDW, 42, Melody only
>>> BLOR, 208, Text and chord symbols
>>> CALA, 2, Text only
>>> HAWD, 143, Text only

Children of the Wilderness Moan for Bread
> Uh wunnuh wey moseyen' 'e mus be dead
>> Death
>>> GUL, 5, d, Text only
>>> HUTS, 7, d, Melody and additional historical information

Children We All Shall Be Free
> Children we all shall be free
>> Faith/Assurance
>>> BOAS, 50, Solo voice with piano accompaniment
>>> CHET, 235, Text only
>>> DETR, 107, Choral unaccompanied with additional historical information
>>> MARS, 130, Choral unaccompanied with additional historical information
>>> PIKJ, 170, Choral unaccompanied with additional historical information
>>> SAAT2, 19, d, Solo voice with piano accompaniment
>>> SEWJ, 13, Choral arrangement
>>> SEWJC, 13, Choral unaccompanied with additional historical information

Children You'll Be Called On
> Children you'll be called on to march
>> Faith/Assurance
>>> MAR3, 174, Choral unaccompanied with additional historical information
>>> MARS, 140, Choral unaccompanied with additional historical information
>>> PETL, 114, d, Text only

PIKJ, 180, Melody only
SEWJ, 19, Melody only
SEWJC, 19, Melody only

Chilly Water
Chilly water chilly water hallelujah to dat Lamb
Rituals of Preparation for Renewal/Regeneration
FRAS, 14, Solo voice with piano accompaniment
GREF, 92, Solo voice with piano accompaniment
HAWD, 99, Text only
HERB, 8, d, Text only
JOHJB, ii, 114, d, Solo voice with piano accompaniment and
additional historical information
MAR3, 298, Choral unaccompanied with additional historical
information
MARS, 264, Choral unaccompanied with additional historical
information
PETL, 54, d, Text only

Choose You a Seat and Set Down
Lordy jes' give me a lone white robe
Heaven
LOMJO, 34, d, Melody only
LOMJO2, 34, d, Melody only

Christ Is All
I don't possess houses or lands
Jesus
CLES, 180, Choral with piano accompaniment and additional
historical information

Christians Hold Up Your Heads
Christians hold up your heads
Praise
PETL, 217, d, Text only
WORF, 29, Choral unaccompanied with additional historical
information

Christians Hymn of the Crucifixion

Repent sinner hammer ring

Easter

BARO, 39, d, Melody only

Church Bell Tolling Ding Dong

Don't you hear that mournful soun' hear de church bell tollin'

Church

JOHRR, 66, d, Solo voice with piano accompaniment and additional historical information

Church of God

Church of God that sound so sweet

Church

ARM, 199, d, Choral unaccompanied with additional historical information

FENC, 27, d, Choral unaccompanied with additional historical information

FENR, 27, d, Choral unaccompanied with additional historical information

PETL, 54, d, Text only

City Called Heaven

I am a poor pilgrim of sorrow I'm tossed in dis wide worl' alone

Heaven

BOAT, 21, d, Solo voice with piano accompaniment

CALA, 2, Text only

CHET, 236, Text only

CLES, 135, Choral with piano accompaniment and additional historical information

HERB, 9, d, Text only

LOYS, 31, d, Solo voice with piano accompaniment

PETL, 7, d, Text only

City of Babylon

Goodby city o' Babylon yo Kingdom must come

Deliverance

KENMM, 133, d, Solo voice with piano accompaniment and additional historical information

Climb Up Ye Little Children
Climb up ye little children climb up ye older people
Heaven
Genesis 28:10–12*
SANH, 27, d, Uses Tonic Sol-fa notation

Climbing High Mountains
Climbing high mountains trying to get home
Songs of Spiritual Journey
KINC, 1, Solo voice with piano accompaniment and additional historical information
PATN, 57, d, Solo voice with piano accompaniment

Climbing Jacob's Ladder — see — Jacob's Ladder

Climbing Up the Mountain
Climbin' up d'mountain children
Deliverance
ALTSH, 29, d, Solo voice with piano accompaniment
ALTSL, 29, d, Solo voice with piano accompaniment
CALA, 3, d, Text only
CHET, 236, d, Text only
CLES, 120, d, Choral with piano accompaniment and additional historical information
LIF, 15, d, Choral with piano accompaniment and additional historical information

Coffin to Bind Me Down
Coffin de coffin to bind me down
Death
BARO, 22, d, Melody only

Cold Icy Hand
Sinner sinner you better pray
Death
BARO, 8, d, Melody only

Come All of God's Children
Come all of God's children in the field

Faith/Assurance
John 4:35#
    MAR3, 292, Choral unaccompanied with additional historical information
    MARS, 258, Choral unaccompanied with additional historical information
    SANH, 28, Uses Tonic Sol-fa notation

Come Along
Come along I am sorry for to leave you
    Songs of Spiritual Journey
        BARO, 13, d, Melody only

Come Along Moses
Come along Moses
    Songs of Spiritual Journey
    Exodus 14:16; Psalms 43:1, 35:1+
        ALLS, 104, Melody only

Come and Go
Come an' go to that lan' where I'm boun'
    Heaven
        ANDW, 8, d, Choral arrangement
        SILS, 14, d, Solo voice with piano accompaniment

Come and Go with Me (1)
This old world is not my home
    Songs of Spiritual Journey
        MCIB, 42, d, Melody and additional historical information
        PETL, 383, d, Text only

Come and Go with Me (2)
Come and go with me to that land
    Songs of Spiritual Journey
        BALS, 66, d, Choral unaccompanied with additional historical information
        HUTS, 11, d, Melody and additional historical information
        LUE, 12, d, Melody, chord symbols, and piano accompaniment
        PETL, 345, d, Text only

Come by Here — see — Kum ba Yah

Come Down
Come down
Deliverance
PETL, 160, d, Text only

Come Down Angels
Come down angels trouble the water
Songs of Spiritual Journey
John 5:4, 7; Luke 7:48–50*
MAR3, 268, Choral unaccompanied with additional historical information
MARS, 234, Choral unaccompanied with additional historical information
PATN, 83, d, Solo voice with piano accompaniment
PETL, 266, d, Text only
SANH, 29, Uses Tonic Sol-fa notation
TAYA, 31, d, Solo voice with piano accompaniment

Come Down My Lord
Come down come down my Lord
Jesus
Revelation 20:12, 19:11–16*
SANH, 30, Uses Tonic Sol-fa notation

Come Down Sinner
Come down come down come down sinner
Admonition/Judgment
DETR, 132, Choral unaccompanied with additional historical information
FENR, 138, Choral unaccompanied with additional historical information
PETL, 55, d, Text only

Come Go with Me
Old Satan is a busy old man
Songs of Spiritual Journey
ALLS, 57, Melody only
CHET, 236, Text only
PETL, 345, d, Text only

Come Here Jesus If You Please
No harm have I done you on my knees
Suffering
PETL, 7, d, Text only

Come Here Lord
Come here Lord
Faith/Assurance
HERB, 9, Text only
JOHJB, ii, 176, d, Solo voice with piano accompaniment and
additional historical information
PETL, 7, d, Text only

Come Let Us All Go Down
By and by we'll all go down
Songs of Spiritual Journey
PETL, 345, d, Text only

Come Let Us All Go Down — see — Good Old Way

Come On In My Room
Come on in my room Jesus is my doctor
Faith/Assurance
Luke 24:29^
AAH, 525, Choral with piano accompaniment and additional
historical information

Come On Sinner — see — I'm All Wore Out Toiling for the Lord

Come Out the Wilderness (1)
I am leaning on the Lord I am leaning on the Lord
Deliverance
Mark 1:4–5; Luke 3:3#
UNI, 416, Melody only

Come Out the Wilderness (2)
Tell me how did you feel whem you come out of the wilderness
Deliverance
Mark 1:4–5; Luke 3:3#
AAH, 367, d, Choral with piano accompaniment and additional
historical information

CLES, 136, d, Choral with piano accompaniment and additional historical information
GUL, 84, d, Text only

Come Sinner Come
Won't you come won't you come
Admonition/Judgment
ODUN, 78, Text only; Source includes additional historical information

Come to Jesus
Come to Jesus come to Jesus just now
Jesus
CHET, 236, Text only

Come to Me
Come to me ye who are hard opprest
Faith/Assurance
CHET, 237, Text only
JACL, 1, Choral with piano accompaniment and additional historical information

Come Trembling Down
Come trembling down go shouting home
Faith/Assurance
PETL, 56, d, Text only

Come unto Me
Come to me can't you hear what my Lord said
Admonition/Judgment
DETD4, 20, Choral unaccompanied with additional historical information
GRIN, 50, Melody only
PETL, 308, d, Text only

Comfort in Heaven
There's comfort in Heaven and I feel it in my soul
Heaven
BARO, 12, d, Melody only

Coming Again By and By
Ain't no more dodging in the bushes iner Gawd's army
  Admonition/Judgment
    MCIB, 64, d, Melody and additional historical information
    PETL, 115, d, Text only

Coming Down the Line
Comin' down de line my Lord
  Aspiration
    MCIB, 71, d, Melody and additional historical information
    PETL, 266, d, Text only

Coming Here Tonight
Brother I never know I comin' here tonight
  Deliverance
    BALS, 36, d, Melody only
    PETL, 346, d, Text only

Communion
Let us break bread together
  Praise
    DETD4, 7, Choral unaccompanied with additional historical information

Conviction of the Wise Men in Jerusalem
Little boy how old are you
  Jesus
    KENMM, 41, d, Text only; Source includes additional historical information

Cotton Needs Picking
Cotton needs a-pickin' so bad
  Work Songs
    ANDW, 46, d, Melody only

Couldn't Hear Nobody Pray — see — I Couldn't Hear Nobody Pray

Cross Me Over
Yonder come er sister all dressed in black

Death
>MCIB, 75, d, Melody and additional historical information
>ODUN, 89, Text only; Source includes additional historical information
>PETL, 384, d, Text only

Crowned Him Lord of All
We will crownd Him Lord of all
>Jesus
>>BARO, 29, d, Melody only

Crucifixion — see — He Never Said a Mumbling Word

Cruel Jews
Cruel Jews just look at Jesus
>Jesus
>>MCIB, 38, Melody and additional historical information
>>PETL, 8, d, Text only

Daniel — see — Didn't My Lord Deliver Daniel

Daniel Daniel Servant of the Lord
King cried
>Deliverance
>Daniel 6:18–22; Jonah 2:10+
>>HERB, 10, Text only
>>PETL, 56, d, Text only

Daniel Saw the Stone (1)
Daniel saw the stone rolling
>Jesus
>Daniel 2:34, 45; 6:10, 22; Matthew 11:5+
>>DETD1, 9, Choral unaccompanied with additional historical information
>>DETR, 54, Choral unaccompanied with additional historical information
>>FENR, 157, Choral unaccompanied with additional historical information

JOHJB, ii, 162, d, Solo voice with piano accompaniment and additional historical information
JONF, 91, Melody only
PETL, 115, d, Text only
SANH, 31, Uses Tonic Sol-fa notation

Daniel Saw the Stone (2)

Daniel saw the stone hewn out of the mountain
Jesus
Daniel 2:34, 45; 6:10, 22; Matthew 11:5+
CHET, 237, Text only
PETL, 209, d, Text only

Daniel's in the Lion's Den

Lord Daniel's in de lion's den
Prayer
Daniel 3:23, 6:16; Jonah 2:1–2+
BALS, 42, d, Choral unaccompanied with additional historical information
MCIB, 77, d, Melody and additional historical information
PETL, 160, d, Text only

Danville Chariot

Swing low sweet chariot pray let me enter in
Death
ARM, 183, Choral unaccompanied with additional historical information
FENC, 11, Choral unaccompanied with additional historical information
FENR, 11, Choral unaccompanied with additional historical information
PETL, 161, d, Text only

Dark Was the Night

Oh oh ah ah oh ah
Suffering
COUN, 251, Melody only

Day I Left My Home

Day I lef' huh my mother's hous' huh
Work Songs
ODUN, 259, d, Text only; Source includes additional historical
information

Day of Judgment

And the moon will turn to blood
Admonition/Judgment
ALLS, 53, Melody only
PETL, 267, d, Text only

Death Ain't Nothing but a Robber

Death ain't nothin' but a robber don't you see
Death
CHET, 237, Text only
GUL, 12, d, Text only
HUTS, 17, d, Melody and additional historical information
PETL, 8, d, Text only

Death Come to My House He Didn't Stay Long

Hallelu o my Lord I'm gwineter see my mother again
Death
JOHJB, ii, 108, d, Solo voice with piano accompaniment and
additional historical information
PETL, 384, d, Text only

Death Is in This Land

Death is in this land
Death
ODUN, 109, d, Text only; Source includes additional historical
information

Death's Going to Lay His Cold Icy Hands on Me (1)

Cryin' oh Lord cryin'
Death
CHET, 237, d, Text only
JOHHG, 35, d, Solo voice with piano accompaniment
JOHHH, 42, d, Solo voice with piano accompaniment

JOHJB, ii, 96, d, Solo voice with piano accompaniment and additional historical information

PETL, 385, d, Text only

Death's Going to Lay His Cold Icy Hands on Me (2)

Death t'row thy sting away

Death

MCIB, 73, d, Melody and additional historical information

PETL, 385, d, Text only

Death's Going to Lay His Cold Icy Hands on Me (3)

Death is going to lay his cold icy hands on me

Death

BALS, 75, d, Melody only

JOHJB, ii, 93, d, Solo voice with piano accompaniment and additional historical information

PETL, 161, d, Text only

PRI4, 26, d, Solo voice with piano accompaniment

Deep River

Deep river Lord I want to pass over into camp ground

Heaven

Deuteronomy 11:31*

SANH, 32, Uses Tonic Sol-fa notation

Deep River

Deep river my home is over Jordan deep river Lord I want to cross over into campground

Heaven

Deuteronomy 11:31*

AAH, 605, Choral with piano accompaniment and additional historical information

ANDW, 3, Choral arrangement

APPA, 160, Solo voice with piano accompaniment

BAYF, 5, d, Solo voice with piano accompaniment and chord symbols

BECK, 48, Solo voice with piano accompaniment

BELT, 11, Uses Tonic Sol-fa notation

BLOR, 208, Text and chord symbols

BOAS, 52, Solo voice with piano accompaniment
BOYFB2, 26, d, Solo voice with piano accompaniment
BRYW, 27, Melody only
BUR2H, 16, d, Solo voice with piano accompaniment
BUR2L, 16, d, Solo voice with piano accompaniment
BURA, 11, d, Solo voice with piano accompaniment
BURC1, 7, d, Solo voice with piano accompaniment
BURS, 74, d, Solo voice with piano accompaniment
CALA, 6, Melody only
CHAT, 19, Solo voice with piano accompaniment
CHET, 238, Text only
CHIA, 4, Melody only
CLES, 115, Choral with piano accompaniment and additional historical information
DANF, 14, Melody only
DETR, 167, Melody only
FISS, 20, d, Solo voice with piano accompaniment and additional historical information
FIST, 2, Solo voice with piano accompaniment
FREC, 3, Solo voice with piano accompaniment
GREF, 3, Solo voice with piano accompaniment
GREF, 94, Solo voice with piano accompaniment
GUIU, 30, Solo voice with piano accompaniment
HAWD, 157, Text only
HAY1H, 48, Solo voice with piano accompaniment
HAY1L, 4, Solo voice with piano accompaniment
HAYMF, 24, d, Solo voice with piano accompaniment and additional historical information
HAYMS, 24, d, Solo voice with piano accompaniment and additional historical information
HELC, 18, d, Solo voice with piano accompaniment
HERB, 10, Text only
HOGDH, 3, d, Solo voice with piano accompaniment and additional historical information
HOGDL, 3, d, Solo voice with piano accompaniment and additional historical information
JOHJB, i, 100, d, Solo voice with piano accompaniment and additional historical information
JOHRA, 38, Solo voice with piano accompaniment

Did You Hear How They Crucified My Lord
Did you hear how they crucified my Lord

Easter
> DETR, 104, d, Melody only
> FENR, 141, d, Choral unaccompanied with additional historical information
> SLA, 16, d, Melody only

Did You Hear My Jesus

If you want to get to Heaven come along come along
> Songs of Spiritual Journey
>> ARMH, 230, d, Choral unaccompanied with additional historical information
>> DETR, 134, d, Choral unaccompanied with additional historical information
>> FENC, 58, Choral unaccompanied with additional historical information
>> FENR, 58, Choral unaccompanied with additional historical information
>> PETL, 346, d, Text only

Did You Hear When Jesus Rose

Mary set her table in spite of all her foes children did you hear when Jesus rose
> Easter
>> AFR, 23, Solo voice with piano accompaniment
>> CHET, 235, d, Text only
>> HAYMF, 123, d, Solo voice with piano accompaniment and additional historical information
>> HAYMS, 123, d, Solo voice with piano accompaniment and additional historical information
>> PETL, 383, d, Text only

Didn't It Rain (1)

Didn't it rain some fo'ty days fo'ty nights when de rain kept a-fallin
> Admonition/Judgment
>> BUR2H, 62, d, Solo voice with piano accompaniment
>> BUR2L, 62, d, Solo voice with piano accompaniment
>> BURC2, 33, d, Solo voice with piano accompaniment
>> BURS, 26, d, Solo voice with piano accompaniment
>> CHET, 266, Text only

HALC, 6, Choral with piano accompaniment and additional historical information

PATN, 61, d, Solo voice with piano accompaniment

PETL, 287, d, Text only

SPAG, 41, d, Solo voice with piano accompaniment and chord symbols

WALSH, 210, d, Solo voice with piano accompaniment

WALSL, 210, d, Solo voice with piano accompaniment

Didn't It Rain (2)

Didn't it rain oh didn't it rain
Admonition/Judgment
PETL, 287, d, Text only

Didn't It Rain (3)

Didn't it rain children rain the whole night long?
Admonition/Judgment
BONI, 9, d, Solo voice with piano accompaniment

BRUS, 19, d, Solo voice with piano accompaniment

HAWD, 55, Text only

LANC, 3, Melody, chord symbols, and additional historical information

LOMAF, 477, Melody, chord symbols, and additional historical information

LUE, 16, Melody, chord symbols, and piano accompaniment

PETL, 267, d, Text only

Didn't My Lord Deliver Daniel

Didn't my Lord deliver Daniel and why not every man
Deliverance
Daniel 6:1–24; Jonah 1:15–2:10*
BAYF, 30, d, Solo voice with piano accompaniment and chord symbols

BLOR, 208, Text and chord symbols

BOAT, 29, d, Solo voice with piano accompaniment

BOY3S, 24, Solo voice with piano accompaniment

BRON, 3, d, Solo voice with piano accompaniment

BRYW, 17fc, Melody only

BUR2H, 22, d, Solo voice with piano accompaniment

BUR2L, 22, d, Solo voice with piano accompaniment

BURC2, 12, d, Solo voice with piano accompaniment

BURS, 184, d, Solo voice with piano accompaniment

CHAT, 23, Solo voice with piano accompaniment

CHET, 239, Text only

CHIA, 2, Melody only

CLASS, 7, d, Solo voice with piano accompaniment and additional historical information

CLES, 106, Choral with piano accompaniment and additional historical information

FREC, 42, Solo voice with piano accompaniment

GUIU, 62, Solo voice with piano accompaniment

HAYMF, 45, d, Solo voice with piano accompaniment and additional historical information

HAYMS, 45, d, Solo voice with piano accompaniment and additional historical information

HERB, 10, Text only

JACL, 73, Choral with piano accompaniment and additional historical information

JOHJB, i, 148, d, Solo voice with piano accompaniment and additional historical information

JOHRA, 10, Solo voice with piano accompaniment

JONF, 158, Melody only

LANC, 17, Melody, chord symbols, and additional historical information

LIES, 24, Solo voice with piano accompaniment

LIF, 182, Choral with piano accompaniment and additional historical information

LLOA, 140, Solo voice with piano accompaniment

LUEB, 18, Melody, chord symbols, and piano accompaniment

MARS, 134, Choral unaccompanied with additional historical information

MIL3, 4, Solo voice with piano accompaniment

NAA, 5, Melody and chord symbols

PETL, 162, d, Text only

PIKJ, 174, Melody only

SANH, 33, Uses Tonic Sol-fa notation

SEWJ, 16, Melody only

SEWJC, 16, Melody only

SILSP, 48, Solo voice with piano accompaniment

SKEG, 20, d, Solo voice with piano accompaniment and chord symbols

SNYS, 42, d, Solo voice with piano accompaniment

SPAG, 12, d, Solo voice with piano accompaniment and chord symbols

STIT, 87, d, Solo voice with piano accompaniment and additional historical information

WAL14H, 12, Solo voice with piano accompaniment

WAL15H, 12, Solo voice with piano accompaniment

WAL15L, 12, Solo voice with piano accompaniment

WALSH, 154, d, Solo voice with piano accompaniment

WALSL, 154, Solo voice with piano accompaniment

WIES, 200, Solo voice with piano accompaniment

Didn't Old Pharaoh Get Lost

Isaac a ransom while he lay upon an altar

Songs of Spiritual Journey

Exodus 4:21, 5:1–2, 16:4; Genesis 22:9, 37:28; James 2:21+

CHET, 239, d, Text only

HERB, 11, d, Text only

JOHJB, i, 60, d, Solo voice with piano accompaniment and additional historical information

MARS, 179, Choral unaccompanied with additional historical information

PETL, 210, d, Text only

PIKJ, 219, Choral unaccompanied with additional historical information

SEWJC, 64, Choral unaccompanied with additional historical information

Didn't You Hear

Didn't you hear my Lord when He called

Faith/Assurance

COUN, 241, Melody only

COUNS, 4, Solo voice with piano accompaniment and additional historical information

Die in the Field

What you say seekers about dat gospel war
Death
JOHJB, i, 68, d, Solo voice with piano accompaniment and additional historical information
PETL, 115, d, Text only
PIKJ, 179, Choral unaccompanied with additional historical information

Dig Deep Children

Dig deep children
Aspiration
LOGR, 33, Melody only

Divers Never Gave Nothing to the Poor

Divers never gave nothing to the poor
Aspiration
Luke 16:20–31+
KENMM, 51, d, Text only; Source includes additional historical information

Dives and Lazarus

Wo' his purple an' linen too
Aspiration
Luke 16:19–25+
LOMJA, 583, d, Melody only

Do Don't Touch My Garment Good Lord

Do don't touch my garment good Lawd
Songs of Spiritual Journey
BALS, 8, d, Choral unaccompanied with additional historical information
JOHJB, ii, 68, d, Solo voice with piano accompaniment and additional historical information
LOYS, 21, d, Solo voice with piano accompaniment
PETL, 211, d, Text only

Do Don't You Weep for the Baby

Do don't you weep for the baby

Suffering
    FISS, 30, d, Solo voice with piano accompaniment and additional historical information
    PETL, 8, d, Text only

Do Lord Remember Me

Do Lord do Lord do remember me
Aspiration
Luke 23:40–43#
    BLOR, 208, Text and chord symbols
    BOAS, 54, Solo voice with piano accompaniment
    BRYI, 41, d, Melody only
    CALA, 7, Melody only
    CHET, 240, Text only
    CLES, 119, Choral with piano accompaniment and additional historical information
    GRIN, 68, Melody only
    HAWD, 146, Text only
    HERB, 12, d, Text only
    JACL, 69, Choral with piano accompaniment and additional historical information
    LIES, 29, Solo voice with piano accompaniment
    LIF, 164, Choral with piano accompaniment and additional historical information
    MCIB, 186, d, Melody and additional historical information
    MCIB, 82, Melody and additional historical information
    MCIS, 24, Solo voice with piano accompaniment
    NAA, 6, Melody and chord symbols
    ODUN, 92, Text only; Source includes additional historical information
    PETL, 9, d, Text only
    PETL, 57, d, Text only
    UNI, 527, Melody only

Do What the Spirit Say Do

We going to do what the spirit say
Aspiration
    NAA, 38, Melody and chord symbols

Do You Think I'll Make a Soldier
  Do you think I'll make a soldier
    Faith/Assurance
      SIX, 46, Solo voice with piano accompaniment

Does You Call That Religion
  Does you call dat religion no no no
    Admonition/Judgment
    Acts 16:31; 2 Corinthians 12:20; Ephesians 4:29–31+
      JOHRR, 85, d, Solo voice with piano accompaniment and additional historical information
      NILS, 2, d, Solo voice with piano accompaniment and additional historical information

Don't Be Weary Traveler
  Don't be weary traveller come along home to Jesus
    Rituals of Preparation for Renewal/Regeneration
      ALLS, 75, Melody only
      BURS, 18, d, Solo voice with piano accompaniment
      CHET, 240, d, Text only
      DETR, 113, Melody only
      FENR, 127, Choral unaccompanied with additional historical information
      FISS, 32, d, Solo voice with piano accompaniment and additional historical information
      HERB, 13, Text only
      PETL, 308, d, Text only

Don't Call the Roll
  Don't call the roll John till I get there
    Heaven
      DANF, 61, Melody only
      DETD1, 19, Choral unaccompanied with additional historical information
      DETR, 119, d, Choral unaccompanied with additional historical information
      FENR, 150, d, Choral unaccompanied with additional historical information
      GUL, 83, d, Text only
      PETL, 163, d, Text only

Don't Come Oh Lord
  Don't come oh Lord in the mawnin
    Deliverance
      LOGR, 27, Melody only

Don't Get Weary
  My brethren don't get weary
    Faith/Assurance
      BALS, 87, d, Melody only
      DETR, 114, Choral unaccompanied with additional historical
        information
      PETL, 58, d, Text only

Don't Leave Me Lord
  Don't leave me Lord
    Aspiration
      DETR, 31, Melody only
      FENR, 117, Choral unaccompanied with additional historical
        information
      PETL, 58, d, Text only

Don't Let It Be Said Too Late
  My mother she's gone she's gone
    Heaven
      BOAS, 46, Solo voice with piano accompaniment
      HAWD, 106, Text only

Don't Let the Wind Blow Here No More
  Don't let the wind don't let the wind
    Admonition/Judgment
      BALS, 39, d, Choral unaccompanied with additional historical
        information
      PETL, 267, d, Text only

Don't Let Your Elder Condemn You
  Leaduh leaduuh do(n)' let yuh elduh condemn yuh
    Faith/Assurance
      GUL, 15, d, Text only

Don't Stay Away — see — Brothers Don't Stay Away

Don't You Grieve After Me (1)
Who is that a-coming
Death
MAR3, 250, Choral unaccompanied with additional historical
information
MARS, 216, Choral unaccompanied with additional historical
information
PETL, 59, d, Text only

Don't You Grieve After Me (2)
When I'm dead and buried don't you grieve after me
Death
GUL, 19, d, Text only
MCIB, 91, Melody and additional historical information
PETL, 116, d, Text only

Don't You Grieve for Me — see — Angel's Waiting at the Door

Don't You Have Everybody for Your Friend
Don't you have everybody for your friend
Suffering
BALS, 71, d, Melody only
PETL, 347, d, Text only

Don't You Hear the Lambs Crying — see — Hear the Lamb's Crying

Don't You Let Nobody Turn You Around
Don't you let nobody turn you roun'
Faith/Assurance
HAWD, 106, Text only
JOHHG, 10, d, Solo voice with piano accompaniment
JOHHH, 18, d, Solo voice with piano accompaniment
MCLS, 32, d, Solo voice with piano accompaniment
NAA, 8, d, Melody and chord symbols
PETL, 59, d, Text only
WHIF, 60, d, Solo voice with piano accompaniment

Don't You Mind What the Devil Do
Don't yuh min' w'at duh Debble do 'e cyan' git tuh Heben en'e won'
let you

Heaven
    HUTS, 19, d, Melody and additional historical information

Don't You Mind What the People Do
Don'chuh mine' wha' duh Deeble do don'chuh mine'
    Heaven
        GUL, 14, d, Text only

Don't You See — see — I Got a Home in That Rock

Don't You View That Ship Come Sailing
Don't ye view dat ship a come a sailin'
    Deliverance
        ARMH, 226, d, Choral unaccompanied with additional historical information
        CHET, 241, d, Text only
        DETR, 220, d, Choral unaccompanied with additional historical information
        FENC, 54, d, Choral unaccompanied with additional historical information
        FENR, 54, d, Choral unaccompanied with additional historical information
        PETL, 163, d, Text only

Don't You Want to Go
Brother don't you want to go
    Songs of Spiritual Journey
        BARO, 31, d, Melody only

Don't You Weep After Me — see — Mother Don't You Weep

Don't You Weep When I'm Gone — see — Mother Don't You Weep

Don't You Wish You Were in Heaven
Don't you wish you were in Hebben today
    Heaven
        MCIB, 97, d, Melody and additional historical information
        PETL, 385, d, Text only

Done Been Sanctified
One day I'se a-walking along
Deliverance
BARO, 31, d, Melody only

Done Found My Lost Sheep
Done foun' my los' sheep
Faith/Assurance
BOAT, 87, d, Solo voice with piano accompaniment
CHET, 240, d, Text only
GREF, 16, d, Solo voice with piano accompaniment
HALC, 10, d, Choral with piano accompaniment and additional historical
HERB, 13, d, Text only
JOHJB, i, 167, d, Solo voice with piano accompaniment and additional historical information
PETL, 57, d, Text only

Done Found the Way At Last
Been a long time praying for this-a way
Death
MCIB, 92, d, Melody and additional historical information
PETL, 58, d, Text only

Done Made My Vow to the Lord
Done made my vow to the Lord and I will never go back
Songs of Spiritual Journey
Matthew 21:28–32#
BOAT, 34, d, Solo voice with piano accompaniment
BRUT, 13, d, Solo voice with piano accompaniment and additional historical information
CALA, 5, Text only
JACL, 42, Choral with piano accompaniment and additional historical information
LIF, 123, Choral with piano accompaniment and additional historical information
MCIS, 11, Solo voice with piano accompaniment
NAA, 7, Melody and chord symbols
PATN, 1, d, Solo voice with piano accompaniment

BOAS, 23, Solo voice with piano accompaniment
CALA, 5, Text only
DANF, 46, d, Melody only
FRAS, 16, Solo voice with piano accompaniment
GREF, 68, d, Solo voice with piano accompaniment
GUIU, 54, Solo voice with piano accompaniment
HERB, 14, Text only
JACL, 43, Choral with piano accompaniment and additional historical information
LIF, 210, Choral with piano accompaniment and additional historical information
LUEB, 20, Melody, chord symbols, and piano accompaniment
PETL, 163, d, Text only
SIX, 61, Solo voice with piano accompaniment
SLA, 33, Choral arrangement
SNES, 1, Solo voice with piano accompaniment

Down in Hell

Down in Hell

Admonition/Judgment

DETD3, 24, Choral unaccompanied with additional historical information

Down in the Valley on My Praying Knees

Down een duh walley on muh prayin' knee

Prayer

GUL, 16, d, Text only
HUTS, 21, d, Melody and additional historical information

Down in the Valley to Pray (1)

Brother didn't conscience come and tell you go down in the valley to pray

Prayer

Luke 11:1; Psalms 23:2*

BARO, 4, d, Melody only
PETL, 350, d, Text only

Down in the Valley to Pray (2)

As I went down in the valley to pray

Prayer
Luke 11:1; Psalms 23:2*
    ALTAH, 5, Solo voice with piano accompaniment
    ALTAL, 2, Solo voice with piano accompaniment
    BECK, 20, Solo voice with piano accompaniment
    HAY1H, 20, Solo voice with piano accompaniment
    SANH, 23, Uses Tonic Sol-fa notation

Down on Me

Down on me down on me
    Suffering
        PETL, 10, d, Text only
        WORJT, 10, Choral unaccompanied with additional historical information

Downward Road

Well brother the downward road is crowded
    Admonition/Judgment
        LOMAF, 485, Melody, chord symbols, and additional historical information

Downward Road Is Crowded (1)

Young people who delight in sin downward road is crowded with unbelievin souls
    Admonition/Judgment
        CHET, 278, Text only
        DETR, 14, d, Choral unaccompanied with additional historical information
        FENR, 119, Choral unaccompanied with additional historical information
        ODUN, 73, Text only; Source includes additional historical information
        PETL, 10, d, Text only

Downward Road Is Crowded (2)

Downward road is crowded crowded the wind blows east
    Admonition/Judgment
        PETL, 347, d, Text only

Draw Level

Draw lebble de ainjul am a comin' down
   Work Songs
      GUL, 17, d, Text only
      HUTS, 23, d, Melody and additional historical information

Drinking of the Wine

If my mother ask you for me
   Jesus
      GUL, 18, d, Text only
      ODUN, 136, d, Text only; Source includes additional historical
         information

Drive Satan Away

Takes a pu'e in heart to drive Satan away
   Rituals of Preparation for Renewal/Regeneration
      HALC, 70, Melody only
      PETL, 309, d, Text only

Dry Bones (1)

Down in de valley de sperret spoke
   Rituals of Preparation for Renewal/Regeneration
      BUR4H, 18, d, Solo voice with piano accompaniment and addi-
         tional historical information
      BUR4L, 18, d, Solo voice with piano accompaniment and addi-
         tional historical information
      KENM, 48, Solo voice with piano accompaniment and additional
         historical information

Dry Bones (2)

God called Ezekiel by his word
   Rituals of Preparation for Renewal/Regeneration
      CHET, 242, Text only
      HAYMF, 33, d, Solo voice with piano accompaniment and addi-
         tional historical information
      HAYMS, 34, d, Solo voice with piano accompaniment and addi-
         tional historical information
      LUEB, 22, Melody, chord symbols, and piano accompaniment
      PETL, 348, d, Text only

Dry Bones (3)

Dem bones dem dry bones I hear the word of the Lord
Work Songs
BONR, 132, d, Solo voice with piano accompaniment
CALA, 6, Text only
CHAT, 26, Solo voice with piano accompaniment
TAYA, 43, d, Solo voice with piano accompaniment

Dry Bones Going to Rise (1)

Some go to meeting to sing and shout
Rituals of Preparation for Renewal/Regeneration
MCIB, 62, d, Melody and additional historical information
ODUN, 102, d, Text only; Source includes additional historical information
PETL, 309, d, Text only

Dry Bones Going to Rise (2)

All them bones all them bones in the morning all them bones
Rituals of Preparation for Renewal/Regeneration
HERB, 15, d, Text only

Dum-A-Lum

I was way down a-yonder a-by myself
Songs of Spiritual Journey
HALC, 9, Choral with piano accompaniment and additional historical information on the spiritual
PETL, 386, d, Text only

Dust and Ashes

Dust dust and ashes fly over on my grave
Heaven
Luke 24:1–6; Mark 15:45, 16:1–6; Matthew 27:35, 57–60, 28:1–6+
ARMH, 251, d, Choral unaccompanied with additional historical information
BALS, 92, d, Melody only
DETR, 213, d, Choral unaccompanied with additional historical information
FENC, 79, d, Choral unaccompanied with additional historical information

FENR, 79, d, Choral unaccompanied with additional historical information

Eagle's Wings
Lord I wish I had an eagle's wings
Songs of Spiritual Journey
BALS, 38, d, Choral unaccompanied with additional historical information
PETL, 386, d, Text only

Early in the Morning
I meet little Rosa early in the morning I'm goin' rise
Heaven
ALLS, 44, Melody only
ODUN, 260, d, Text only; Source includes additional historical information
PETL, 60, d, Text only

Elder You Say You Love King Jesus
Elder you say you love King Jesus
Jesus
Mark 12:30*
SANH, 34, Uses Tonic Sol-fa notation

Elijah Rock
Elijah rock shout shout
Deliverance
HERB, 16, d, Text only
PETL, 60, d, Text only

End of That Morning
Gambler get up o' yo' knees
Admonition/Judgment
HALC, 25, d, Choral with piano accompaniment and additional historical information

End of the World
The fields are all white the harvest is near
Admonition/Judgment
MCKF, 12, Solo voice with piano accompaniment

Enlisted in the Field of Battle
    Pray on my brudder don't you get tired
        Work Songs
            HALC, 32, d, Choral with piano accompaniment and additional historical information on the spiritual
            PETL, 133, d, Text only

Enlisted Soldiers
    Hark listen to the trumpeters
        Work Songs
            DETR, 180, Choral unaccompanied with additional historical information
            FENR, 145, Choral unaccompanied with additional historical information
            PETL, 117, d, Text only

Even Me
    Lord I hear show'rs of blessing
        Aspiration
            CLES, 174, Choral with piano accompaniment and additional historical information

Every Day
    Well the horse wheel rolling
        Admonition/Judgment
            ODUN, 119, Text only; Source includes additional historical information

Every Day Will Be Sunday
    By and by by and by good Lord
        Deliverance
            PETL, 164, d, Text only

Every Hour in the Day
    One cold freezing morning I lay this body down
        Prayer
            ALLS, 58, Melody only
            PETL, 10, d, Text only

Every Little Step Goes Higher
Every little step goes higher higher higher
Songs of Spiritual Journey
DITT, 47, Choral arrangement
PETL, 387, d, Text only

Every Time I Feel the Spirit
Every time I feel the Spirit moving in my heart I will pray
Deliverance
John 4:24^
AAH, 325, Choral with piano accompaniment and additional historical information
ALBGH, 22, Solo voice with piano accompaniment
ALBGL, 22, Solo voice with piano accompaniment
ANDW, 22, d, Choral arrangement
BALS, 88, d, Melody only
BONF, 1, d, Solo voice with piano accompaniment and additional historical information
BONF, 9, d, Solo voice with piano accompaniment and additional historical information
BROS, 16, d, Solo voice with piano accompaniment
BRYI, 18, d, Melody only
BURA, 6, d, Solo voice with piano accompaniment
BURC2, 17, d, Solo voice with piano accompaniment
BURS, 5, d, Solo voice with piano accompaniment
CALA, 8, Melody only
CHAT, 32, d, Solo voice with piano accompaniment
CHET, 242, Text only
CHIA, 6, Melody only
CLES, 121, Choral with piano accompaniment and additional historical information
DETR, 169, Choral unaccompanied with additional historical information
DITT, 10, Choral arrangement
FENR, 169, d, Choral unaccompanied with additional historical information
FISS, 39, d, Solo voice with piano accompaniment and additional historical information
FIST, 6, Solo voice with piano accompaniment

Everybody Got to Die
Everybody who am living everybody got to die
Death
CHAT, 31, d, Solo voice with piano accompaniment

Everybody Wants to Know Just How I Die
Everybody who is living got to die the rich and the poor the great
and the small
Death
PETL, 348, d, Text only
BALS, 22, d, Melody only

Everybody Who Is Living (Has) Got to Die (1)
Eb'rybawdy who is libbin' gawt'uh die gawt'uh die
Death
GUL, 21, d, Text only
HUTS, 25, d, Melody and additional historical information

Everybody Who Is Living (Has) Got to Die (2)
Everybody who is living (has) got to die the rich and the poor the
great and the small
Death
HUTS, 27, d, Melody and additional historical information

Everywhere I Go My Lord
Everywhere I go everywhere I go my Lord
Jesus
COUN, 247, Melody only

Ezekiel Saw the Wheel (1)
Wheel oh wheel Ezekiel saw the wheel of time every spoke was
humankind
Rituals of Preparation for Renewal/Regeneration
Ezekiel 1:15–21, 10:10*
HAWD, 91, Text only
JOHJB, ii, 144, d, Solo voice with piano accompaniment and
additional historical information
PETL, 387, d, Text only
SPAG, 63, d, Solo voice with piano accompaniment and chord
symbols

Ezekiel Saw the Wheel (2)
Ezekiel saw the wheel way up in the middle of the air
Rituals of Preparation for Renewal/Regeneration
Ezekiel 1:15–21, 10:10*
AAH, 484, d, Choral with piano accompaniment and additional historical information
ALTSH, 2, Solo voice with piano accompaniment
ALTSL, 2, Solo voice with piano accompaniment
ANDW, 10, d, Choral arrangement
BONI, 6, d, Solo voice with piano accompaniment
CALA, 9, d, Melody only
CHET, 242, d, Text only
CHIA, 8, Melody only
CLES, 84, d, Choral with piano accompaniment and additional historical information
DETR, 60, d, Choral unaccompanied with additional historical information
FENR, 164, d, Choral unaccompanied with additional historical information
HAYMF, 26, d, Solo voice with piano accompaniment and additional historical information
HAYMS, 26, d, Solo voice with piano accompaniment and additional historical information
HERB, 16, d, Text only
JOHRA, 35, d, Solo voice with piano accompaniment
KINS, 22, d, Solo voice with piano accompaniment
LANC, 14, Melody, chord symbols, and additional historical information
LIF, 224, Choral with piano accompaniment and additional historical information
MIL3, 36, Solo voice with piano accompaniment
PETL, 387, d, Text only
PETL, 388, d, Text only
SANH, 35, Uses Tonic Sol-fa notation
WARE, 34, d, Solo voice with piano accompaniment and additional historical information
WHIF, 85, d, Solo voice with piano accompaniment

Ezekiel's Wheel
Zekus wheel oh my soul

Rituals of Preparation for Renewal/Regeneration
Ezekiel 1:15–21, 10:10*
GRIN, 32, Melody only

Face the Rising Sun
We will all sing tugedduh on dat day
Admonition/Judgment
GUL, 29, d, Text only
HUTS, 31, d, Melody and additional historical information

Fairest Lord Jesus
Fairest Lord Jesus ruler of all nature
Jesus
NAA, 30, Melody and chord symbols

Faith of Our Fathers
Faith of our fathers
Faith/Assurance
NAA, 31, Melody and chord symbols

Fare Ye Well
Fare you well my brother
Rituals of Preparation for Renewal/Regeneration
ALLS, 47, Melody only
CHET, 242, d, Text only
HAWD, 132, d, Text only
HERB, 17, Text only
PETL, 310, d, Text only

Farewell My Brother
Farewell my brother farewell forever
Death
MARS, 185, Choral unaccompanied with additional historical information
PETL, 164, d, Text only

Farewell My Dear Mother
Farewell my dear mother

Fire

Fi-yer Lord fi-yer gonna burna ma soul
> Faith
>> JOHHH, 56, d, Solo voice with piano accompaniment

Fire Song

My lovin' sister when the world's on fire
> Faith/Assurance
>> HALU, 5, Solo voice with piano accompaniment
>> SIX, 7, Solo voice with piano accompaniment

Fisherman Peter

Fisherman Peter on the sea
> Faith/Assurance
>> DITT, 37, Choral arrangement

Five of Them Were Wise — see — There Were Ten Virgins

Fix Me Jesus

Fix me fix me Jesus fix me for my long white robe
> Rituals of Preparation for Renewal/Regeneration
> 1 John 1:9; Revelation 6:11, 7:9–14+
>> AAH, 436, Choral with piano accompaniment and additional historical information
>> ANDM, 78, d, Solo voice with piano accompaniment
>> BALS, 83, d, Choral unaccompanied with additional historical information
>> BRUO, 30, d, Solo voice with piano accompaniment and additional historical information
>> CALA, 10, Melody only
>> CLES, 122, Choral with piano accompaniment and additional historical information
>> CREO, 17, Solo voice with piano accompaniment
>> DITT, 45, Choral arrangement
>> HAIS, 25, Solo voice with piano accompaniment
>> HAIS, 28, Solo voice with piano accompaniment
>> HERB, 17, d, Text only
>> LIF, 125, Choral with piano accompaniment and additional historical information

PETL, 310, d, Text only
RUPM, 81, Solo voice with piano accompaniment
UNI, 655, Melody only

Flood Comes Creeping
Flood come uh-creepin' up tuh Norah do'
Admonition/Judgment
GUL, 31, d, Text only
HUTS, 35, d, Melody and additional historical information

Fold My Hands and Tie My Feet
And when I come to die
Death
LOGR, 14, Melody only

Follow Me
When I was a seeker good Lord when I was a seeker King Jesus took-a me in
Songs of Spiritual Journey
PATN, 29, d, Solo voice with piano accompaniment

Footprints of Jesus
Footprints of Jesus leading the way
Jesus
CLES, 200, Choral with piano accompaniment and additional historical information on the spiritual

For I Ain't Going to Die No More
When I'm on my sick bed nobody visit me
Death
PARS, 190, d, Text only

For My Lord
Tell Jesus done done all I can
Faith/Assurance
ODUN, 90, Text only; Source includes additional historical information

For the Lord
Fo' de Lord
Faith/Assurance
HALC, 42, d, Choral with piano accompaniment and additional historical information
PETL, 164, d, Text only

Forty Days and Nights
They call Bro' Noah a foolish man
Suffering
Genesis 7:7, 12+
ODUN, 127, d, Text only; Source includes additional historical information

Four and Twenty Elders
See for and twenty elders on there knees
Prayer
Judges 7:5; Revelation 4:10, 5:8, 5:14, 19:14+
BOAS, 70, Solo voice with piano accompaniment
CHET, 243, Text only
DANF, 25, Melody only
DETR, 71, Choral unaccompanied with additional historical information
FENR, 105, Choral unaccompanied with additional historical information
HAWD, 149, Text only
PETL, 249, d, Text only
TOBB, 17, Melody only

Foxes Have Holes in the Ground
Foxes have holes in the ground and the birds have nests in the air
Songs of Spiritual Journey
SANH, 127, Uses Tonic Sol-fa notation

Free At Last
Free at last thank God Almighty I'm free at last
Deliverance
Psalm 118:5; 1 Thessalonians 4:13–18#
CALA, 11, Melody only
CHET, 243, Text only

GLAS, 49, Melody and chord symbols
GUIU, 57, Solo voice with piano accompaniment
HERB, 18, d, Text only
JACL, 51, Choral with piano accompaniment and additional historical information
KENM, 38, d, Melody only
LIF, 230, Choral with piano accompaniment and additional historical information
LLOA, 139, Solo voice with piano accompaniment
MCIB, 95, d, Melody and additional historical information
PETL, 212, d, Text only
SLA, 40, Choral arrangement
TAYA, 38, d, Solo voice with piano accompaniment
WORJF, 46, d, Text only; Source includes additional historical information

Free Free My Lord
Moon come down like a piper's stem
Aspiration
ODUN, 68, Text only; Source includes additional historical information

Freedom Train Coming
Hear that-a freedom train a-coming
Deliverance
CLES, 92, d, Choral with piano accompaniment and additional historical information

From Every Graveyard
Just behold that number
Death
MARS, 129, Choral unaccompanied with additional historical information
PETL, 268, d, Text only
PIKJ, 169, Choral unaccompanied with additional historical information
SEWJ, 12, Choral arrangement
SEWJC, 12, Choral unaccompanied with additional historical information

Gabriel's Trumpet Going to Blow
Gabriel's trumpet going to blow
Admonition/Judgment
PETL, 268, d, Text only
MARS, 195, Choral unaccompanied with additional historical information

Galman Day
Galman day and a one two dun k'am die
Faith/Assurance
LOGR, 29, Melody only

Gambler Get Up Off of Your Knees
Gambler get up off your knees
Admonition/Judgment
HERB, 60, d, Text only
JOHJB, i, 122, d, Solo voice with piano accompaniment and additional historical information
PETL, 287, d, Text only

General Roll
I'll be there I'll be there in the morning
Heaven
BARO, 29, d, Melody only
MARS, 172, Choral unaccompanied with additional historical information
PETL, 212, d, Text only
PIKJ, 212, Melody only
SEWJC, 53, Melody only

General Roll Call
Come my brethren one and all
Heaven
DETR, 166, Choral unaccompanied with additional historical information
FENC, 91, Choral unaccompanied with additional historical information
FENR, 91, Choral unaccompanied with additional historical information
PETL, 349, d, Text only

Get in the Union

Get in the union Jesus is a listening

Admonition/Judgment

ODUN, 85, Text only; Source includes additional historical information

Get On Board Little Children

Gospel train is a-coming get on board little children

Deliverance

ANDW, 12, Choral arrangement

APPA, 162, Solo voice with piano accompaniment

BRYA, 25, Melody, chord symbols, and additional historical information

BRYI, 24, d, Melody only

BURA, 34, d, Solo voice with piano accompaniment

BURS, 115, d, Solo voice with piano accompaniment

CALA, 4, d, Text only

CHAT, 21, Solo voice with piano accompaniment

CHET, 243, Text only

CLES, 116, Choral with piano accompaniment and additional historical information

DETR, 131, d, Choral unaccompanied with additional historical information

FENR, 134, Choral unaccompanied with additional historical information

HAWD, 90, Text only

JOHJB, i, 126, d, Solo voice with piano accompaniment and additional historical information

JOHRA, 21, d, Solo voice with piano accompaniment

MIL3, 40, d, Solo voice with piano accompaniment

PATN, 51, d, Solo voice with piano accompaniment

PETL, 171, d, Text only

SILS, 58, d, Solo voice with piano accompaniment and additional historical information

SIMA, 27, d, Solo voice with piano accompaniment

SIX, 42, d, Solo voice with piano accompaniment

SLA, 29, d, Choral arrangement

SNYS, 50, d, Solo voice with piano accompaniment

TOBB, 28, d, Melody only

Get On Board Little Children — see also — Gospel Train

Get On Board Old Ship of Zion
Git on board o' ship o' Zion
Deliverance
Psalm 48:12–14^
AAH, 349, d, Choral with piano accompaniment and additional
historical information
CALA, 13, d, Text only
CHET, 280, d, Text only
KENMM, 141, d, Text only; Source includes additional historical
information

Get on the Boat Little Children
Jes you git on de boat little chillun
Faith/Assurance
MCIB, 69, d, Melody and additional historical information
PETL, 60, d, Text only

Get on the Evening Train
Gwine to git on de evening train
Songs of Spiritual Journey
BARO, 33, d, Melody only

Get Right Stay Right
Get right stay right be ready when yo Jesus come
Heaven
JOHRR, 51, d, Solo voice with piano accompaniment and addi-
tional historical information

Get Your Ticket
Get yo' ticket
Admonition/Judgment
GRIN, 48, d, Melody only
PETL, 272, d, Text only

Getting Ready to Die
Getting ready to die
Death

Isaiah 35:10; Revelation 21:1–14*
    MARS, 172, Choral unaccompanied with additional historical information
    PETL, 213, d, Text only
    PIKJ, 212, Melody only
    SANH, 38, Uses Tonic Sol-fa notation
    SEWJC, 53, Melody only

Gideon's Band — see — Band of Gideon

Gift of God Is Eternal Life
Gif' ob Gawd is eternal life
    Rituals of Preparation for Renewal/Regeneration
        MCIB, 81, d, Melody and additional historical information
        PETL, 61, d, Text only

Give Me a Clean Heart
Give me a clean heart so I may serve
    Aspiration
        CLES, 182, Choral with piano accompaniment and additional historical information

Give Me Jesus (1)
Give-er me Jesus you may have all-er dis worl'
    Faith/Assurance
    Matthew 16:26#
        MCIB, 102, d, Melody and additional historical information

Give Me Jesus (2)
I heard my mother say give me Jesus
    Faith/Assurance
    Matthew 16:26#
        AAH, 561, Choral with piano accompaniment and additional historical information
        CLES, 165, Choral with piano accompaniment and additional historical information
        HERB, 19, Text only
        WORF, 40, Choral unaccompanied with additional historical information

Give Me Jesus (3)

   In the morning when I rise in the morning when I rise
     Faith/Assurance
     Matthew 16:26#
        ALBGH, 4, Solo voice with piano accompaniment
        ALBGL, 4, Solo voice with piano accompaniment
        CALA, 12, Melody only
        HAIS, 31, Solo voice with piano accompaniment
        HELC, 41, d, Solo voice with piano accompaniment
        HOGDH, 11, d, Solo voice with piano accompaniment and additional historical information
        JACL, 117, Choral with piano accompaniment and additional historical information
        JOHHH, 49, d, Solo voice with piano accompaniment
        LIF, 91, Choral with piano accompaniment and additional historical information
        SEV, 305, Choral with piano accompaniment and additional historical information

Give Me Jesus (4)

   When I am alone give me Jesus
     Faith/Assurance
     Matthew 16:26#
        LABC, 18, Solo voice with piano accompaniment
        MILF, 17, d, Solo voice with piano accompaniment
        BALF, 6, Solo voice with cello accompaniment

Give Me Jesus (5)

   When I come to die
     Faith/Assurance
     Matthew 16:26#
        BOAT, 38, d, Solo voice with piano accompaniment
        BURS, 30, d, Solo voice with piano accompaniment
        CHAT, 36, Solo voice with piano accompaniment
        CHET, 244, Text only
        DANF, 24, Melody only
        FISS, 46, d, Solo voice with piano accompaniment and additional historical information
        GUIU, 33, Solo voice with piano accompaniment

HAY1L, 53, Solo voice with piano accompaniment

JOHJB, i, 160, d, Solo voice with piano accompaniment and additional historical information

MAR3, 174, Choral unaccompanied with additional historical information

MARS, 140, Choral unaccompanied with additional historical information

PETL, 61, d, Text only

PIKJ, 180, Melody only

SEWJ, 19, Melody only

SEWJC, 19, Melody only

WARE, 36, d, Solo voice with piano accompaniment and additional historical information

Give Me Jesus When I Die

Soon in de mornin' give me Jesus when I die

Faith/Assurance

MCIB, 115, d, Melody and additional historical information

PETL, 62, d, Text only

Give Me That Old Time Religion — see — Old Time Religion

Give Me the Wings

Give me the wings oh good Lord

Deliverance

MAR3, 297, Choral unaccompanied with additional historical information

MARS, 263, Choral unaccompanied with additional historical information

WORJT, 14, Choral unaccompanied with additional historical information

Give Me the Wings for to Move Along

Gimme de wings my good Lord de wings of love

Deliverance

JOHRS, 11, Solo voice with piano accompaniment

Give Me Your Hand

Give me your hand give me your hand all I want is the love of God

Aspiration

> BOAS, 18, Solo voice with piano accompaniment
>
> BOAT, 42, d, Solo voice with piano accompaniment
>
> DETD1, 14, Choral unaccompanied with additional historical information
>
> HERB, 20, d, Text only
>
> JOHJB, ii, 86, d, Solo voice with piano accompaniment and additional historical information
>
> LOYS, 58, d, Solo voice with piano accompaniment
>
> PETL, 63, d, Text only

Give Up the World (1)

Sun give a light in the Heaven all around

> Rituals of Preparation for Renewal/Regeneration
>
> > ALLS, 27, Melody only
> >
> > PETL, 166, d, Text only

Give Up the World (2)

My brother wont you give up the world

> Rituals of Preparation for Renewal/Regeneration
>
> > HALC, 73, Melody only
> >
> > PETL, 311, d, Text only

Give Way Jordan

Give way Jordan

> Aspiration
>
> > ARMH, 195, d, Choral unaccompanied with additional historical information
> >
> > CHIA, 14, d, Melody only
> >
> > DETR, 96, Choral unaccompanied with additional historical information
> >
> > FENC, 23, Choral unaccompanied with additional historical information
> >
> > FENR, 23, Choral unaccompanied with additional historical information
> >
> > HAYMF, 38, d, Solo voice with piano accompaniment and additional historical information
> >
> > HAYMS, 38, d, Solo voice with piano accompaniment and additional historical information

PETL, 138, d, Text only
PETL, 165, d, Text only

Glad I Got Religion
I'm so glad
Faith/Assurance
ODUN, 70, Text only; Source includes additional historical information

Glory and Honor (1)
Got glory an' honor praise Jesus
Praise
MCIB, 104, d, Melody and additional historical information
PETL, 63, d, Text only

Glory and Honor (2)
Live humble humble humble yourselves
Songs of Spiritual Journey
FENC, 87, Choral unaccompanied with additional historical information
FENR, 87, Choral unaccompanied with additional historical information
PETL, 349, d, Text only

Glory Bound
When I reach the top of the mountain and can touch the brightest star
Heaven
BECK, 34, Solo voice with piano accompaniment
HAY1H, 34, Solo voice with piano accompaniment

Glory Glory Hallelujah
Glory glory hallelujah since I laid my burden
Praise
Psalm 55:22^
AAH, 500, Choral with piano accompaniment and additional historical information
BALS, 53, d, Choral unaccompanied with additional historical information
BOAS, 3, Solo voice with piano accompaniment

CALA, 13, Melody only
CHET, 266, Text only
CLES, 98, Choral with piano accompaniment and additional historical information
HELC, 50, d, Solo voice with piano accompaniment
JOHHT, 76, d, Solo voice with piano accompaniment
MCLS, 38, Solo voice with piano accompaniment
WARE, 38, d, Solo voice with piano accompaniment and additional historical information

Glory Hallelujah to the New-Born King

Tell me who do you call de Wonderful Counsellor
Christmas
JOHHT, 80, d, Solo voice with piano accompaniment

Glow Within

You've gotta get a glory in the work you do
Work Songs
CHAT, 121, Solo voice with piano accompaniment

Go and I Go with You

Go and I will go with you
Faith/Assurance
ODUN, 135, d, Text only; Source includes additional historical information

Go and Tell Mary and Martha

Go and tell Mary and Martha yes Jesus is risen
Easter
Matthew 28:5–7; Mark 16:6–7; Luke 24:5–12; John 11:23–40#
AAH, 284, Choral with piano accompaniment and additional historical information

Go Chain the Lion Down (1)

Go chain the lion down before the Heaven doors close
Heaven
MARS, 174, Choral unaccompanied with additional historical information

PETL, 118, d, Text only
PIKJ, 214, Melody only
SEWJC, 59, Melody only

Go Chain the Lion Down (2)
Go chain the lion down
  Heaven
    PETL, 166, d, Text only

Go Down Death
Sperrit say I want yuh fo' to go down death
  Deliverance
    KENM, 60, Solo voice with piano accompaniment and additional
      historical information

Go Down in the Lonesome Valley — see — Lonesome Valley

Go Down Moses (1)
Go down Moses 'way down in Egypt's lan'
  Deliverance
  Exodus 3–15#
    CHET, 244, Text only
    HAWD, 50, Text only
    JOHRA, 6, Solo voice with piano accompaniment
    JORS, 13, d, Text only
    MCIB, 235, d, Melody and additional historical information
    PETL, 166, d, Text only
    PRI4, 40, Solo voice with piano accompaniment
    SCHG, 10, Solo voice with piano accompaniment

Go Down Moses (2)
When Israel was in Egypt's land let my people go
  Deliverance
  Exodus 3–15#
    AAH, 543, Choral with piano accompaniment and additional
      historical information
    ANDW, 13, Choral arrangement
    APPA, 174, Solo voice with piano accompaniment

BALF, 4, Solo voice with piano accompaniment

BAYF, 12, d, Solo voice with piano accompaniment and chord symbols

BELT, 19, Uses Tonic Sol-fa notation

BOAT, 48, d, Solo voice with piano accompaniment

BOYE, 18, Solo voice with piano accompaniment

BRYW, 13, Melody only

BUCS, 8, Instrumental Ensemble accompaniment

BUR2H, 26, d, Solo voice with piano accompaniment

BUR2L, 26, d, Solo voice with piano accompaniment

BURC2, 21, d, Solo voice with piano accompaniment

BURS, 42, d, Solo voice with piano accompaniment

CALA, 14, Melody only

CHAT, 38, Solo voice with piano accompaniment

CHIA, 16, Melody only

CLES, 112, Choral with piano accompaniment and additional historical information

CLES, 212, Choral with piano accompaniment and additional historical information

DANF, 33, Melody only

DETD1, 15, Choral unaccompanied with additional historical information

DETR, 108, Choral unaccompanied with additional historical information

FENR, 153, Choral unaccompanied with additional historical information

FISS, 99, d, Solo voice with piano accompaniment and additional historical information

FRAS, 28, Solo voice with piano accompaniment

FREC, 18, Solo voice with piano accompaniment

GAIF, 213, Solo voice with piano accompaniment

GLAS, 23, Melody and chord symbols

GREF, 41, Solo voice with piano accompaniment

GUIU, 22, Solo voice with piano accompaniment

HAYMF, 22, d, Solo voice with piano accompaniment and additional historical information

HAYMS, 22, d, Solo voice with piano accompaniment and additional historical information

HERB, 22, Text only

WALSL, 166, d, Solo voice with piano accompaniment
WARE, 40, d, Solo voice with piano accompaniment and additional historical information
WHIF, 75, d, Solo voice with piano accompaniment
WIES, 209, Solo voice with piano accompaniment

Go Elijah

Go 'Lija and git yo' horses
Deliverance
LOGR, 22, d, Melody only

Go in the Wilderness

I wait upon the Lord
Faith/Assurance
ALLS, 14, Melody only
CHET, 245, Text only
PETL, 168, d, Text only

Go Mary and Toll the Bell (1)

Go Mary and toll the bell who's all them come dressed in white
Death
DETR, 153, d, Choral unaccompanied with additional historical information
FENR, 113, d, Choral unaccompanied with additional historical information
GREF, 24, d, Solo voice with piano accompaniment
HALC, 14, d, Choral with piano accompaniment and additional historical information
PETL, 215, d, Text only

Go Mary and Toll the Bell (2)

Go Mary and toll the bell go John and call the roll
Death
DANF, 51, Melody only
PETL, 215, d, Text only

Go On Brother

Go on brother go on go on

Heaven
    DETS, 8, Solo voice with piano accompaniment
    OWEN, 14, Solo voice with piano accompaniment

Go Round Go Round

Go round go round look at de mornin' star
Deliverance
    PETL, 217, d, Text only
    BALS, 27, d, Melody only

Go Tell It on the Mountain (1)

Go tell it go tell it go tell it on the mountain that Jesus Christ is born
Christmas
Luke 2:6–20^
    AAH, 202, Choral with piano accompaniment and additional historical information
    ALBGH, 28, Solo voice with piano accompaniment
    ALBGL, 28, Solo voice with piano accompaniment
    ALTRH, 30, Solo voice with piano accompaniment
    ALTRL, 30, Solo voice with piano accompaniment
    ALTSH, 46, Solo voice with piano accompaniment
    ALTSL, 46, Solo voice with piano accompaniment
    ANDW, 40, Choral arrangement
    BAP, 82, Choral with piano accompaniment and additional historical information
    BAP1, 95, Choral with piano accompaniment and additional historical information
    BOAT, 53, d, Solo voice with piano accompaniment
    BOCH, 205, Choral with piano accompaniment and additional historical information
    BONI, 3, d, Solo voice with piano accompaniment
    BUCS, 16, Instrumental Ensemble accompaniment
    CALA, 16, Melody only
    CHET, 245, Text only
    CLES, 75, Choral with piano accompaniment and additional historical information
    FRAS, 32, Solo voice with piano accompaniment
    GUIU, 36, Solo voice with piano accompaniment
    HELC, 2, d, Solo voice with piano accompaniment

Go Tell It on the Mountain (2)
When I was a seeker I sought both night and day
Christmas
Luke 2:6–20^

HAY1L, 10, Solo voice with piano accompaniment
PETL, 351, d, Text only
SLA, 14, Choral arrangement
SPAG, 19, d, Solo voice with piano accompaniment and chord symbols
TOBB, 15, Melody only
WALCH, 210, Solo voice with piano accompaniment
WALCL, 210, Solo voice with piano accompaniment
WALSH, 170, Solo voice with piano accompaniment
WALSL, 170, Solo voice with piano accompaniment

God Don't Like It
Well God don't like it
Admonition/Judgment
LOMJO, 28, Melody only
LOMJO2, 28, Melody only

God Got Plenty O' Room — see — Plenty Good Room

God Has Smiled on Me
God has smiled on me He has set me free
Praise
CLES, 196, Choral with piano accompaniment and additional historical information

God Is a God
God is a God God don't never change
Praise
CHET, 246, Text only
CLES, 140, Choral with piano accompaniment and additional historical information
HAIS, 33, Solo voice with piano accompaniment
HAIS, 37, Solo voice with piano accompaniment
HAIS, 41, Solo voice with piano accompaniment
HERB, 21, Text only
PETL, 63, d, Text only
WHAG, 1, Solo voice with piano accompaniment

God Knows It's Time
God knows it's time
Admonition/Judgment
ODUN, 71, Text only; Source includes additional historical information

God Moves on the Water
God moves on the water
Praise
LOMJO, 26, Melody only
LOMJO2, 26, Melody only

God's Amazing Grace
I was but young but I recall
Praise
CLES, 195, Choral with piano accompaniment and additional historical information

God's Going to Set This World on Fire
God's gonna set this world on fire
Faith/Assurance
BOAS, 4, Solo voice with piano accompaniment
COLS, 78, d, Solo voice with piano accompaniment
HAWD, 135, Text only
PETL, 269, d, Text only

God's Going to Straighten Them
We got deacons in de church
Admonition/Judgment
PETL, 268, d, Text only
WORJA, 230, d, Choral unaccompanied with additional historical information

God's Going to Trouble the Water — see — Wade in the Water

God's Going to Wake Up the Dead
Goin' to wake up the dead
Death
ODUN, 75, Text only; Source includes additional historical information

God's Got Plenty of Room — see — Plenty Good Room

Going Away to See My Lord
Goin' away to see ma Savior
Songs of Spiritual Journey
MCIB, 65, d, Melody and additional historical information
PETL, 388, d, Text only

Going Down to Jordan
Halleluyer to the Lam'
Praise
ODUN, 124, d, Text only; Source includes additional historical
information

Going Home — see — I'm Going Home

Going Home in the Chariot
Going home in the chariot in the morning
Admonition/Judgment
HERB, 23, Text only
PETL, 213, d, Text only

Going Lay Down My Life for My Lord
Lord giv' me mer trumpet an' tole me ter blow
Aspiration
ODUN, 91, d, Text only; Source includes additional historical
information

Going Over on the Other Side of Jordan
I'm jes' a-goin' over on de other side of Jordan
Songs of Spiritual Journey
BARO, 5, d, Melody only

Going to Follow
Titty Mary you know I am going to follow
Songs of Spiritual Journey
ALLS, 18, Melody only
PETL, 350, d, Text only

Going to Ride Up in the Chariot

Going to ride up in the chariot

Heaven

2 Kings 2:11–12*

BRON, 10, d, Solo voice with piano accompaniment

GREF, 56, d, Solo voice with piano accompaniment

HAWD, 101, Text only

JOHJB, ii, 121, d, Solo voice with piano accompaniment and additional historical information

PATN, 65, d, Solo voice with piano accompaniment

PETL, 167, d, Text only

PETL, 389, d, Text only

PIKJ, 178, d, Melody only

SANH, 39, Uses Tonic Sol-fa notation

SEWJ, 20, d, Melody only

SEWJC, 20, d, Melody only

WHAG, 11, Solo voice with piano accompaniment

Going to Roll in My Jesus' Arms

Gwine to roll in my Jesus' arms

Rituals of Preparation for Renewal/Regeneration

HALC, 5, d, Choral with piano accompaniment and additional historical information

PETL, 312, d, Text only

WHIF, 32, d, Solo voice with piano accompaniment

Going to Set Down and Rest Awhile

Going to set down and rest a while

Faith/Assurance

CHET, 246, Text only

FISS, 49, d, Solo voice with piano accompaniment and additional historical information

PETL, 65, d, Text only

Going to Shout All Over God's Heaven

I've got a robe you've got a robe all of God's children got a robe

Heaven

Revelation 7:9–10#

ANDW, 17, d, Choral arrangement

BAYF, 2, d, Solo voice with piano accompaniment and chord symbols

BELT, 14, Uses Tonic Sol-fa notation

BOAS, 67, Solo voice with piano accompaniment

BRUT, 30, d, Solo voice with piano accompaniment and additional historical information

BURC1, 10, d, Solo voice with piano accompaniment

BURS, 79, d, Solo voice with piano accompaniment

CALA, 14, Text only

CHAT, 47, Solo voice with piano accompaniment

CLES, 82, Choral with piano accompaniment and additional historical information

CREO, 13, d, Solo voice with piano accompaniment

DETR, 126, d, Choral unaccompanied with additional historical information

FENR, 168, d, Choral unaccompanied with additional historical information

FISS, 41, d, Solo voice with piano accompaniment and additional historical information

FIST, 8, d, Solo voice with piano accompaniment

FREC, 26, d, Solo voice with piano accompaniment

GREF, 28, d, Solo voice with piano accompaniment

GUL, 42, d, Text only

HALC, 58, d, Melody only

HAWD, 44, Text only

HAYMF, 70, d, Solo voice with piano accompaniment and additional historical information

HAYMS, 70, d, Solo voice with piano accompaniment and additional historical information

HERB, 25, d, Text only

JOHJB, i, 71, d, Solo voice with piano accompaniment and additional historical information

JOHRA, 54, d, Solo voice with piano accompaniment

JORS, 48, d, Text only

KENM, 155, d, Solo voice with piano accompaniment and additional historical information

LUEB, 46, Melody, chord symbols, and piano accompaniment

MACS, 41, d, Melody only

MIL3, 35, d, Solo voice with piano accompaniment

PETL, 213, d, Text only

BONR, 148, d, Solo voice with piano accompaniment
DETR, 34, d, Choral unaccompanied with additional historical information
FENC, 44, d, Choral unaccompanied with additional historical information
FENR, 44, d, Choral unaccompanied with additional historical information
PETL, 389, d, Text only

Going Up (2)

If you wanna know where I'm going
Heaven
CLES, 181, d, Choral with piano accompaniment and additional historical information

Going Up (3)

Yes I'm gwine up gwine all the way
Heaven
JOHJB, i, 118, d, Solo voice with piano accompaniment and additional historical information

Gold Band

Going to march away in the gold band
Aspiration
ALLS, 83, Melody only
PETL, 269, d, Text only
SILSP, 44, Solo voice with piano accompaniment

Golden Altar

John saw the holy number sitting on the golden
Faith/Assurance
ALLS, 77, Melody only
PETL, 65, d, Text only

Golden Slippers

Oh my golden slippers am a-laid away
Heaven
SKEG, 24, d, Solo voice with piano accompaniment and chord symbols

SPAG, 44, d, Solo voice with piano accompaniment and chord symbols

Gone Along
My good old auntie's gone along
Death
BARO, 8, d, Melody only

Good Bye
Good bye my brother
Praise
ALLS, 47, Melody only
ALLS, 52, Melody only
PETL, 65, d, Text only
PETL, 169, d, Text only

Good Bye Brothers
Good bye brothers good bye sisters
Faith/Assurance
Acts 20:38*
MAR3, 249, Choral unaccompanied with additional historical information
MARS, 215, Choral unaccompanied with additional historical information
PETL, 66, d, Text only
SANH, 41, Uses Tonic Sol-fa notation

Good Bye City of Babylon
Good bye city o' Babylon
Deliverance
KENMM, 12, d, Melody only

Good Bye Mother
Good bye Mother good bye
Death
LOMJA, 592, Melody only

Good Lord Done Been Here
Adam in the garden Eve disobeyed

Admonition/Judgment
Genesis 3:6; Proverbs 7:5; Revelation 15:2–3+
KENMM, 28, d, Text only; Source includes additional historical information
MCIB, 55, d, Melody and additional historical information
PETL, 66, d, Text only

Good Lord I Done Done — see — Lord I Done Done

Good Lord I Done Good
Good Lord I done good
Songs of Spiritual Journey
PETL, 350, d, Text only

Good Lord Shall I Be the One
Good Lord shall I be de one
Aspiration
CHET, 246, d, Text only
DETR, 32, Melody only
FENR, 123, d, Choral unaccompanied with additional historical information
HALC, 48, d, Choral with piano accompaniment and additional historical information
PETL, 169, d, Text only
PETL, 351, d, Text only

Good Lord When I Die
Good Lord when I die
Heaven
HAWD, 89, Text only
WORJF, 63, d, Text only; Source includes additional historical information

Good Morning Everybody
Good morning everybody
Praise
PETL, 216, d, Text only
WORF, 3, Choral unaccompanied with additional historical information

Good News
Good news good news
Heaven
HAWD, 22, Text only
HERB, 26, d, Text only
PETL, 216, d, Text only

Good News Angels Bring the Tidings
Good news good news angels bring the tidings
Heaven
Luke 2:8–14*
BALS, 10, d, Choral unaccompanied with additional historical information
SANH, 42, Uses Tonic Sol-fa notation

Good News in the Kingdom
Good news in the Kingdom an' I won't die no more
Praise
ANDW, 14, d, Choral arrangement
GUIU, 59, d, Solo voice with piano accompaniment

Good News Member
Good news member
Praise
ALLS, 97, Melody only
PETL, 216, d, Text only

Good News the Chariot's Coming
Good news the chariot's coming
Deliverance
2 Kings 2:11–12; Revelation 7:9, 15:2*
ALTRH, 36, d, Solo voice with piano accompaniment
ALTRL, 36, d, Solo voice with piano accompaniment
ANDW, 15, Choral arrangement
ARMH, 224, d, Choral unaccompanied with additional historical information
BOAS, 29, Solo voice with piano accompaniment
CALA, 15, Melody only
CHET, 247, Text only

CHIA, 18, Melody only

CLES, 124, Choral with piano accompaniment and additional historical information

DETR, 90, d, Choral unaccompanied with additional historical information

FENC, 52, d, Choral unaccompanied with additional historical information

FENR, 52, d, Choral unaccompanied with additional historical information

HAYMF, 79, d, Solo voice with piano accompaniment and additional historical information

HAYMS, 79, d, Solo voice with piano accompaniment and additional historical information

LUEB, 40, d, Melody, chord symbols, and piano accompaniment

MAR3, 282, Choral unaccompanied with additional historical information

MARS, 248, Choral unaccompanied with additional historical information

PETL, 169, d, Text only

SANH, 43, Uses Tonic Sol-fa notation

SKEG, 16, d, Solo voice with piano accompaniment and chord symbols

SLA, 26, d, Choral arrangement

STIT, 79, d, Solo voice with piano accompaniment and additional historical information

WORJF, 49, d, Text only; Source includes additional historical information

WORJF, 49, d, Text only; Source includes additional historical information

Good Old Chariot (1)

In the morning when I rise

Jesus

ODUN, 93, Text only; Source includes additional historical information

Good Old Chariot (2)

Good old chariot swing so low

JOHHT, 74, d, Solo voice with piano accompaniment
JORS, 55, d, Text only
KENMM, 40, d, Text only; Source includes additional historical information
LABC, 22, Solo voice with piano accompaniment
MARS, 150, Choral unaccompanied with additional historical information
MCIB, 107, Melody and additional historical information
ODUN, 113, Text only; Source includes additional historical information
PETL, 170, d, Text only
PIKJ, 190, Choral unaccompanied with additional historical information
SAAT, 1, d, Solo voice with piano accompaniment
SANH, 129, Uses Tonic Sol-fa notation
SEWJC, 36, Choral unaccompanied with additional historical information
SPAG, 11, d, Solo voice with piano accompaniment and chord symbols
WAL14H, 24, Solo voice with piano accompaniment
WAL15H, 24, Solo voice with piano accompaniment
WAL15L, 24, Solo voice with piano accompaniment
WAL25H, 12, Solo voice with piano accompaniment
WAL25L, 12, Solo voice with piano accompaniment
WALSH, 174, d, Solo voice with piano accompaniment
WALSL, 174, d, Solo voice with piano accompaniment
WIES, 194, d, Solo voice with piano accompaniment

Gospel Train — see also — Get On Board Little Children

Got a Home At Last
Good Lord in dat Heab'm
Heaven
JESM, 74, d, Solo voice with piano accompaniment and additional historical information

Got Glory and Honor
Got glory an' honor praise Jesus

Praise
KENMM, 73, d, Solo voice with piano accompaniment and additional historical information

Got My Letter
Got me letter
Rituals of Preparation for Renewal/Regeneration
PETL, 313, d, Text only
WORJA, 224, Choral unaccompanied with additional historical information

Got Religion All Around the World — see — Christians Hold Up Your Heads

Got to Go to Judgment
Got to go to judgememt stand your trial
Admonition/Judgment
PETL, 269, d, Text only

Got to Take the Children out of Pharaoh's Hand
Oh Lawd trouble een duh lan'
Deliverance
GUL, 34, d, Text only
HUTS, 37, d, Melody and additional historical information

Gotta Meet the Judgment
All Uh do gottuh meet duh jedgement
Admonition/Judgment
GUL, 33, d, Text only

Grace Before Meat
Thou art great and Thou art good
Praise
DETR, 179, Choral unaccompanied with additional historical information
FENR, 143, Choral unaccompanied with additional historical information
MAR3, 245, Choral unaccompanied with additional historical information

MARS, 211, Choral unaccompanied with additional historical information

Grade Song

Well I tole my captain my feet wus cold
Work Songs
ODUN, 252, Text only; Source includes additional historical information

Grave Sinking Down

It was sad when the grave sinking down
Death
GUL, 35, d, Text only
HUTS, 39, d, Melody and additional historical information

Graveyard

Who is going to lay this body
Death
ALLS, 15, Melody only
PETL, 11, d, Text only

Great Big Stars

Great big stars 'way up yonder
Heaven
BRYA, 45, Melody, chord symbols, and additional historical information

Great Camp Meeting — see — Walk Together Children

Great Day

Great day the righteous marching
Praise
Psalm 51:18#
BOAS, 36, Solo voice with piano accompaniment
BRUT, 44, d, Solo voice with piano accompaniment and additional historical information
CALA, 8, Text only
CHET, 247, Text only
CLES, 142, Choral with piano accompaniment and additional historical information

HERB, 28, Text only

JOHHT, 14, d, Solo voice with piano accompaniment

JOHJB, ii, 56, d, Solo voice with piano accompaniment and additional historical information

LIF, 5, Choral with piano accompaniment and additional historical information

MIL3, 38, Solo voice with piano accompaniment

NAA, 16, Melody and chord symbols

NEW, 487, Choral with piano accompaniment and additional historical information

OKS1, 27, Solo voice with piano accompaniment

PATN, 53, d, Solo voice with piano accompaniment

PETL, 119, d, Text only

SCHG, 1, Solo voice with piano accompaniment

SIX, 34, Solo voice with piano accompaniment

SPAG, 20, d, Solo voice with piano accompaniment and chord symbols

STIT, 53, d, Solo voice with piano accompaniment and additional historical information

WARE, 46, d, Solo voice with piano accompaniment and additional historical information

Great Day for Me

Great day for me great day for me I am so happy

Praise

COUNS, 17, Solo voice with piano accompaniment and additional historical information

Great Gittin' Up Mornin' — see — In That Great Getting Up Morning

Great Judgment Day

Lord I want to go to Heaven fer to stan'my trials

Admonition/Judgment

ODUN, 99, Text only; Source includes additional historical information

Green Trees

Green trees rocky road

Work Songs

ANDW, 44, Choral arrangement

Grey Goose

Well one Monday mornin'
Work Songs
ANDW, 45, d, Melody only

Guide My Feet

Guide my feet while I run this race
Songs of Spiritual Journey
Luke 1:78–79^
AAH, 131, Choral with piano accompaniment and additional historical information
CALA, 9, Text only
PATN, 35, d, Solo voice with piano accompaniment
PETL, 172, d, Text only

Guide My Head — see — Guide My Feet

Hail Hail

Hail hail I'll tell you when I get over
Praise
MARS, 261, Choral unaccompanied with additional historical information
MAR3, 295, Choral unaccompanied with additional historical information

Hail Hail Hail

Children hail hail hail I'm going to join the saints above
Praise
ARMH, 177, d, Choral unaccompanied with additional historical information
BRYI, 23, d, Melody only
DETR, 185, Choral unaccompanied with additional historical information
FENC, 4, Choral unaccompanied with additional historical information
FENR, 5, Choral unaccompanied with additional historical information
PETL, 218, d, Text only

Hail John's Army Bend Down and Died
Hail John's army ben' down an' die
Jesus
MCIB, 99, Melody and additional historical information
PETL, 172, d, Text only

Hail Mary
I want some valiant soldier here
Suffering
ALLS, 45, Melody only
PETL, 119, d, Text only

Hail Sinners Hail-lo
You will wish you had religion in dat army by and by
Admonition/Judgment
LOGR, 16, Melody only

Hail the Crown
Some have crippled and some come lame
Praise
FISS, 68, d, Solo voice with piano accompaniment and additional
historical information
KREA, 158, d, Choral with piano accompaniment and additional
historical information
PETL, 351, d, Text only

Hail the King of Babylon
Hail de King of Babylon
Praise
JOHHG, 34, d, Solo voice with piano accompaniment
JOHHH, 45, d, Solo voice with piano accompaniment

Half Has Never Been Told
Truth that frees is from above
Faith/Assurance
KENMM, 37, d, Text only; Source includes additional historical
information

Hallelu

Hallelu

Praise

WORJA, 225, Choral unaccompanied with additional historical information

Hallelu Hallelu (1)

One day as another hallelu hallelu

Praise

ALLS, 50, Melody only

PETL, 218, d, Text only

Hallelu Hallelu (2)

Hallelu' hallelu' hallelu' hallelujah praise ye the Lord!

Praise

LUEB, 42, d, Melody, chord symbols, and piano accompaniment

Halleluiah to the Lamb

Halleluiah to de Lamb ob Gawd

Praise

MCIB, 110, d, Melody and additional historical information

Hallelujah (1)

Hallelujah hallelujah I do belong to the band

Praise

HERB, 28, Text only

PETL, 218, d, Text only

WORF, 47, Choral unaccompanied with additional historical information

Hallelujah (2)

Hallelujah and a hallelujah Lord I been down into the sea

Praise

JOHHG, 8, Solo voice with piano accompaniment

JOHHH, 16, d, Solo voice with piano accompaniment

JOHJB, i, 172, d, Solo voice with piano accompaniment and additional historical information

PETL, 313, d, Text only

Hallelujah King Jesus
Hallelujah King Jesus
Praise
JOHHG, 39, Solo voice with piano accompaniment
JOHHH, 47, d, Solo voice with piano accompaniment

Hallelujah to the Lamb
Hallelujah to the Lamb
Praise
PETL, 270, d, Text only

Hammer Keeps Ringing
Hammer keeps ringing
Death
PETL, 12, d, Text only

Hammering
Those cruel people those cruel people
Suffering
CHET, 247, Text only
PETL, 12, d, Text only

Hammering Judgment
Don't you hear God talking
Admonition/Judgment
HALC, 60, Melody only
PETL, 270, d, Text only

Hand Me Down My Silver Trumpet
Han' me down Yo' silvah trumpet
Songs of Spiritual Journey
ANDW, 47, d, Choral arrangement
BONF, 16, d, Solo voice with piano accompaniment and additional
historical information
BONF, 22, d, Solo voice with piano accompaniment and additional
historical information
GUL, 37, d, Text only
HAWD, 56, Text only

CHET, 247, Text only

CLES, 107, Choral with piano accompaniment and additional historical information

DETR, 222, Choral unaccompanied with additional historical information

FENC, 41, Choral unaccompanied with additional historical information

FENR, 41, Choral unaccompanied with additional historical information

FREC, 24, Solo voice with piano accompaniment

HAWD, 30, Text only

HERB, 29, Text only

LOMJA, 600, Melody only

LUEB, 85, Melody, chord symbols, and piano accompaniment

MARS, 207, Choral unaccompanied with additional historical information

PETL, 12, d, Text only

SILSP, 24, Solo voice with piano accompaniment

SNYS, 7, d, Solo voice with piano accompaniment

Hard Trials (2)

Ain't dat hard trials tribulation very great

Suffering

MCIB, 105, Melody and additional historical information

PETL, 352, d, Text only

Hard Trials (3)

Been a lis'nin' all de night long

Suffering

BURS, 157, d, Solo voice with piano accompaniment

DANF, 36, Melody only

Has Anybody Here Seen My Lord

Has anybody here seen my Jesus

Deliverance

FISS, 63, d, Solo voice with piano accompaniment and additional historical information

PETL, 173, d, Text only

Have You Got Good Religion
Have you got religion cert'nly Lord
Songs of Spiritual Journey
CHET, 248, Text only
JACL, 120, Choral with piano accompaniment and additional historical information
LUEB, 44, Melody, chord symbols, and piano accompaniment

Have You Seen the Vessel
Hab' Ile een duh wessel 'en duh bride groom come
Jesus
GUL, 36, d, Text only

He Arose
They crucified my Savior and nailed Him to the cross
Easter
John 20:1, 11; Matthew 27:59, 28:2*
AAH, 280, Choral with piano accompaniment and additional historical information
BOAS, 56, Solo voice with piano accompaniment
CHET, 248, Text only
JACL, 40, Choral with piano accompaniment and additional historical information
SIX, 35, Solo voice with piano accompaniment
WARE, 49, d, Solo voice with piano accompaniment and additional historical information

He Does Believe
E dat belieb' 'e dat belieb'
Faith/Assurance
GUL, 38, d, Text only

He Is King of Kings
He is King of kings He is Lord of lords
Jesus
John 1:14#
CALA, 9, Text only
CHET, 248, Text only

DETR, 146, Choral unaccompanied with additional historical information

DETR, 151, Choral unaccompanied with additional historical information

FENC, 96, Choral unaccompanied with additional historical information

FENR, 99, Choral unaccompanied with additional historical information

HERB, 30, Text only

JACL, 79, Choral with piano accompaniment and additional historical information

PETL, 220, d, Text only

SANH, 147, Uses Tonic Sol-fa notation

WORJA, 218, Choral unaccompanied with additional historical information

WORJF, 68, d, Text only; Source includes additional historical information

He Is Waiting

Why does you tarry sinner

Admonition/Judgment

ODUN, 83, Text only; Source includes additional historical information

He Knows Just How Much We Can Bear

We are our Heavenly Father's children

Suffering

CLES, 202, Choral with piano accompaniment and additional historical information

He Never Said a Mumbling Word (1)

They crucified my Lord and He never said mumbalin' word

Easter

Matthew 27:35; John 19:23–34#

ANDM, 71, d, Solo voice with piano accompaniment

BONR, 152, d, Solo voice with piano accompaniment

BOYFM, 42, d, Solo voice with piano accompaniment

CALA, 3, Text only

CALA, 18, d, Melody only

CHAT, 39, d, Solo voice with piano accompaniment

CHET, 248, d, Text only

CLES, 101, d, Choral with piano accompaniment and additional historical information

DETD2, 21, d, Choral unaccompanied with additional historical information

GREF, 36, d, Solo voice with piano accompaniment

GUIU, 42, Solo voice with piano accompaniment

JACL, 34, Choral with piano accompaniment and additional historical information

JOHHH, 52, d, Solo voice with piano accompaniment

JOHJB, i, 174, d, Solo voice with piano accompaniment and additional historical information

KENM, 126, d, Solo voice with piano accompaniment and additional historical information

LIF, 33, d, Choral with piano accompaniment and additional historical information

LOMJA, 587, Melody only

LOMJF, 448, d, Solo voice with piano accompaniment and additional historical information

PARS, 165, d, Text only; Source includes additional historical information

RAIJ, 80, d, Solo voice with piano accompaniment

RUPM, 73, Solo voice with piano accompaniment

SPAG, 21, d, Solo voice with piano accompaniment and chord symbols

UNI, 291, d, Melody only

WIES, 191, Solo voice with piano accompaniment

He Never Said a Mumbling Word (2)

Wasn't it a pitty an' a shame

Easter

Matthew 27:35; John 19:23–34#

BOAS, 12, Solo voice with piano accompaniment

BOAT, 25, d, Solo voice with piano accompaniment

FISS, 1, d, Solo voice with piano accompaniment and additional historical information

HAYMF, 121, d, Solo voice with piano accompaniment and additional historical information

HAYMS, 121, d, Solo voice with piano accompaniment and additional historical information
HOGDH, 6, d, Solo voice with piano accompaniment and additional historical information
HOGDL, 6, d, Solo voice with piano accompaniment and additional historical information

He Never Said a Mumbling Word (3)

They led Him to Pilate's bar not a word not a word not a word not a word
Easter
Matthew 27:35; John 19:23–34#
HERB, 31, d, Text only
PETL, 15, d, Text only

He Raised Poor Lazarus

He raise a poor Lazarus
Jesus
John 11:42–43; Matthew 9:35+
CHET, 267, Text only
DETR, 66, Choral unaccompanied with additional historical information
FENR, 116, Choral unaccompanied with additional historical information
PETL, 69, d, Text only

He Rose from the Dead (1)

They crucified my Savior and nailed Him to the cross
Easter
Mark 1:15, 16:8*
CLES, 168, Choral with piano accompaniment and additional historical information
UNI, 316, Melody only

He Rose from the Dead (2)

He rose He rose He rose
Easter
Mark 1:15, 16:8*
GUL, 22, d, Text only
MARS, 209, Choral unaccompanied with additional historical information

PETL, 221, d, Text only
SANH, 45, Uses Tonic Sol-fa notation

He'll Understand and Say Well Done

If when you give the best of your service
Heaven
CLES, 178, Choral with piano accompaniment and additional historical information
NAA, 39, Melody and chord symbols

He's a Mighty Good Leader

He's a mighty good leader
Jesus
PETL, 69, d, Text only
WORJA, 231, Choral unaccompanied with additional historical information

He's Got His Eyes on Me

He's got His eyes on me
Admonition/Judgment
HAWD, 51, Text only

He's Got His Eyes on You

He's got His eyes on you
Admonition/Judgment
BOAS, 60, Solo voice with piano accompaniment
HERB, 31, Text only
PETL, 272, d, Text only

He's Got the Whole World in His Hands

He's got the whole world in His hands
Praise
Genesis 1:1; Job 12:10; Psalm 95:4#
AAH, 150, Choral with piano accompaniment and additional historical information
AFR, 32, Choral arrangement
ANDW, 36, Melody only
APPA, 165, Solo voice with piano accompaniment
BOAS, 68, Solo voice with piano accompaniment

He's Just the Same Today

When Moses an' his soldiers fum Egypt's lan'

Songs of Spiritual Journey

Daniel 6:16, 22; Exodus 12:51, 14:10, 21–22+

BURS, 106, d, Solo voice with piano accompaniment

CHAT, 40, d, Solo voice with piano accompaniment

CHET, 249, d, Text only

HALC, 30, d, Choral with piano accompaniment and additional historical information

JOHJB, i, 80, d, Solo voice with piano accompaniment and additional historical information

LABC, 44, Solo voice with piano accompaniment

PETL, 70, d, Text only

WALSH, 161, d, Solo voice with piano accompaniment

WALSL, 161, d, Solo voice with piano accompaniment

He's the Lily of the Valley

He's the lily of the valley

Jesus

Ephesians 6:15; Habakkuk 3:8; Revelation 19:11–16; Romans 10:15*

CHET, 249, Text only

DETR, 145, Choral unaccompanied with additional historical information

FISS, 74, d, Solo voice with piano accompaniment and additional historical information

GREF, 23, d, Solo voice with piano accompaniment

GRIN, 96, Melody only

HAWD, 10, Text only

MARS, 163, Choral unaccompanied with additional historical information

PETL, 70, d, Text only

PETL, 71, d, Text only

PIKJ, 203, Choral unaccompanied with additional historical information

SANH, 47, Uses Tonic Sol-fa notation

SEWJC, 48, Choral unaccompanied with additional historical information

WIES, 206, d, Solo voice with piano accompaniment

He's the Lord of Lords
He is the Lord of lords
Jesus
Genesis 32:26; Acts 16:25; Revelation 19:16, 1:8*
FENR, 96, Choral unaccompanied with additional historical information
MARS, 148, Choral unaccompanied with additional historical information
PETL, 313, d, Text only
PIKJ, 188, Choral unaccompanied with additional historical information
SEWJC, 33, Choral unaccompanied with additional historical information

Heal Me Jesus
Lord I'm sick an' I want to be healed
Aspiration
ODUN, 139, Text only; Source includes additional historical information

Healing Waters
Healin' waters done move
Rituals of Preparation for Renewal/Regeneration
LOMJA, 581, d, Melody only

Hear Gabriel Blow in That Morn
Didn't yo know pilgrim
Admonition/Judgment
HALC, 45, d, Melody only
PETL, 271, d, Text only

Hear Me Praying
Lord oh hear me praying
Prayer
HERB, 62, Text only
JOHJB, ii, 166, d, Solo voice with piano accompaniment and additional historical information
PETL, 352, d, Text only

PETL, 366, d, Text only

SIX, 10, Solo voice with piano accompaniment

Hear the Angels Singing

Sing all de way my Lord hear de angels singin'

Heaven

ARMH, 246, d, Choral unaccompanied with additional historical information

CHET, 249, d, Text only

DETR, 206, d, Choral unaccompanied with additional historical information

FENC, 74, d, Choral unaccompanied with additional historical information

FENR, 74, d, Choral unaccompanied with additional historical information

MAR3, 307, d, Choral unaccompanied with additional historical information

PETL, 219, d, Text only

Hear the Lamb's Crying

You hear the lamb's a crying

Suffering

John 21:15–17*

ARMH, 210, d, Choral unaccompanied with additional historical information

BALS, 30, d, Melody only

BOAT, 141, d, Solo voice with piano accompaniment

BRON, 8, d, Solo voice with piano accompaniment

BURS, 167, d, Solo voice with piano accompaniment

CHET, 285, d, Text only

CLES, 128, d, Choral with piano accompaniment and additional historical information

DETR, 224, d, Choral unaccompanied with additional historical information

FENC, 38, d, Choral unaccompanied with additional historical information

FENR, 38, d, Choral unaccompanied with additional historical information

HAYMF, 110, d, Solo voice with piano accompaniment and additional historical information

HAYMS, 110, d, Solo voice with piano accompaniment and additional historical information
HERB, 97, d, Text only
JONF, 359, Melody only
PETL, 9, d, Text only
PETL, 13, d, Text only
SANH, 149, d, Uses Tonic Sol-fa notation

Heave Away
Heave away heave away
Work Songs
ALLS, 61, Melody only

Heave-A-Hora
Hey slip de him slip slide him
Work Songs
ODUN, 265, Text only; Source includes additional historical information

Heaven (1)
Well there are sinners here and sinners there
Heaven
ODUN, 98, Text only; Source includes additional historical information

Heaven (2)
I got a-shoes you got a-shoes
Heaven
SIX, 55, d, Solo voice with piano accompaniment

Heaven Heaven — see — Going to Shout All Over God's Heaven

Heaven Bell Ring
My Lord my Lord what shall I do
Admonition/Judgment
ALLS, 20, d, Melody only
PETL, 271, d, Text only

Heaven Bells
Mother I believe

Heaven
  ALLS, 79, Melody only
  PETL, 272, d, Text only

Heaven Bells Ringing and I'm Going Home
Heav'n bells a-ringin' and I'm a-goin' home
  Heaven
    BARO, 20, d, Melody only

Heaven Bells Ringing in My Soul
Nobody knows who I am
  Heaven
    BARO, 10, d, Melody only
    FISS, 70, d, Solo voice with piano accompaniment and additional
      historical information
    PETL, 14, d, Text only

Heaven Bound Light of Mine
This little light of mine I'm gonna let it shine
  Songs of Spiritual Journey
    BECK, 25, d, Solo voice with piano accompaniment
    HAY1H, 25, Solo voice with piano accompaniment

Heaven Is a Beautiful Place (1)
Heaven is a beautiful place I believe
  Heaven
    BALS, 16, d, Choral unaccompanied with additional historical
      information
    CARS, 2, Solo voice with piano accompaniment
    PETL, 68, d, Text only

Heaven Is a Beautiful Place (2)
Heaven is a beautiful place I know
  Heaven
    GRIN, 22, Melody only
    PETL, 68, d, Text only

Heaven Is Going to Be My Home
I am trampin' I am trampin'

Heaven
> BALS, 55, d, Choral unaccompanied with additional historical information
> PETL, 353, d, Text only

Heaven Is Shining
Heaven is shining run moaner run Heaven is shining
> Heaven
>> ARMH, 219, d, Choral unaccompanied with additional historical information
>> DETR, 94, d, Choral unaccompanied with additional historical information
>> FENC, 47, d, Choral unaccompanied with additional historical information
>> FENR, 47, d, Choral unaccompanied with additional historical information
>> MCIB, 109, d, Melody and additional historical information
>> PETL, 220, d, Text only
>> PETL, 238, d, Text only

Heaven Is So High
Heaven is so high you can't get over it
> Heaven
>> LUEB, 48, Melody, chord symbols, and piano accompaniment

Heaven-Bound Soldier
Hold out your light you Heaven-bound soldier
> Songs of Spiritual Journey
>> HERB, 29, Text only
>> JOHJB, i, 54, d, Solo voice with piano accompaniment and additional historical information
>> PETL, 353, d, Text only

Heavy Burdens — see — Trying to Get Home

Hell and Heaven
I been 'buked an' I been scorned
> Satan
>> LOMJA, 588, Melody only

Here's One

Talk about a child who do love Jesus here's one here's one
Aspiration
ALBGH, 14, Solo voice with piano accompaniment
ALBGL, 14, Solo voice with piano accompaniment
LABC, 4, Solo voice with piano accompaniment
SNES, 1, Solo voice with piano accompaniment

Hide Me

When this world is all on fire
Admonition/Judgment
GRIN, 66, d, Melody only
PETL, 273, d, Text only

Hint to the Wise

Don't you remember one mornin'
Work Songs
ODUN, 257, Text only; Source includes additional historical
information

His Eye Is on the Sparrow

Why should I feel discouraged
Faith/Assurance
JACL, 3, Choral with piano accompaniment and additional his-
torical information

His Love Comes Trickling Down

When Jesus died upon the cross
Jesus
LOGR, 31, d, Melody only

His Name So Sweet

Lawd I jes come from de fountain
Jesus
BOAT, 64, d, Solo voice with piano accompaniment
CALA, 10, Text only
CHET, 250, Text only
CLES, 90, Choral with piano accompaniment and additional
historical information
JOHHH, 63, d, Solo voice with piano accompaniment

LIF, 127, Choral with piano accompaniment and additional historical information

WARE, 52, d, Solo voice with piano accompaniment and additional historical information

Ho Every One That Thirsts

Ho everyone that thirsts the King of Heav'n His table spreads

Deliverance

DETD4, 16, Choral unaccompanied with additional historical information

MCKF, 5, Solo voice with piano accompaniment

Ho-Ho

Ain't it dinner ho ho

Work Songs

ODUN, 261, Text only; Source includes additional historical information

Hold On (1)

Keep your hand on-a that plow hold on

Work Songs

CALA, 10, Text only

CHET, 250, Text only

CLES, 86, Choral with piano accompaniment and additional historical information

HERB, 32, Text only

PETL, 173, d, Text only

WARE, 54, d, Solo voice with piano accompaniment and additional historical information

Hold On (2)

Noah let me come in

Work Songs

BONI, 12, d, Solo voice with piano accompaniment

NILS, 8, d, Solo voice with piano accompaniment and additional historical information

Hold Out

Your religion never make you shame

Faith/Assurance

BALS, 66, d, Choral unaccompanied with additional historical information

PETL, 120, d, Text only

Hold Out to the End (1)

I'm going to hold out to the end

Faith/Assurance

GREF, 50, d, Solo voice with piano accompaniment

MCIB, 112, d, Melody and additional historical information

PETL, 120, d, Text only

WORF, 27, Choral unaccompanied with additional historical information

Hold Out to the End (2)

All them Mount Zion member

Faith/Assurance

ALLS, 57, Melody only

PETL, 120, d, Text only

Hold Out Your Light

Hold out your light you Heaven bound soldier

Heaven

GREF, 32, d, Solo voice with piano accompaniment

GUL, 57, d, Text only

HALC, 37, d, Choral with piano accompaniment and additional historical information

MCLS, 54, Solo voice with piano accompaniment

PETL, 390, d, Text only

Hold the Light

Hol' de light angels lookin' at me

Faith/Assurance

JOHHH, 132, d, Solo voice with piano accompaniment

Hold the Wind Don't Let It Blow

Hold the wind hold the wind

Songs of Spiritual Journey

BONR, 158, d, Solo voice with piano accompaniment

JOHJB, ii, 178, d, Solo voice with piano accompaniment and additional historical information
LOMAF, 474, Melody, chord symbols, and additional historical information
PETL, 121, d, Text only

Hold Your Light

What make old Satan to follow me
Songs of Spiritual Journey
ALLS, 10, Melody only
PETL, 121, d, Text only

Holy Baby

Children go and I will send thee
Faith/Assurance
LOMAF, 482, Melody, chord symbols, and additional historical information

Holy Bible

Holy Bible Holy Bible book divine
Suffering
PETL, 16, d, Text only
WORF, 6, Choral unaccompanied with additional historical information

Holy Holy You Promised to Answer Prayer

Holy Holy You promised to answer prayer
Prayer
BALS, 14, d, Choral unaccompanied with additional historical information
DITT, 8, Choral arrangement
PETL, 16, d, Text only

Holy Is My God

Holy is my God
Rituals of Preparation for Renewal/Regeneration
HALC, 44, Choral with piano accompaniment and additional historical information
PETL, 314, d, Text only

Holy Lord — see — Oh Holy Lord

Holy Savior — see — Oh Holy Savior

Home in That Rock — see — I Got a Home in That Rock

Home on the Rock
One ob dese mawnin' at duh risin' ob duh sun
Deliverance
HUTS, 43, d, Melody and additional historical information

Honor Honor
King Jesus lit the candle by de water side
Jesus
CHET, 250, Text only
JOHHH, 68, d, Solo voice with piano accompaniment
JOHHH, 73, d, Solo voice with piano accompaniment

Hope I Join the Band
Sinner goin' to sing 'roun'
Faith/Assurance
MCIB, 117, d, Melody and additional historical information
PETL, 71, d, Text only

Hosannah
Hosannah in the highest blessed is He that cometh in the name of
the Lord
Deliverance
LOYS, 36, d, Solo voice with piano accompaniment

House That's Built Without Hands
I want a house what's built without hands
Faith/Assurance
MCIB, 114, d, Melody and additional historical information
PETL, 72, d, Text only

How Can I Pray
How can I pray
Prayer

Luke 6:12; Psalms 38:4, 42:5*
    BALS, 18, d, Choral unaccompanied with additional historical information
    PETL, 314, d, Text only
    SANH, 48, Uses Tonic Sol-fa notation

How I Got Over
How I got over how I got over
    Praise
        CLES, 188, Choral with piano accompaniment and additional historical information

How Long
When de clouds hang heavy an' it look like rain
    Death
        CHET, 250, Text only
        KENM, 93, d, Solo voice with piano accompaniment and additional historical information
        PETL, 16, d, Text only

How Long Has the Train Been Gone
How long de train been gone
    Deliverance
        BALS, 12, d, Choral unaccompanied with additional historical information
        JOHHT, 17, d, Solo voice with piano accompaniment
        PETL, 174, d, Text only
        WHIF, 54, d, Solo voice with piano accompaniment

How Long Watchman
My Lawd done jes' like 'e said how long watch-e-man how long
    Work Songs
    Genesis 6:14–22, 7:12, 9:13–14; Jonah 1:17+
        BARO, 36, d, Melody only
        GUL, 41, d, Text only

How You Do Believer
How you do believer how you do today

Songs of Spiritual Journey
BALS, 75, d, Choral unaccompanied with additional historical information
PETL, 390, d, Text only

Howdy Howdy
An' a howdy howdy brother
Praise
BAR, 4, Melody only
DANF, 40, Melody only

Humble
Humble humble humble
Aspiration
PETL, 315, d, Text only

Humble Yourself
Live humble humble Lord
Praise
HAWD, 33, Text only

Humble Yourself the Bell Done Ring
Live a-humble humble humble yourselves the bell's done rung
Praise
CALA, 20, Text only
HERB, 33, Text only
JOHJB, ii, 183, d, Solo voice with piano accompaniment and additional historical information
MAR3, 301, Choral unaccompanied with additional historical information
PETL, 274, d, Text only

Hunting for a City
I am hunting for a city
Faith/Assurance
ALLS, 18, Melody only
PETL, 174, d, Text only

Hunting for the Lord
Hunt until you find Him

Faith/Assurance
>ALLS, 13, Melody only
>PETL, 122, d, Text only

Hush Hush Amen — see — Hush Somebody's Calling My Name

Hush Hush Somebody's Calling My Name — see — Hush Somebody's Calling My Name

Hush Somebody's Calling My Name
Hush hush somebody's callin' mah name
Death
Isaiah 43:1, 7; 1 Samuel 3:1–10*
>AAH, 556, d, Choral with piano accompaniment and additional historical information
>BOAS, 64, d, Solo voice with piano accompaniment
>CALA, 11, d, Text only
>CHET, 250, d, Text only
>CLES, 100, d, Choral with piano accompaniment and additional historical information
>GUIU, 14, Solo voice with piano accompaniment
>HERB, 33, Text only
>JOHRR, 46, d, Solo voice with piano accompaniment and additional historical information
>LIF, 128, d, Choral with piano accompaniment and additional historical information
>LOYS, 11, d, Solo voice with piano accompaniment
>PETL, 292, d, Text only
>SANH, 49, Uses Tonic Sol-fa notation
>SIX, 4, Solo voice with piano accompaniment

Hymn to Parnassus
You are not higher than your lowest thought
Admonition/Judgment
>DETS, 10, Solo voice with piano accompaniment

Hypocrite and the Concubine
Hypocrite and the concubine
Jesus
>PETL, 221, d, Text only

I Ain't Going to Die No More
Ain't I glad oh ain't I glad
Praise
Revelations 21:4*
MARS, 171, Choral unaccompanied with additional historical information
PETL, 221, d, Text only
PIKJ, 211, Melody only
SANH, 89, Uses Tonic Sol-fa notation
SEWJC, 57, Melody only

I Ain't Going to Grieve My Lord No More
I in't going to grief my Lord no mo'
Deliverance
BALS, 64, d, Choral unaccompanied with additional historical information
DITT, 14, d, Choral arrangement
PETL, 353, d, Text only

I Ain't Going to Study War No More (1)
Going to lay down my sword and shield
Aspiration
BRYI, 32, d, Melody only
CALA, 27, Text only
CHET, 276, Text only
CLES, 138, Choral with piano accompaniment and additional historical information
DETD3, 29, Choral unaccompanied with additional historical information
HAWD, 145, Text only
PETL, 252, d, Text only
TOBB, 22, Melody only

I Ain't Going to Study War No More (2)
Going to lay down my burden
Aspiration
ANDW, 37, Choral arrangement
BURS, 68, d, Solo voice with piano accompaniment
CHAT, 12, d, Solo voice with piano accompaniment

Death

    BALS, 68, d, Choral unaccompanied with additional historical information

    PETL, 72, d, Text only

I Am Seeking for a City

I am seeking for a city hallelujah

Aspiration

Hebrews 11:16*

    ARMH, 228, d, Choral unaccompanied with additional historical information

    BAYF, 26, d, Solo voice with piano accompaniment and chord symbols

    BOAS, 73, Solo voice with piano accompaniment

    BURS, 129, d, Solo voice with piano accompaniment

    CALA, 21, Text only

    CHET, 251, Text only

    CHIA, 26, Melody only

    CLES, 175, Choral with piano accompaniment and additional historical information

    DETD2, 17, Choral unaccompanied with additional historical information

    DETR, 36, d, Choral unaccompanied with additional historical information

    FENC, 56, Choral unaccompanied with additional historical information

    FENR, 56, Choral unaccompanied with additional historical information

    FREC, 28, Solo voice with piano accompaniment

    HAIS, 4, d, Solo voice with piano accompaniment

    HAIS, 9, d, Solo voice with piano accompaniment

    HAIS, 14, d, Solo voice with piano accompaniment

    HAWD, 113, Text only

    JOHHG, 28, Solo voice with piano accompaniment

    JOHHH, 36, d, Solo voice with piano accompaniment

    MCIS, 21, Solo voice with piano accompaniment

    PETL, 123, d, Text only

    SANH, 51, Uses Tonic Sol-fa notation

SILSP, 30, d, Solo voice with piano accompaniment
WALSH, 178, d, Solo voice with piano accompaniment
WALSL, 178, Solo voice with piano accompaniment

I Am the Light of the World
Hallelujah good Lord
Praise
ODUN, 64, d, Text only; Source includes additional historical information

I Am the True Vine
I am the true vine
Praise
PETL, 315, d, Text only

I Am the Truth and the Light
Laz'reth is dead oh bless Gawd
Praise
MCIB, 120, d, Melody and additional historical information
PETL, 222, d, Text only

I and Satan Had a Race
I and Satan had a race
Satan
ALLS, 40, Melody only
PETL, 122, d, Text only

I Believe I'll Go Back Home
I believe I'll go back home
Rituals of Preparation for Renewal/Regeneration
GRIN, 36, Melody only
HERB, 34, Text only
PETL, 316, d, Text only

I Believe This Is Jesus
I believe this is Jesus
Jesus
PETL, 72, d, Text only

I Can't Stay Behind (2)
>I can't stay behind the roses bloom
>>Heaven
>>>PETL, 175, d, Text only

I Cannot Stay Here by Myself
>My mother and my father both are dead
>>Suffering
>>>ODUN, 115, Text only; Source includes additional historical information

I Come This Night
>I come this night for to sing and pray
>>Songs of Spiritual Journey
>>John 15:18–19; 1 John 3:13*
>>>SANH, 53, Uses Tonic Sol-fa notation

I Couldn't Hear Nobody Pray
>And I couldn't hear nobody pray
>>Prayer
>>Joshua 3:1–17; Psalm 23:4*
>>>AAH, 487, Choral with piano accompaniment and additional historical information
>>>ANDW, 9, Choral arrangement
>>>BAYF, 25, d, Solo voice with piano accompaniment and chord symbols
>>>BOAS, 32, Solo voice with piano accompaniment
>>>BRUS, 15, d, Solo voice with piano accompaniment
>>>BUR2H, 12, d, Solo voice with piano accompaniment
>>>BUR2L, 12, d, Solo voice with piano accompaniment
>>>BURA, 30, d, Solo voice with piano accompaniment
>>>BURS, 83, d, Solo voice with piano accompaniment
>>>CALA, 12, Text only
>>>CHAT, 42, Solo voice with piano accompaniment
>>>CHET, 252, Text only
>>>CLES, 78, Choral with piano accompaniment and additional historical information
>>>DETR, 202, Choral unaccompanied with additional historical information

FENR, 160, Choral unaccompanied with additional historical information

GREF, 44, Solo voice with piano accompaniment

GUL, 8, d, Text only

HAWD, 34, Text only

HERB, 34, Text only

JACL, 54, Choral with piano accompaniment and additional historical information

JOHHT, 30, d, Solo voice with piano accompaniment

JOHJB, i, 89, d, Solo voice with piano accompaniment and additional historical information

JOHRA, 46, Solo voice with piano accompaniment

LIF, 171, Choral with piano accompaniment and additional historical information

LOMAF, 473, Melody, chord symbols, and additional historical information

LUEB, 10, Melody, chord symbols, and piano accompaniment

MIL3, 28, Solo voice with piano accompaniment

OKS1, 19, d, Solo voice with piano accompaniment

PAYN, 3, Solo voice with piano accompaniment

PETL, 17, d, Text only

SANH, 22, Uses Tonic Sol-fa notation

SCHG, 5, Solo voice with piano accompaniment

SIX, 15, Solo voice with piano accompaniment

SLA, 12, Choral arrangement

SNYS, 20, d, Solo voice with piano accompaniment

WALSH, 150, Solo voice with piano accompaniment

WALSL, 150, d, Solo voice with piano accompaniment

WIES, 193, Solo voice with piano accompaniment

WORJF, 24, d, Text only; Source includes additional historical information

WORJF, 51, d, Text only; Source includes additional historical information

I Do Know God Don't Lie

I do know God don't lie

Faith/Assurance

BALS, 72, d, Melody only

PETL, 73, d, Text only

I Do Love the Lamb
What makes my sister shout so bold
Praise
LOGR, 15, d, Melody only

I Don't Care for Riches
I don't care for riches
Heaven
ODUN, 108, Text only; Source includes additional historical information

I Don't Care What the World May Do
Hallelujah glory hallelujah truly I'm going
Praise
CLES, 176, Choral with piano accompaniment and additional historical information on the spiritual

I Don't Feel No-Ways Tired — see — I Am Seeking for a City

I Don't Feel Weary
I don't feel weary and noways tired
Praise
ALLS, 70, Melody only
PETL, 124, d, Text only

I Don't Intend to Die in Egypt Land
I cannot stay away
Songs of Spiritual Journey
Exodus 16:3; Numbers 14:1–2, 21:5+
HALC, 66, Choral with piano accompaniment and additional historical information
PETL, 128, d, Text only
RAIJ, 86, Solo voice with piano accompaniment

I Don't Want to Stay Here No Longer
Swing low sweet chariot pray let me enter in
Aspiration
BURP, 3, d, Solo voice with piano accompaniment

DETR, 38, Choral unaccompanied with additional historical information

SANH, 107, Uses Tonic Sol-fa notation

I Don't Want You Go On and Leave Me

I'm comin' yes Lord I'm comin'

Songs of Spiritual Journey

BARO, 23, d, Melody only

I Done Been Home

I done been home I done try on my robe

Songs of Spiritual Journey

HALC, 43, Choral with piano accompaniment and additional historical information

PETL, 390, d, Text only

I Done Done What You Told Me to Do — see — I Done What You Told Me to Do

I Done What You Told Me to Do

Lord I've done what you told me to do

Deliverance

CARS, 22, d, Solo voice with piano accompaniment

DETD1, 24, Choral unaccompanied with additional historical information

HALC, 21, Choral with piano accompaniment and additional historical information

HAWD, 152, d, Text only

JOHJB, i, 180, d, Solo voice with piano accompaniment and additional historical information

PETL, 280, d, Text only

PETL, 354, d, Text only

I Feel Like Dying in This Army

I feel like dyin' in de service ob ma Lord

Songs of Spiritual Journey

MCIB, 131, d, Melody and additional historical information

PETL, 354, d, Text only

I Feel Like My Time Ain't Long (1)
Went to the graveyard the other day
Death
CHET, 252, Text only
HERB, 35, Text only
LOMJO, 31, Melody only
LOMJO2, 31, Melody only
PETL, 18, d, Text only

I Feel Like My Time Ain't Long (2)
I feel like I feel like my time ain't long
Death
CLES, 148, Choral with piano accompaniment and additional historical information
JOHJB, ii, 174, d, Solo voice with piano accompaniment and additional historical information
PETL, 275, d, Text only

I Fold Up My Arms and I Wonder
Guide me oh Thou great Jehovah
Prayer
Isaiah 58:11; Psalm 23:2; John 6:50–51; Revelation 7:17+
KENM, 111, d, Solo voice with piano accompaniment and additional historical information

I Found Jesus Over in Zion
I found Jesus over in Zion
Songs of Spiritual Journey
GRIN, 88, Melody only
PETL, 391, d, Text only

I Going Put On My Golden Shoes
In the morning
Heaven
ODUN, 107, d, Text only; Source includes additional historical information

I Going Try the Air
One morning soon my Lord

Heaven
ODUN, 106, d, Text only; Source includes additional historical information

I Got a Hiding Place
I got a hidin' place
Faith/Assurance
GRIN, 90, d, Melody only
PETL, 391, d, Text only

I Got a Home
I got a home where liars can't go
Heaven
ODUN, 95, Text only; Source includes additional historical information

I Got a Home in That Rock
I got a home in de rock don't yuh see
Faith/Assurance
BALF, 1, d, Solo voice with cello accompaniment
BECK, 41, Solo voice with piano accompaniment
BONI, 20, d, Solo voice with piano accompaniment
BURS, 21, d, Solo voice with piano accompaniment
CHAT, 44, d, Solo voice with piano accompaniment
CHET, 252, Text only
DITT, 16, d, Choral arrangement
GUL, 39, d, Text only
HAWD, 100, Text only
HAY1H, 41, Solo voice with piano accompaniment
HERB, 36, Text only
JOHDT, 24, Instrumental Ensemble accompaniment
JOHJB, i, 96, d, Solo voice with piano accompaniment and additional historical information
KENM, 88, d, Solo voice with piano accompaniment and additional historical information
OWEN, 9, d, Solo voice with piano accompaniment
PETL, 73, d, Text only
PETL, 395, d, Text only
RAI, 62, Solo voice with piano accompaniment

STIT, 67, d, Solo voice with piano accompaniment and additional historical information
TOBB, 8, Melody only
WHIF, 104, d, Solo voice with piano accompaniment
WORJT, 15, d, Choral unaccompanied with additional historical information

I Got a Key to the Kingdom
I got a key to the Kingdom
Heaven
GRIN, 98, Melody only
PETL, 393, d, Text only

I Got a Letter This Morning
I got a letter this mornin' aye Lawd
Praise
BALS, 27, d, Melody only
PETL, 222, d, Text only

I Got a Light
I got a light the light that shineth
Faith/Assurance
DETD1, 3, Choral unaccompanied with additional historical information

I Got a Mother in the Bright Shining World
I got a mother in the bright shinin' world
Heaven
BALS, 76, d, Choral unaccompanied with additional historical information
PETL, 74, d, Text only

I Got a New Name
I got a new name over in Zion
Praise
PETL, 317, d, Text only

I Got a Robe — see — Going to Shout All Over God's Heaven

Praise
> BALS, 24, d, Melody only
> PETL, 318, d, Text only

I Have Another Building

I know I have another building
> Heaven
> > WORF, 26, Choral unaccompanied with additional historical information

I Have Another Building — see also — I Know I Have Another Building

I Heard a Voice Couldn't Tell Where

I been in some strange lan' so far from home
> Songs of Spiritual Journey
> > MCIB, 135, Melody and additional historical information
> > PETL, 355, d, Text only

I Heard from Heaven Today

Hurry on my weary soul
> Heaven
> > ALLS, 2, Melody only
> > PETL, 223, d, Text only

I Heard from Heaven Today — see also — Peter Go Ring Them Bells

I Heard of a City Called Heaven

My mother has reached the bright glory
> Heaven
> > WHIF, 118, d, Solo voice with piano accompaniment

I Heard the Angels Singing

Who is that yonder all dressed in red
> Praise
> > ODUN, 140, d, Text only; Source includes additional historical information
> > PARS, 140, d, Melody only

I Heard the Preaching of the Elder
I heard the preaching of the elder
Admonition/Judgment
Genesis 7:14; Jonah 1:17+
DETR, 62, Choral unaccompanied with additional historical information
JOHJB, ii, 90, d, Solo voice with piano accompaniment and additional historical information
PATN, 16, d, Solo voice with piano accompaniment
PETL, 355, d, Text only
WORF, 33, Choral unaccompanied with additional historical information

I Hope I'll Join the Band
Ride up in the chariot
Heaven
WORJF, 63, d, Text only; Source includes additional historical information

I Hope My Mother Will Be There
I hope my mother will be there in that beautiful world on high
Heaven
ARMH, 218, d, Choral unaccompanied with additional historical information
DETD1, 13, Choral unaccompanied with additional historical information
DETD3, 19, Choral unaccompanied with additional historical information
DETR, 130, Choral unaccompanied with additional historical information
FENC, 46, Choral unaccompanied with additional historical information
FENR, 46, Choral unaccompanied with additional historical information
PETL, 75, d, Text only

I Know de Udder Worl' Is Not — see — Run Mary Run

I Know I Have Another Building
I know I have another buildin' children
Faith/Assurance
PETL, 75, d, Text only
SIX, 18, Solo voice with piano accompaniment
WHIF, 16, d, Solo voice with piano accompaniment
WORJF, 61, d, Text only; Source includes additional historical information

I Know I Would Like to Read
I know I would like to read
Aspiration
DETR, 40, Choral unaccompanied with additional historical information
FENR, 148, Choral unaccompanied with additional historical information
PETL, 176, d, Text only

I Know I've Been Changed
I know uh bin change
Deliverance
GUL, 44, d, Text only

I Know It Was the Blood
I know it was the blood for me
Jesus
CHET, 253, Text only

I Know My Jesus Loves Me
I know my Jesus loves me o my Lord
Faith/Assurance
HALC, 36, Choral with piano accompaniment and additional historical information
PETL, 223, d, Text only

I Know My Road Is Rough and Rocky
I know my road is rough an' rocky
Songs of Spiritual Journey
WORJT, 8, Choral unaccompanied with additional historical information

I Know My Time Ain't Long
    Lightnin' flashin' and the thunder rollin'
      Death
          ODUN, 119, Text only; Source includes additional historical information

I Know That My Redeemer Lives
    I know I know my Lord
      Faith/Assurance
          MAR3, 276, Choral unaccompanied with additional historical information
          MARS, 242, Choral unaccompanied with additional historical information
          PETL, 75, d, Text only

I Know the Lord
    I know the Lord I know the Lord
      Faith/Assurance
          ANDW, 18, Choral arrangement

I Know the Lord Laid His Hands on Me
    I know the Lord
      Faith/Assurance
      Luke 4:40; Matthew 11:5; Revelation 1:17*
          AAH, 360, Choral with piano accompaniment and additional historical information
          BOAS, 73, Solo voice with piano accompaniment
          BOAT, 73, d, Solo voice with piano accompaniment
          BROS, 9, d, Solo voice with piano accompaniment
          BRYI, 15, d, Melody only
          BURS, 90, d, Solo voice with piano accompaniment
          CHET, 252, Text only
          CLES, 166, Choral with piano accompaniment and additional historical information
          DANF, 31, Melody only
          DETD1, 29, Choral unaccompanied with additional historical information
          DETR, 207, Choral unaccompanied with additional historical information

FENR, 166, Choral unaccompanied with additional historical information

FISS, 76, d, Solo voice with piano accompaniment and additional historical information

GREF, 48, d, Solo voice with piano accompaniment

HALC, 74, Choral with piano accompaniment and additional historical information

HAWD, 114, Text only

HERB, 36, Text only

JACL, 103, Choral with piano accompaniment and additional historical information

JOHJB, ii, 164, d, Solo voice with piano accompaniment and additional historical information

JORS, 57, d, Text only

LIF, 131, Choral with piano accompaniment and additional historical information

MCLS, 42, Solo voice with piano accompaniment

MIL3, 8, Solo voice with piano accompaniment

PETL, 356, d, Text only

SANH, 96, Uses Tonic Sol-fa notation

SIX, 53, Solo voice with piano accompaniment

WORF, 7, Choral unaccompanied with additional historical information

WORJF, 64, d, Text only; Source includes additional historical information

I Know When I'm Going Home

Old Satan told me to my face

Songs of Spiritual Journey

ALLS, 30, Melody only

PETL, 125, d, Text only

I Look Down the Road

I look down duh road en duh road so lawnsome

Songs of Spiritual Journey

GUL, 45, d, Text only

HUTS, 45, d, Melody and additional historical information

I Look for Jesus All My Days

And when I found Him this is what He said

Jesus
> ODUN, 79, Text only; Source includes additional historical information

I Looked Down the Road
> Uh look down duh road en duh road look foggy
>> Songs of Spiritual Journey
>>> HUTS, 87, d, Melody and additional historical information

I Love Everybody
> I love everybody I love everybody in my heart
>> Praise
>>> COUNS, 27, Solo voice with piano accompaniment and additional historical information

I Love My Blessed Savior
> I love my blessed Savior
>> Suffering
>>> BALS, 78, d, Melody only
>>> PETL, 18, d, Text only

I Love the Lord
> I love the Lord
>> Jesus
>>> PETL, 125, d, Text only

I Mean to Lift Up the Standard for My King
> I mean to lift up a standard for my King
>> Songs of Spiritual Journey
>>> GRIN, 30, Melody only
>>> PETL, 394, d, Text only

I Must Walk My Lonesome Valley — see — Lonesome Valley

I Never Felt Such Love in My Soul Before
> I never felt such love in my soul before
>> Songs of Spiritual Journey
>>> PETL, 357, d, Text only

I Saw the Beam in My Sister's Eye
 Saw the beam in my sister's eye
  Faith/Assurance
   ALLS, 17, Melody only
   CHET, 253, Text only
   PETL, 358, d, Text only

I Saw the Light
 I saw de light
  Heaven
   WHIF, 94, d, Solo voice with piano accompaniment

I Shall Not Be Moved
 When my cross is heavy I shall not be moved
  Faith/Assurance
  Psalm 16:8^
   AAH, 479, Choral with piano accompaniment and additional
    historical information
   BOAS, 9, Solo voice with piano accompaniment
   CHET, 253, Text only
   HAWD, 141, Text only
   JACL, 110, Choral with piano accompaniment and additional
    historical information

I Stood on the River of Jordan
 I stood on the River of Jordan to see that ship come sailin' over
  Death
   BRYA, 24, Melody, chord symbols, and additional historical
    information
   BUR2H, 38, d, Solo voice with piano accompaniment
   BUR2L, 38, d, Solo voice with piano accompaniment
   BURC2, 25, d, Solo voice with piano accompaniment
   BURS, 95, d, Solo voice with piano accompaniment
   CALA, 20, d, Melody only
   CHET, 253, d, Text only
   CLES, 149, d, Choral with piano accompaniment and additional
    historical information
   HAWD, 46, d, Text only

SPAG, 25, d, Solo voice with piano accompaniment and chord
symbols
WALSL, 182, Solo voice with piano accompaniment
WALSH, 182, Solo voice with piano accompaniment

I Stood Outside the Gate
I stood outside the gate
Aspiration
GRIN, 76, Melody only
PETL, 22, d, Text only

I Thank God I'm Free At Last — see — Free At Last

I Thought I Had a Friend
I thought I had a friend was true
Work Songs
ODUN, 250, Text only; Source includes additional historical
information

I Want God's Heaven to Be Mine
Yes I want God's Heaven to be mine
Aspiration
JOHJB, ii, 88, d, Solo voice with piano accompaniment and addi-
tional historical information
PETL, 358, d, Text only
PRI4, 100, d, Solo voice with piano accompaniment

I Want Jesus to Walk with Me
I want Jesus to walk with me
Jesus
John 12:35+
AAH, 563, Choral with piano accompaniment and additional
historical information
BOAS, 40, Solo voice with piano accompaniment
CALA, 22, Melody only
CHET, 253, Text only
CLES, 95, Choral with piano accompaniment and additional
historical information

HAWD, 110, Text only

JACL, 17, Choral with piano accompaniment and additional historical information

JORS, 61, d, Text only

LOYS, 63, d, Solo voice with piano accompaniment

NEW, 500, Choral with piano accompaniment and additional historical information

SEV, 624, Choral with piano accompaniment and additional historical information

WARE, 58, d, Solo voice with piano accompaniment and additional historical information

I Want Jesus to Walk with Me

I'm going to live with Jesus

Heaven

PIKJ, 213, Melody only

MARS, 173, Choral unaccompanied with additional historical information

I Want King Jesus

Wan' King Jedus fuh stan' muh bawn'

Jesus

GUL, 87, d, Text only

HUTS, 89, d, Melody and additional historical information

I Want to Be a Christian — see — Lord I Want to Be a Christian

I Want to Be Ready

I want to be ready

Aspiration

Revelation 21:2^

AAH, 600, Choral with piano accompaniment and additional historical information

ANDW, 21, Choral arrangement

BAYF, 38, d, Solo voice with piano accompaniment and chord symbols

BLOR, 212, Text and chord symbols

BUR2H, 41, d, Solo voice with piano accompaniment

BUR2L, 41, d, Solo voice with piano accompaniment

I Want to Be Ready — see also — Walk in Jerusalem Just Like John

I Want to Climb Up Jacob's Ladder — see — Jacob's Ladder

I Want to Die Easy When I Die
  I want to die easy when I die
    Death
        ANDW, 39, Melody only
        BALS, 20, d, Melody only
        BRUT, 37, d, Solo voice with piano accompaniment and additional
            historical information
        HAWD, 11, Text only
        HERB, 43, Text only
        JOHJB, ii, 46, d, Solo voice with piano accompaniment and addi-
            tional historical information
        OKS1, 32, Solo voice with piano accompaniment
        PATN, 96, d, Solo voice with piano accompaniment
        RAGS, 8, d, Solo voice with piano accompaniment

I Want to Die like Lazarus
  I want to die like-a Lazarus die
    Death
        ALLS, 98, Melody only
        PETL, 321, d, Text only

I Want to Die Shouting
  Amazing grace how sweet the sound I want to die a-shouting
    Death
        BARO, 12, d, Melody only

I Want to Go Home
  There's no rain to wet you
    Suffering
        ALLS, 46, Melody only
        PETL, 24, d, Text only

I Want to Go Where Jesus Is
  I want to go where Jesus is to play upon the golden harp
    Heaven
        BARO, 13, d, Melody only

I Want to Join the Band
  What is that up yonder I see

Aspiration
> ALLS, 95, Melody only
> PETL, 178, d, Text only

I Want to Live So God Can Use Me

I wanta live so God can use me
Aspiration
> CALA, 13, d, Text only
> GRIN, 62, Melody only
> PETL, 320, d, Text only

I Want to See Jesus in the Morning

In de mornin' o in de mornin'
Rituals of Preparation for Renewal/Regeneration
> MCIB, 144, d, Melody and additional historical information
> PETL, 321, d, Text only

I Want Two Wings to Veil My Face — see — Two Wings

I Wants to Climb Up Jacob's Ladder — see — Jacob's Ladder

I Went to the Hillside

I went to the hillside I went to pray
Deliverance
2 Corinthians 4:17; Mark 6:46; Revelation 2:17, 3:12*
> SANH, 65, Uses Tonic Sol-fa notation

I Will Be There in the Morning — see — I'll Be There in the Morning

I Will Overcome

I will overcome
Faith/Assurance
> PETL, 178, d, Text only

I Will Pray

Every time I feel the Spirit
Prayer
> PETL, 322, d, Text only

I Will Sleep Away
When I die I will sleep away
Death
LOGR, 28, Melody only

I Will Trust in the Lord
I will trust in the Lord till I die
Faith/Assurance
Psalm 56:4^
AAH, 391, Choral with piano accompaniment and additional historical information
UNI, 464, Melody only

I Wish I Been There
My mother you follow Jesus
Aspiration
ALLS, 29, Melody only
PETL, 132, d, Text only

I Wish I Had Been There — see — I Wish I Been There

I Wish I Had Died in Egypt Land
I can't stay away
Songs of Spiritual Journey
Exodus 16:3; Numbers 14:1–2, 21:5+
GREF, 26, d, Solo voice with piano accompaniment
JOHRS, 13, Solo voice with piano accompaniment
PETL, 24, d, Text only
WORF, 32, Choral unaccompanied with additional historical information

I Wish I Have Had an Eagle's Wings
I wish I have had an eagle's wings
Songs of Spiritual Journey
DITT, 6, Choral arrangement
PETL, 396, d, Text only

I Won't Die No More
Singin' 'way in de Hebben I won't die no mo'

I'll Fly Away
Some bright morning when this life is over I'll fly away
Heaven
CLES, 183, Choral with piano accompaniment and additional historical information
HAWD, 9, Text only
LUEB, 53, Melody, chord symbols, and piano accompaniment
TRAH, 70, Melody, chord symbols, and piano accompaniment

I'll Hear the Trumpet Sound — see — You May Bury Me in the East

I'll Make Me a Man
God walked around and looked around on all that He made He looked at His sun
Aspiration
Genesis 1:1–27, 2:7+
HAYMF, 16, d, Solo voice with piano accompaniment and additional historical information
HAYMS, 17, d, Solo voice with piano accompaniment and additional historical information
PETL, 224, d, Text only

I'll Meet You Way Up Yonder
I'll meet you way up yonder
Heaven
GREF, 13, d, Solo voice with piano accompaniment
HALC, 18, Choral with piano accompaniment and additional historical information
PETL, 176, d, Text only

I'll Reach to Heaven
King Jesus will be mine I'm mom' done working with crosses
Heaven
BONR, 124, d, Solo voice with piano accompaniment

I'm a Child of Grace
I'm a child of grace
Faith/Assurance
WHIF, 112, d, Solo voice with piano accompaniment

I'm a Poor Little Orphan
I'm a poor li'l orphan in this worl' good Lord can't stay here by myself
Suffering
JESM, 50, d, Solo voice with piano accompaniment and additional historical information
TAYA, 35, d, Solo voice with piano accompaniment

I'm a Poor Wayfaring Stranger — see — Pilgrim's Song

I'm a Soldier in the Army of the Lord
I'm a soldier in the army of the Lord
Faith/Assurance
BOAS, 78, Solo voice with piano accompaniment
GRIN, 60, Melody only
GUL, 47, d, Text only
HAWD, 133, Text only
JORS, 39, d, Text only
MCIB, 55, d, Melody and additional historical information
MCLS, 36, Solo voice with piano accompaniment
PETL, 125, d, Text only
PETL, 130, d, Text only

I'm a Soldier of the Cross
I'm a soldier of de cross in de ahmy o' my Lawd
Aspiration
KENM, 146, d, Solo voice with piano accompaniment and additional historical information

I'm A-Rolling — see — I'm Rolling

I'm All Wore Out Toiling for the Lord
I'm all wore out a-toiling for the Lord
Suffering
FISS, 84, d, Solo voice with piano accompaniment and additional historical information
PETL, 19, d, Text only

I'm Almost Done Traveling
Yes I'm bound to carry my soul to my Jesus

Death
>   MCIB, 137, d, Melody and additional historical information
>   PETL, 76, d, Text only

I'm an Everyday Witness (1)
I'm a witness for my Lord
>   Songs of Spiritual Journey
>   PETL, 393, d, Text only

I'm an Everyday Witness (2)
I'm a witness faw mah Lawd
>   Songs of Spiritual Journey
>   GRIN, 58, Melody only

I'm Crossing Jordan
Well I'm crossing Jordan River
>   Heaven
>   COUN, 258, Melody only

I'm Going Back with Jesus
I'm going back with Jesus when He comes
>   Deliverance
>   PETL, 176, d, Text only

I'm Going Down to the River of Jordan
I'm a travelin' to the land I'm goin' down to de Ribbuh of Jerdan oh yes
>   Songs of Spiritual Journey
>   BALS, 82, d, Melody only
>   PETL, 225, d, Text only

I'm Going Home
I sought my Lord in the wilderness
>   Songs of Spiritual Journey
>   ALLS, 84, Melody only
>   CREO, 10, d, Solo voice with piano accompaniment
>   HAWD, 169, Text only
>   PETL, 126, d, Text only

I'm Going Home on a Cloud
    One dese fine mawnin's at break of day
        Songs of Spiritual Journey
            KENM, 65, d, Solo voice with piano accompaniment and additional historical information

I'm Going to Do All I Can
    I'm going to do all I can for my Lord
        Aspiration
            PETL, 126, d, Text only
            WORJF, 109, d, Text only; Source includes additional historical information

I'm Going to Eat at the Welcome Table
    I'm a going to eat at the welcome table
        Faith/Assurance
            BRYA, 20, Melody, chord symbols, and additional historical information
            DITT, 22, Choral arrangement
            JACL, 55, Choral with piano accompaniment and additional historical information
            PETL, 76, d, Text only
            SILS, 16, d, Solo voice with piano accompaniment

I'm Going to Join the Band
    I'm going to join the band hallelujah
        Songs of Spiritual Journey
            BARO, 28, d, Melody only
            PETL, 356, d, Text only
            WORF, 12, Melody only

I'm Going to Join the Great Association
    I'm going to join the great association
        Heaven
        Revelation 7:9*
            CHET, 279, Text only
            DETR, 122, d, Choral unaccompanied with additional historical information

> FENC, 1, d, Choral unaccompanied with additional historical information
>
> FENR, 1, d, Choral unaccompanied with additional historical information
>
> GREF, 39, d, Solo voice with piano accompaniment
>
> MAR3, 305, d, Choral unaccompanied with additional historical information
>
> PETL, 239, d, Text only
>
> PRI4, 71, d, Solo voice with piano accompaniment
>
> SANH, 56, d, Uses Tonic Sol-fa notation

I'm Going to Lay Down My Heavy Load

Oh! bye an' bye bye an' bye
> Death
> > PRI4, 62, d, Solo voice with piano accompaniment

I'm Going to Lay Down My Life for My Lord

For my Lord for my Lord
> Faith/Assurance
> > WORF, 36, Choral unaccompanied with additional historical information

I'm Going to Live with Jesus

I'm going to live with Jesus
> Heaven
> > PETL, 76, d, Text only
> > SEWJC, 58, Melody only

I'm Going to Rest from All My Labor

I gwine t' res' from all my labuh w'en I dead
> Death
> > HUTS, 41, d, Melody and additional historical information

I'm Going to See My Loving Father When I Get Home

I'm goin' to see my lovin' Father when I get home
> Heaven
> > PETL, 226, d, Text only
> > BALS, 21, d, Melody only

I'm Going to Sing

I'm gonna sing when the Spirit says a-sing

Praise

ANDW, 30, d, Melody only

BARO, 27, d, Melody only

BRYA, 37, d, Melody, chord symbols, and additional historical information

BRYI, 11, d, Melody only

CALA, 19, d, Melody only

CHET, 255, d, Text only

CLES, 81, d, Choral with piano accompaniment and additional historical information

FRAS, 40, d, Solo voice with piano accompaniment

GUIU, 74, d, Solo voice with piano accompaniment

LIF, 117, d, Choral with piano accompaniment and additional historical information

LUEB, 97, d, Melody, chord symbols, and piano accompaniment

MAR3, 278, Choral unaccompanied with additional historical information

MARS, 244, Choral unaccompanied with additional historical information

NEW, 134, d, Choral with piano accompaniment and additional historical information

PETL, 226, d, Text only

SANH, 97, d, Uses Tonic Sol-fa notation

UNI, 333, d, Melody only

WORJA, 226, d, Choral unaccompanied with additional historical information

I'm Going to Sit at the Welcome Table

I'm going to sit at the welcome table

Praise

GUL, 89, Text only

HUTS, 91, Melody and additional historical information

PRI4, 104, d, Solo voice with piano accompaniment

TOBB, 35, Melody only

I'm Going to Stay in the Battlefield
  I'm going to stay in the battlefield
    Aspiration
      MCIB, 122, d, Melody and additional historical information
      PETL, 126, d, Text only

I'm Going to Tell God All My Troubles
  I'm going to tell God all my troubles
    Suffering
      JOHHH, 91, d, Solo voice with piano accompaniment
      PETL, 20, d, Text only

I'm Going to Wait Until the Holy Ghost Comes
  I'm goin' to wait
    Rituals of Preparation for Renewal/Regeneration
      BALS, 52, d, Choral unaccompanied with additional historical information
      PETL, 318, d, Text only

I'm Going to Walk with Jesus by Myself
  I am goin' to walk with Jesus by myself
    Songs of Spiritual Journey
      BARO, 30, d, Melody only

I'm Going Up to Heaven Anyhow
  Anyhow anyhow anyhow my Lord
    Heaven
      CALA, 8, d, Text only
      HERB, 37, Text only
      JOHJB, ii, 126, d, Solo voice with piano accompaniment and additional historical information
      PETL, 127, d, Text only

I'm Going Where There Ain't No More Dying
  Joshua fought the battle 'round Jericho's wall
    Faith/Assurance
    Joshua 6:1–20+
      MCIB, 127, d, Melody and additional historical information
      PETL, 20, d, Text only

I'm Gonna Rest from All My Labor
I gwine res' from all muh labuh w'en I dead
Faith/Assurance
GUL, 43, d, Text only

I'm in Trouble
I'm in trouble Lord
Suffering
ALLS, 94, Melody only

I'm in Your Care
Oh Lord I'm in your care
Jesus
BOAS, 72, Solo voice with piano accompaniment
HAWD, 70, Text only

I'm Just Going Over Jordan
I'm just a-goin'
Songs of Spiritual Journey
FISS, 88, d, Solo voice with piano accompaniment and additional
historical information

I'm Just Going Over There
I'm just a-goin' over there
Songs of Spiritual Journey
HERB, 38, Text only
PETL, 395, d, Text only
WORJA, 221, d, Choral unaccompanied with additional historical
information

I'm Looking for My Jesus (Can't Stay Away)
Steal away in prayer I'm looking for my Jesus
Jesus
JOHRR, 56, d, Solo voice with piano accompaniment and addi-
tional historical information

I'm Mighty Tired
I'se mighty tired
Death
FENC, 80, d, Choral unaccompanied with additional historical
information

I'm on My Journey Home
Sister when you pray you must pray to the Lord
Heaven
Psalm 125:1; Mark 1:10; John 1:51; Acts 7:56+
ODUN, 99, Text only; Source includes additional historical information

I'm Rolling (1)
I'm a rolling I'm a rolling
Suffering
John 15:18–19; 1 John 3:13*
BAYF, 42, d, Solo voice with piano accompaniment and chord symbols
CHET, 254, Text only
DANF, 6, d, Melody only
FENR, 94, d, Choral unaccompanied with additional historical information
FISS, 86, d, Solo voice with piano accompaniment and additional historical information
HERB, 37, Text only
PETL, 19, d, Text only
PIKJ, 173, Choral unaccompanied with additional historical information
SEWJC, 14, Choral unaccompanied with additional historical information

I'm Rolling (2)
I'm a-rollin thro an unfriendly world
Suffering
John 15:18–19; 1 John 3:13*
ANDW, 19, Choral arrangement
BRYI, 38, d, Melody only
CLES, 150, Choral with piano accompaniment and additional historical information
DETR, 185, Choral unaccompanied with additional historical information
FENC, 94, Choral unaccompanied with additional historical information
FIST, 16, Solo voice with piano accompaniment

I'm Running for My Life

I'm running for my life

Suffering

I'm Running On

I'm runnin' on I'm runnin' on

Aspiration

I'm So Glad (1)

I'm so glad the angels brough the tidings down

Heaven

Luke 2:8–14*

SAAT2, 1, d, Solo voice with piano accompaniment
SANH, 57, Uses Tonic Sol-fa notation

I'm So Glad (2)

I'm so glad dun jes got out ob dat Egypt lan'
Heaven
Luke 2:8–14*
MCIB, 139, Melody and additional historical information
PETL, 177, d, Text only

I'm So Glad (3)

I'm so glad I'm so glad
Heaven
Luke 2:8–14*
GLAS, 17, Melody and chord symbols
MARS, 155, Choral unaccompanied with additional historical information
PETL, 227, d, Text only
PETL, 318, d, Text only
PIKJ, 195, Choral unaccompanied with additional historical information
SEWJC, 40, Choral unaccompanied with additional historical information

I'm So Glad (4)

I am so glad I've been in the grave and rose again
Heaven
Luke 2:8–14*
WORF, 28, Choral unaccompanied with additional historical information

I'm So Glad I Got My Religion in Time

I'm so glad I got my religion in time
Faith/Assurance
CHET, 255, Text only

I'm So Glad Jesus Lifted Me

I'm so glad Jesus lifted me

Faith/Assurance
> CALA, 15, Text only
> JACL, 6, Choral with piano accompaniment and additional historical information
> LIF, 105, Choral with piano accompaniment and additional historical information

I'm So Glad Troubles Don't Last Always
I'm so glad trouble don't last alway
> Faith/Assurance
>> BOAS, 17, Solo voice with piano accompaniment
>> CHET, 255, Text only
>> DETR, 235, Melody only
>> HAWD, 20, Text only
>> WHIF, 14, d, Solo voice with piano accompaniment

I'm Traveling to the Grave
I'm a traveling to the grave
> Death
> 1 Corinthians 15:55*
>> DETR, 187, d, Melody only
>> DETS, 17, d, Solo voice with piano accompaniment
>> FENC, 95, d, Choral unaccompanied with additional historical information
>> FENR, 95, d, Choral unaccompanied with additional historical information
>> FREC, 16, d, Solo voice with piano accompaniment
>> MARS, 146, d, Choral unaccompanied with additional historical information
>> PETL, 177, d, Text only
>> PIKJ, 186, d, Melody only
>> SEWJ, 27, d, Choral arrangement
>> SEWJC, 27, d, Melody only
>> SILSP, 16, d, Solo voice with piano accompaniment

I'm Traveling to the Land
I'm a travelin' to the land

Songs of Spiritual Journey
> BALS, 63, d, Choral unaccompanied with additional historical information
>
> PETL, 225, d, Text only

I'm Troubled in Mind (1)

I am a-troubled in the mind I ask my Lord what shall I do
Suffering
2 Corinthians 4:8–11, 12:8–9*
> ALLS, 30, d, Melody only
>
> HAYMS, 69, d, Solo voice with piano accompaniment and additional historical information
>
> HERB, 37, d, Text only
>
> PETL, 21, d, Text only

I'm Troubled in Mind (2)

I'm troubled in mind if Jesus won't help me I surely will die
Suffering
2 Corinthians 4:8–11, 12:8–9*
> BOAT, 77, d, Solo voice with piano accompaniment
>
> BRUS, 28, d, Solo voice with piano accompaniment
>
> CHIA, 28, Melody only
>
> DANF, 43, Melody only
>
> DETR, 236, Melody only
>
> FISS, 90, d, Solo voice with piano accompaniment and additional historical information
>
> HAYMF, 68, d, Solo voice with piano accompaniment and additional historical information
>
> JOHJB, i, 120, d, Solo voice with piano accompaniment and additional historical information
>
> KINS, 24, d, Melody only
>
> MARS, 173, Choral unaccompanied with additional historical information
>
> PETL, 76, d, Text only
>
> PIKJ, 213, Melody only
>
> SANH, 58, Uses Tonic Sol-fa notation
>
> SEWJC, 58, Melody only
>
> SIX, 59, Solo voice with piano accompaniment

SNYS, 44, d, Solo voice with piano accompaniment

WORJF, 51, d, Text only; Source includes additional historical information

I'm Troubled Lord

I'm troubled about my soul when I get up in the Kingdom won't be troubled no more
  Suffering
    JOHR, 10, Solo voice with piano accompaniment

I'm Walking on Borrowed Land

I'm walking on borrowed land poor sinner aint got no home
  Deliverance
    JOHRS, 8, Solo voice with piano accompaniment

I'm Working on the Building

I'm working on the building for my Lord
  Praise
    PETL, 127, d, Text only
    PRI4, 156, d, Solo voice with piano accompaniment

I've a Message from My Lord

I've a message f'om ma Lord halleluiah
  Praise
    MCIB, 146, d, Melody and additional historical information
    PETL, 229, d, Text only

I've Been in the Storm So Long

I've been in de storm so long children
  Suffering
    BURS, 162, d, Solo voice with piano accompaniment
    CHET, 255, d, Text only
    CHIA, 24, melody only
    CLES, 144, d, Choral with piano accompaniment and additional historical information
    FISS, 94, d, Solo voice with piano accompaniment and additional historical information
    FREC, 46, Solo voice with piano accompaniment

HERB, 42, Text only

JOHRA, 22, d, Solo voice with piano accompaniment

JOHRR, 37, d, Solo voice with piano accompaniment and additional historical information

MAR3, 208, Choral unaccompanied with additional historical information

MARS, 174, Choral unaccompanied with additional historical information

PATN, 8, d, Solo voice with piano accompaniment

PETL, 23, d, Text only

SILSP, 58, Solo voice with piano accompaniment

WHII, 24, d, Solo voice with piano accompaniment

WHII, 33, d, Solo voice with piano accompaniment

WORJT, 3, Choral unaccompanied with additional historical information

I've Been Listening All Night Long

I've been a list'ning all de night long

Suffering

John 1:29*

ARMH, 247, d, Choral unaccompanied with additional historical information

BALS, 84, d, Choral unaccompanied with additional historical information

DETR, 170, d, Choral unaccompanied with additional historical information

FENC, 75, d, Choral unaccompanied with additional historical information

FENR, 108, d, Choral unaccompanied with additional historical information

GREF, 72, d, Solo voice with piano accompaniment

MARS, 144, d, Choral unaccompanied with additional historical information

MCIB, 126, d, Melody and additional historical information

PETL, 5, d, Text only

PETL, 17, d, Text only

PETL, 23, d, Text only

PIKJ, 184, d, Choral unaccompanied with additional historical information

Revelation 7:17; Romans 3:24, 5:15; Zechariah 13:1*
    JACL, 98, Choral with piano accompaniment and additional historical information
    JOHRR, 98, d, Solo voice with piano accompaniment and additional historical information
    MARS, 137, Choral unaccompanied with additional historical information
    PETL, 319, d, Text only
    PIKJ, 177, Choral unaccompanied with additional historical information
    SANH, 63, Uses Tonic Sol-fa notation
    SEWJ, 18, Choral arrangement
    SEWJC, 18, Choral unaccompanied with additional historical information

If Anybody Ask You Who I Am
If anybody ask you who I am
    Faith/Assurance
        BENF, 2, Solo voice with piano accompaniment
        KENM, 45, d, Melody only

If I Can Only Hold Out
Ef uh can only hol' out ef uh can only hol' out
    Faith/Assurance
        GUL, 26, d, Text only

If I Got My Ticket Can I Ride — see — If I Got My Ticket Lord

If I Had a Hammer
If I had a hammer
    Aspiration
        NAA, 40, Melody and chord symbols

If I Had Died When I Was a Babe
If I had died when I was a babe
    Aspiration
        DETD4, 20, Choral unaccompanied with additional historical information

If I Have My Ticket Lord
If I have my ticket Lord can I ride
Admonition/Judgment
BOAS, 76, d, Solo voice with piano accompaniment
GRIN, 82, d, Melody only
LOMJO, 32, Melody only
LOMJO2, 32, Melody only
PETL, 175, d, Text only
PETL, 276, d, Text only

If I Keep Praying On
I'm going to be a Christian if I keep praying on
Prayer
ODUN, 98, d, Text only; Source includes additional historical information

If I Was a Mourner
If I was a mourner just like you
Admonition/Judgment
ODUN, 73, Text only; Source includes additional historical information

If the Lord Calls You
Ef de Lord calls you
Faith/Assurance
LOGR, 21, d, Melody only

If You Ask Him
He'll lift you up if you ask Him
Faith/Assurance
CLES, 186, Choral with piano accompaniment and additional historical information

If You Can't Come Send One — see — Send One Angel Down

If You Can't Come Send One Angel Down — see — Send One Angel Down

If You Don't Like the Way I Work
If you don't like the way I work jus' pay me off

John 14:2*
>
> BOAS, 58, Solo voice with piano accompaniment
>
> CHET, 256, Text only
>
> DETR, 42, Choral unaccompanied with additional historical information
>
> FENR, 124, Choral unaccompanied with additional historical information
>
> JOHHG, 9, Solo voice with piano accompaniment
>
> JOHHH, 17, d, Solo voice with piano accompaniment
>
> MARS, 198, Choral unaccompanied with additional historical information
>
> PETL, 178, d, Text only
>
> RAGS, 15, Solo voice with piano accompaniment
>
> SANH, 59, Uses Tonic Sol-fa notation
>
> WORJF, 62, d, Text only; Source includes additional historical information
>
> WORJT, 5, Choral unaccompanied with additional historical information

In God We Trust

In God we trust with all our heart and soul
> Faith/Assurance
>
> CLES, 214, Choral with piano accompaniment and additional historical information

In His Hands — see — He's Got the Whole World in His Hands

In My Father's House

I'm on my way up there
> Deliverance
>
> BOAS, 62, Solo voice with piano accompaniment

In My Time of Dying

Een muh time ob dyin' uh don' wa(n)' nobody fuh moan
> Death
>
> GUL, 25, d, Text only

In Some Lonesome Graveyard

I hear' a mighty moanin'

FENC, 63, d, Choral unaccompanied with additional historical information

FENR, 63, d, Choral unaccompanied with additional historical information

HERB, 39, d, Text only

JOHJB, ii, 40, d, Solo voice with piano accompaniment and additional historical information

MAR3, 274, Choral unaccompanied with additional historical information

MARS, 240, Choral unaccompanied with additional historical information

PETL, 278, d, Text only

SLA, 34, Choral arrangement

SPAG, 26, d, Solo voice with piano accompaniment and chord symbols

TOBB, 10, Melody only

WARE, 63, d, Solo voice with piano accompaniment and additional historical information

In That Low Land

Come down 'Ze'kul come down hit meb-be duh las' time
Prayer
GUL, 23, d, Text only
HUTS, 29, d, Melody and additional historical information

In That Morning — see — You May Bury Me in the East

In That Old Field

Throw me any way
Death
PARS, 175, Melody only

In the Army

God knows 'tis a better day an' dis a-coming
Heaven
HALC, 54, d, Choral with piano accompaniment and additional historical information
PETL, 178, d, Text only

In the Army of the Lord — see — I'm a Soldier in the Army of the Lord

In the Fault in Me
Duh fau(l)t een me eh Lawd en' duh fau(l)t een me eh Lawd
Faith/Assurance
GUL, 27, d, Text only

In the Kingdom
My mother has gone to journey away
Heaven
DETR, 92, Choral unaccompanied with additional historical information
FENR, 108, Choral unaccompanied with additional historical information
PETL, 77, d, Text only

In the Mansions Above
Good Lord in the mansions above
Deliverance
ALLS, 59, Melody only
HERB, 41, Text only
PETL, 131, d, Text only

In the Morning
I have been tempted oh yes
Heaven
MCIB, 140, d, Melody and additional historical information
ODUN, 100, Text only; Source includes additional historical information
PETL, 228, d, Text only

In the New Jerusalem
Well in that new Jerusalem
Faith/Assurance
BELS, 114, d, Solo voice with piano accompaniment
PETL, 228, d, Text only

In the River of Jordan
In the River of Jordan

Rituals of Preparation for Renewal/Regeneration
John 1:28*
    BOAS, 82, Solo voice with piano accompaniment
    HAWD, 134, Text only
    MARS, 153, Choral unaccompanied with additional historical
        information
    PETL, 319, d, Text only
    PETL, 331, d, Text only
    PIKJ, 193, Choral unaccompanied with additional historical
        information
    SANH, 60, Uses Tonic Sol-fa notation
    SEWJC, 38, Choral unaccompanied with additional historical
        information

In This Field
Lordy won't you he'p me
    Suffering
        GRIN, 70, Melody only
        PETL, 357, d, Text only

In This Land
Lord help the poor and needy
    Suffering
        PETL, 21, d, Text only

Inching Along — see — Keep Inching Along

Is It True
World of form and changes is just now so confusing
    Faith/Assurance
        KENMM, 45, d, Text only; Source includes additional historical
            information

**Is Massa Going to Sell Us — see — Mother Is Master Going to Sell
Us Tomorrow**

Is There Anybody Here
Is there anybody here that loves my Jesus anybody here that loves my
Lord

Jesus
> BARO, 21, d, Melody only
> BRYW, 25, Melody only
> CARS, 6, Solo voice with piano accompaniment
> CHET, 257, Text only
> DETD4, 19, Choral unaccompanied with additional historical information
> HAWD, 124, Text only
> HERB, 41, Text only
> LIF, 73, Choral with piano accompaniment and additional historical information
> PETL, 22, d, Text only
> SIX, 56, d, Solo voice with piano accompaniment
> TAYA, 28, d, Solo voice with piano accompaniment
> WHAG, 15, Solo voice with piano accompaniment

Israelites Shouting
I wonder where is my sister she is gone away
> Deliverance
>> COUN, 248, Melody only

It Is Me — see — Sanding in the Need of Prayer

It Just Suits Me
John wrote a letter and he wrote it in haste
> Church
>> ODUN, 121, Text only; Source includes additional historical information

It May Be the Last Time
It may be the last time
> Admonition/Judgment
>> GRIN, 42, d, Melody only
>> PETL, 279, d, Text only

It's Alright
It's alright my Jesus said He'll fix it
> Faith/Assurance
> Romans 8:34^

AAH, 526, Choral with piano accompaniment and additional historical information

It's Getting Late in the Evening
Lord it's gettin' late over in the evenin'
Death
COUN, 234, Melody only
COUNS, 29, Solo voice with piano accompaniment and additional historical information
PETL, 289, d, Text only
WORJA, 232, d, Choral unaccompanied with additional historical information

It's Me O Lord — see — Standing in the Need of Prayer

It's Moving Day
It breaks my heart to see my baby part
Work Songs
ODUN, 250, Text only; Source includes additional historical information

Jacob's Ladder (1)
We are climbing Jacob's ladder
Songs of Spiritual Journey
Genesis 28:10–17+
AAH, 464, Choral with piano accompaniment and additional historical information
ANDW, 5, Choral arrangement
BAP, 147, Choral with piano accompaniment and additional historical information
BOCH, 488, Choral with piano accompaniment and additional historical information
BRYW, 11, Melody only
CALA, 29, Text only
CLES, 205, Choral with piano accompaniment and additional historical information
DANF, 19, Melody only
DETD2, 25, Choral unaccompanied with additional historical information

WAL25H, 40, Solo voice with piano accompaniment
WAL25L, 40, Solo voice with piano accompaniment
WALA, 176, Solo voice with piano accompaniment
WALSH, 19, Solo voice with piano accompaniment
WALSL, 19, Solo voice with piano accompaniment
WORJA, 220, Choral unaccompanied with additional historical information

Jacob's Ladder (2)

I want to climb up Jacob's ladder
Songs of Spiritual Journey
Genesis 28:10–17+
ALLS, 96, Melody only
BALS, 61, d, Choral unaccompanied with additional historical information
DITT, 2, Choral arrangement
GUL, 70, d, Text only
PETL, 321, d, Text only
PETL, 359, d, Text only

Jacob's Ladder Long and Tall

Jacob's ladder long an' tall
Jesus
Genesis 28:12–17; John 20:2; Matthew 28:13+
HALC, 16, d, Choral with piano accompaniment and additional historical information
PETL, 322, d, Text only

Jay Gooze

Jay Gooze said-a befo' he died
Work Songs
ODUN, 248, Text only; Source includes additional historical information

Jehovah Hallelujah

Jehova hallelujah
Praise
ALLS, 2, Melody only
PETL, 230, d, Text only

Jehovah Has Triumph Messiah Is King
Tell how He came from nation to nation
Jesus
KENMM, 35, d, Text only; Source includes additional historical information

Jerusalem Morning — see — Sweet Turtle Dove

Jesus Ain't Coming Here to Die No More (1)
But He ain't comin' here t' die no mo'
Jesus
FENR, 151, d, Choral unaccompanied with additional historical information

Jesus Ain't Coming Here to Die No More (2)
Virgin Mary had one son
Jesus
PETL, 230, d, Text only
SIX, 6, d, Solo voice with piano accompaniment

Jesus Done Bless My Soul
One day one day while walking along
Jesus
ODUN, 65, Text only; Source includes additional historical information

Jesus Done Just What He Said
Jesus done just what He said
Jesus
BALS, 25, d, Melody only
PETL, 78, d, Text only

Jesus Going to Make Up My Dying Bed
Don't you worry 'bout me well in the time of dyin' I don't want nobody to mourn
Death
COLS, 80, d, Solo voice with piano accompaniment
HALU, 2, d, Solo voice with piano accompaniment
KENMM, 103, d, Solo voice with piano accompaniment and additional historical information

PARS, 178, d, Melody only
PETL, 78, d, Text only
RAIJ, 74, Solo voice with piano accompaniment

Jesus Got His Business Fix
My soul is a witness for my Lord
Jesus
LOGR, 10, Melody only

Jesus Healed the Sick
Jesus heal' de sick give sight to de blin'
Jesus
KREA, 160, d, Choral with piano accompaniment and additional
historical information

Jesus Is a Rock in a Weary Land
Jesus is a rock in a weary land
Jesus
BOAS, 59, Solo voice with piano accompaniment
HAWD, 116, Text only

Jesus Is Listening
Jesus is li'tening all day long
Prayer
ODUN, 81, Text only; Source includes additional historical
information

Jesus Is Risen from the Dead
In this band we have sweet music
Jesus
PETL, 231, d, Text only
WORF, 35, Choral unaccompanied with additional historical
information

Jesus Locked the Lion's Jaw
Baptist Baptist unbeliever
Jesus
HALC, 19, d, Choral with piano accompaniment and additional
historical information
PETL, 79, d, Text only

Jesus Loves Me
Jesus loves me this I know
Faith/Assurance
CREO, 33, Solo voice with piano accompaniment

Jesus on the Waterside
Heaven bell a ring I know the road
Jesus
ALLS, 28, Melody only
CHET, 258, Text only
FREC, 41, Solo voice with piano accompaniment
PETL, 79, d, Text only
SILSP, 46, Solo voice with piano accompaniment
WHIF, 62, d, Solo voice with piano accompaniment

Jesus Rides That Milk-White Horse
Jesus rides that milk-white horse
Jesus
DITT, 12, Choral arrangement

Jesus Rolling in His Arms
Great God He rules all around the mountain
Faith/Assurance
MCIB, 150, d, Melody and additional historical information
PETL, 79, d, Text only

Jesus Walked This Lonesome Valley
Jesus walked this lonesome valley
Jesus
BOCH, 217, Choral with piano accompaniment and additional historical information
SEV, 151, Choral with piano accompaniment and additional historical information

Jesus Won't You Come By and By
You ride that horse
Jesus
ALLS, 60, Melody only
PETL, 359, d, Text only

Jesus Wore the Crown
Jesus He wore the starry crown
Jesus
ODUN, 108, Text only; Source includes additional historical information

Jesus' Blood Done Make Me Whole
Jesus' blood done make me whole
Jesus
BALS, 79, d, Melody only
CHET, 257, Title only
PETL, 322, d, Text only

Jews Killed Poor Jesus
Jews killed poor Jesus
Easter
John 20:1, 11; Matthew 27:59, 28:2*
MARS, 160, d, Choral unaccompanied with additional historical information
PETL, 13, d, Text only
PIKJ, 200, Choral unaccompanied with additional historical information
SANH, 130, Uses Tonic Sol-fa notation
SEWJC, 45, Choral unaccompanied with additional historical information

Jews They Took Our Savior
Jews they took our Savior
Easter
FISS, 36, d, Solo voice with piano accompaniment and additional historical information
PETL, 24, d, Text only

Job
Job Job what you reckin' your children's dead your servant's dead your daughter's dead
Death
Job 1:18–21+
COUN, 225, Melody only

LOMJO, 14, Melody only
LOMJO2, 14, Melody only

John Brown's Body
John Brown's body lies a-mould'ring in the grave
Death
LUEB, 32, d, Melody, chord symbols, and piano accompaniment
MAR3, 257, Choral unaccompanied with additional historical information
MARS, 223, Choral unaccompanied with additional historical information
SANH, 66, d, Uses Tonic Sol-fa notation
SLA, 36, Choral arrangement

John Done Saw That Number
John done saw that-n number
Church
Revelation 5:8–11, 7:14, 14:3+
GRIN, 38, d, Melody only
LOMJO, 16, Melody only
LOMJO2, 16, Melody only
PETL, 281, d, Text only

John John
John John you will see John
Heaven
PARS, 145, Melody only

John John of the Holy Order
John John with the holy order
Heaven
ALLS, 16, Melody only
PETL, 25, d, Text only

John Saw the Holy Number
John saw oh John saw
Heaven
ARMH, 196, d, Choral unaccompanied with additional historical information

CHET, 258, d, Text only

DETR, 63, Choral unaccompanied with additional historical information

FENC, 24, Choral unaccompanied with additional historical information

FENR, 24, Choral unaccompanied with additional historical information

JESM, 44, d, Solo voice with piano accompaniment and additional historical information

JOHJB, i, 158, d, Solo voice with piano accompaniment and additional historical information

MCIB, 157, d, Melody and additional historical information

PETL, 80, d, Text only

John Saw the Number No Man Could Number

John saw the number that no man could number comin' up on high

Heaven

Revelation 5:9–11, 14:3+

BALS, 46, d, Choral unaccompanied with additional historical information

PETL, 281, d, Text only

John the Bunyan

John de Bunyan o Lord

Songs of Spiritual Journey

HALC, 61, Choral with piano accompaniment and additional historical information

PETL, 359, d, Text only

John Was Writing

My Lord called John while He was a-writin'

Church

Revelation 1:12, 21:2, 5:12+

LOMAF, 480, Melody, chord symbols, and additional historical information

LOMJO, 22, d, Melody only

LOMJO2, 22, d, Melody only

John's Gone Down on the Island
I look away yonder what do I see
Heaven
Revelation 1:9, 21:21+
BURS, 133, d, Solo voice with piano accompaniment

John's on the Island on His Knees
John's on de island on his knees
Heaven
MCIB, 154, d, Melody and additional historical information
PETL, 132, d, Text only

Join the Angel Band
If you look up the road
Heaven
ALLS, 39, Melody only
PETL, 133, d, Text only

Join the Army of the Lord — see — Reign Oh Reign

Join the Heaven with the Angels
Join on join my Lord
Heaven
ODUN, 103, d, Text only; Source includes additional historical information

Join Them
On Sunday morning I seek my Lord
Church
ALLS, 21, d, Melody only
PETL, 80, d, Text only

Jordan's Mills
Jordan's mill's a-grinding
Jesus
PETL, 323, d, Text only

Joshua Fought the Battle of Jericho
Joshua fit de battle of Jericho
Songs of Spiritual Journey
Joshua 6:1–27+

ALBGH, 34, d, Solo voice with piano accompaniment
ALBGL, 34, d, Solo voice with piano accompaniment
ALTRH, 33, Solo voice with piano accompaniment
ALTRL, 33, Solo voice with piano accompaniment
APPA, 168, Solo voice with piano accompaniment
BELT, 23, d, Uses Tonic Sol-fa notation
BONI, 16, d, Solo voice with piano accompaniment
BOYE, 34, Solo voice with piano accompaniment
BRYI, 6, d, Melody only
BUCS, 5, Instrumental Ensemble accompaniment
BURP, 16, d, Solo voice with piano accompaniment
BURS, 192, d, Solo voice with piano accompaniment
CALA, 23, d, Melody only
CHAT, 52, d, Solo voice with piano accompaniment
CHET, 258, d, Text only
CHIA, 30, Melody only
CLES, 96, d, Choral with piano accompaniment and additional historical information
FRAS, 49, d, Solo voice with piano accompaniment
GUIU, 66, Solo voice with piano accompaniment
HAWD, 54, d, Text only
HAY1L, 57, d, Solo voice with piano accompaniment
HERB, 44, Text only
JOHHG, 31, d, Solo voice with piano accompaniment
JOHHH, 39, d, Solo voice with piano accompaniment
JOHJB, i, 56, d, Solo voice with piano accompaniment and additional historical information
JOHRA, 18, d, Solo voice with piano accompaniment
JORS, 22, d, Text only
LANC, 11, d, Melody, chord symbols, and additional historical information
LEU, 60, d, Melody, chord symbols, and piano accompaniment
LIES, 46, d, Solo voice with piano accompaniment
LOMJF, 466, d, Solo voice with piano accompaniment and additional historical information

MIL3, 20, Solo voice with piano accompaniment

NORS, 6, Melody and instrumental ensemble accompaniment

PETL, 231, d, Text only

RUTF, 1, d, Solo voice with piano accompaniment

SILSP, 42, d, Solo voice with piano accompaniment

SKEG, 5, d, Solo voice with piano accompaniment and chord symbols

SPAG, 32, d, Solo voice with piano accompaniment and chord symbols

TOBB, 32, d, Melody only

Joshua the Son of None

Joshua bin duh son ob nun

Faith

GUL, 48, d, Text only

Jubilee

Jubilee jubilee o Lordy jubilee what is the matter with the mourners

Praise

CHET, 258, Text only

CLES, 109, Choral with piano accompaniment and additional historical information

JOHJB, ii, 142, d, Solo voice with piano accompaniment and additional historical information

MIL3, 25, Solo voice with piano accompaniment

PETL, 282, d, Text only

Judgment

Judgment judgment oh how I long to go

Admonition/Judgment

DETR, 158, Choral unaccompanied with additional historical information

Judgment Day Is Rolling Around

Judgment judment judgment day is a-rollin'

Admonition/Judgment

Acts 7:59; 2 Corinthians 5:10*

ARMH, 206, d, Choral unaccompanied with additional historical information

CHET, 259, Text only

FENC, 34, d, Choral unaccompanied with additional historical information

FENR, 34, d, Choral unaccompanied with additional historical information

HERB, 44, Text only

MARS, 149, Choral unaccompanied with additional historical information

PETL, 282, d, Text only

PIKJ, 189, Choral unaccompanied with additional historical information

SANH, 68, Uses Tonic Sol-fa notation

SEWJC, 34, Choral unaccompanied with additional historical information

Judgment Day Is Trying Time

Let yo' light shine judgment day is tryin' time

Admonition/Judgment

MCIB, 158, d, Melody and additional historical information

PETL, 282, d, Text only

Judgment Will Find You So

Just as you live

Admonition/Judgment

MARS, 162, Choral unaccompanied with additional historical information

PETL, 283, d, Text only

PIKJ, 202, Choral unaccompanied with additional historical information

SEWJC, 47, Choral unaccompanied with additional historical information

Just Above My Head

Just above my head

Faith/Assurance

PETL, 179, d, Text only

Just As I Am

Lamb of God just as I am oh lamb of God I come

Aspiration
>> CLES, 208, Choral with piano accompaniment and additional historical information
>> CREO, 31, Solo voice with piano accompaniment
>> SPAG, 29, d, Solo voice with piano accompaniment and chord symbols

Just Behold That Number
Just behold that number
> Heaven
> Revelation 7:9, 14*
>> SANH, 69, Uses Tonic Sol-fa notation

Just Going Over in the Heavenly Land
You can hinder me here
> Heaven
>> BARO, 42, d, Melody only

Just Let Me Get Up in the House — see — Let Me Get Up

Just Let Me Get Up in the House of God — see — Let Me Get Up

Just Now
Sanctify me sanctify me
> Rituals of Preparation for Renewal/Regeneration
>> ALLS, 67, Melody only
>> PETL, 323, d, Text only

Just to Behold His Face
Not just to kneel with the angels nor to see love
> Heaven
>> CLES, 187, Choral with piano accompaniment and additional historical information

Keep in the Middle of the Road
Keep in the middle of the road I hear dem angels a-calling loud
> Songs of Spiritual Journey
>> PETL, 360, d, Text only
>> SIX, 58, d, Solo voice with piano accompaniment

Keep Inching Along

Keep a inchin' along

Songs of Spiritual Journey

John 14:3, 16:33; Mark 14:38*

ANDW, 20, Choral arrangement

CHET, 259, d, Text only

CLES, 93, d, Choral with piano accompaniment and additional historical information

DANF, 37, Melody only

DETR, 10, d, Choral unaccompanied with additional historical information

FENR, 154, d, Choral unaccompanied with additional historical information

FISS, 79, d, Solo voice with piano accompaniment and additional historical information

HALC, 7, d, Choral with piano accompaniment and additional historical information

HAWD, 102, Text only

HERB, 45, d, Text only

JOHJB, i, 134, d, Solo voice with piano accompaniment and additional historical information

JOHHT, 32, d, Solo voice with piano accompaniment

LOMAF, 456, d, Melody, chord symbols, and additional historical information

MARS, 186, Melody, chord symbols, and additional historical information

NAA, 17, Melody and chord symbols

ODUN, 89, d, Text only; Source includes additional historical information

PETL, 128, d, Text only

PETL, 359, d, Text only

SANH, 70, d, Uses Tonic Sol-fa notation

SIX, 49, d, Solo voice with piano accompaniment

WIES, 204, d, Solo voice with piano accompaniment

WORJF, 66, d, Text only; Source includes additional historical information

Keep Me from Sinking Down

Lord oh my good Lord keep me from sinkin' down

Deliverance
Matthew 14:30*
ARMH, 245, d, Choral unaccompanied with additional historical information
CHET, 260, Text only
DANF, 50, Melody only
DETD1, 21, Choral unaccompanied with additional historical information
DETR, 228, d, Choral unaccompanied with additional historical information
FENC, 73, d, Choral unaccompanied with additional historical information
FENR, 73, d, Choral unaccompanied with additional historical information
GREF, 99, d, Solo voice with piano accompaniment
HERB, 45, Text only
JOHJB, i, 156, d, Solo voice with piano accompaniment and additional historical information
MARS, 145, Choral unaccompanied with additional historical information
PETL, 397, d, Text only
PIKJ, 185, Choral unaccompanied with additional historical information
SANH, 99, Uses Tonic Sol-fa notation
SEWJ, 26, Choral arrangement
SEWJC, 26, Choral unaccompanied with additional historical information
STIT, 31, d, Solo voice with piano accompaniment and additional historical information
WORJF, 50, d, Text only; Source includes additional historical information

Keep Moving
Keep a-moving keep a-moving
Songs of Spiritual Journey
John 14:13; 1 Thessalonians 4:16*
MAR3, 303, d, Choral unaccompanied with additional historical information
SANH, 71, d, Uses Tonic Sol-fa notation

Keep Running

Keep un runnin' keep uh runnin'
Faith/Assurance
GUL, 49, d, Text only

Keep the Ark Moving

Let's keep de ark a movin' fer to hear what Jesus
Work Songs
MCIB, 159, d, Melody and additional historical information
PETL, 323, d, Text only

Keep Your Lamps Trimmed

Keep your lamps trimmed and a-burning
Faith/Assurance
BRUT, 18, d, Solo voice with piano accompaniment and additional historical information
CALA, 15, Text only
DANF, 58, Melody only
HERB, 45, d, Text only
MARS, 190, Choral unaccompanied with additional historical information
PETL, 180, d, Text only

Kind Savior

Helleluja kind Saviour let dis warfare be ended
Deliverance
HALC, 59, Choral with piano accompaniment and additional historical information
PETL, 180, d, Text only

King David

King David was good
Jesus
1 Samuel 16:11, 19; 17:34, 49–50+
COUNS, 26, Solo voice with piano accompaniment and additional historical information

King Emanuel (1)

Who do you call de King Emanuel

Jesus
> CHET, 260, Text only
>
> DETR, 147, Choral unaccompanied with additional historical information
>
> FENR, 25, Choral unaccompanied with additional historical information
>
> PETL, 80, d, Text only
>
> WORJF, 68, d, Text only; Source includes additional historical information

King Emanuel (2)

My King Emanuel

Jesus
> ALLS, 26, Melody only
>
> PETL, 231, d, Text only

King Jesus Built Me a House Above

King Jesus built me a house above

Heaven
> PETL, 81, d, Text only
>
> WORJA, 227, Choral unaccompanied with additional historical information

King Jesus Is Listening

King Jesus is alistenin' all day long

Jesus

Psalm 66:19^
> AAH, 364, d, Choral with piano accompaniment and additional historical information
>
> CALA, 16, d, Text only
>
> CHET, 260, d, Text only
>
> CLES, 152, d, Choral with piano accompaniment and additional historical information
>
> DANF, 44, d, Melody only
>
> JACL, 84, d, Choral with piano accompaniment and additional historical information
>
> JOHRR, 54, d, Solo voice with piano accompaniment and additional historical information
>
> SIX, 2, d, Solo voice with piano accompaniment

King Jesus Is My Only Friend
King Jesus is my only friend
Jesus
BALS, 6, d, Choral unaccompanied with additional historical information
PETL, 81, d, Text only

King Jesus Is the Rock
Lead me to the rock lead me to the rock
Jesus
ODUN, 92, Text only; Source includes additional historical information

King Jesus Sitting on the Water Side
Do Lord come show me de way
Jesus
MCIB, 167, d, Melody and additional historical information
PETL, 323, d, Text only

King of Kings
He is King of kings He is Lord of lords
Jesus
ANDW, 23, Choral arrangement
BRYW, 51, Melody only
BUCS, 18, Instrumental Ensemble accompaniment

King Oh King
I pitch my tent on dis camping groun(g)
Praise
GUL, 50, Text only
HUTS, 47, Melody and additional historical information

Kum Ba Yah
Come by here my Lord
Deliverance
2 Chronicles 6:21^
AFR, 43, Melody only
ALTRH, 10, Solo voice with piano accompaniment
ALTRL, 10, Solo voice with piano accompaniment

L'Envoi

I'm a going to travel
   Aspiration

Lamb Beautiful Lamb

Lamb beautiful lamb
   Rituals of Preparation for Renewal/Regeneration

Lamb's Blood Done Washed Me Clean

Let me tell you 'bout Lord Lord Lord
   Deliverance

Land I Am Bound For

Land I am bound for sweet Canaan's happy land

Aspiration
Acts 18:27; Numbers 34:2*
SANH, 110, Uses Tonic Sol-fa notation

Last Call
Gospel train is passing through
Death
KENMM, 38, d, Text only; Source includes additional historical information

Last Supper
Jesus was a-sittin' at the last Passover
Easter
HAYMF, 114, d, Solo voice with piano accompaniment and additional historical information
HAYMS, 115, d, Solo voice with piano accompaniment and additional historical information
PETL, 25, d, Text only

Lay Down Daniel Take Your Rest
Leddown Dan'ul tek yo res'
Faith/Assurance
GUL, 52, d, Text only
HUTS, 51, d, Melody and additional historical information

Lay This Body Down
Graveyard oh graveyard
Death
ALLS, 19, Melody only
CHET, 261, Text only
HERB, 46, Text only
LOMJA, 577, d, Melody only
PETL, 398, d, Text only

Lead Me to the Rock
Lead me lead me my Lord
Deliverance
HERB, 46, Text only
PETL, 324, d, Text only

Lead On O King Eternal
Lead on o King Eternal
Aspiration
NAA, 32, Melody and chord symbols

Lean on the Lord's Side
Poor Daniel he lean on the Lord's side
Deliverence
ALLS, 100, Melody only
PETL, 232, d, Text only

Leaning on That Lamb
Long time mo'ner
Faith/Assurance
JOHHT, 42, d, Solo voice with piano accompaniment

Leaning on the Lord (1)
If you want to see Jesus
Aspiration
DETR, 208, d, Choral unaccompanied with additional historical
information

Leaning on the Lord (2)
Tell me how did you feel when you come out de wilderness
Aspiration
JOHRS, 16, d, Solo voice with piano accompaniment

Leave You in the Hand of a Kind Savior
I'se uh gwine 'uh lebe yuh een duh han'
Deliverance
GUL, 51, d, Text only
HUTS, 49, d, Melody and additional historical information

Let God's Saints Come In
Come down angel and trouble the water
Songs of Spiritual Journey
Exodus 1:8–11, 3:7–10, 14+
ALLS, 76, Melody only
CHEA, 9, Solo voice with piano accompaniment

Let Us Cheer the Weary Traveler

Let us cheer the weary traveller

Like a Feather in the Wind
    We'll sail away to Heaven like a feather in the wind
        Heaven
            LOGR, 30, Melody only

Like a Rough and a Rolling Sea
    Farewell farewell to my only child
        Death
            DETR, 229, Choral unaccompanied with additional historical information

Listed in the Battlefield — see — Enlisted in the Field of Battle

Listen to the Angels
    Where do you think I found my soul
        Aspiration
            DANF, 54, d, Melody only
            LOYS, 41, d, Solo voice with piano accompaniment
            MAR3, 229, Choral unaccompanied with additional historical information
            MARS, 225, Choral unaccompanied with additional historical information
            PETL, 133, d, Text only

Listen to the Lambs
    Listen to de lambs
        Suffering
        Isaiah 40:11; John 21:15*
            BOAS, 79, Solo voice with piano accompaniment
            CHAT, 55, d, Solo voice with piano accompaniment
            CHET, 261, Text only
            DANF, 8, d, Melody only
            DETR, 136, d, Choral unaccompanied with additional historical information
            FENR, 158, d, Choral unaccompanied with additional historical information
            FISS, 102, d, Solo voice with piano accompaniment and additional historical information
            FREC, 12, Solo voice with piano accompaniment

GREF, 20, d, Solo voice with piano accompaniment
HAWD, 130, Text only
HERB, 48, Text only
JOHJB, i, 78, d, Solo voice with piano accompaniment and additional historical information
JOHRA, 44, d, Solo voice with piano accompaniment
LUEB, 64, Melody, chord symbols, and piano accompaniment
PETL, 26, d, Text only
SANH, 75, d, Uses Tonic Sol-fa notation
SILSP, 12, Solo voice with piano accompaniment
SNYS, 56, d, Solo voice with piano accompaniment
STIT, 23, d, Solo voice with piano accompaniment and additional historical information
TOBB, 13, Melody only

Little Black Train Is Coming

God tol' Hezekiah
    Admonition/Judgment
        GRIN, 10, d, Melody only
        LUEB, 38, d, Melody, chord symbols, and piano accompaniment
        PETL, 283, d, Text only

Little Boy

Lit'l boy how ole are you
    Jesus
        HAYMF, 103, d, Solo voice with piano accompaniment and additional historical information
        HAYMS, 103, d, Solo voice with piano accompaniment and additional historical information
        HERB, 49, d, Text only
        PETL, 82, d, Text only

Little Boy Named David

Li'l boy name David shepherd on de mountain
    Faith/Assurance
        1 Samuel 16:19, 17:15, 34, 49–51+
            CHET, 262, d, Text only
            KENMM, 124, d, Solo voice with piano accompaniment and additional historical information

Little Children
Little chillun I believe
Faith/Assurance
LOGR, 7, d, Melody only

Little Children Then Won't You Be Glad
Little children then won't you be glad
Heaven
ALLS, 87, Melody only
PETL, 232, d, Text only

Little Children You Better Believe
Little chillun you better believe
Praise
MCIB, 170, d, Melody and additional historical information
PETL, 325, d, Text only

Little David (1)
Little David play on your harp
Aspiration
Exodus 3:10; 1 Samuel 16:23*
AFR, 28, d, Choral with piano accompaniment
BARO, 26, d, Melody only
BELT, 8, d, Uses Tonic Sol-fa notation
BONR, 166, d, Solo voice with piano accompaniment
BOY3S, 44, Solo voice with piano accompaniment
BRYW, 3, d, Melody only
BURS, 60, d, Solo voice with piano accompaniment
CALA, 25, Melody only
CHAT, 58, Solo voice with piano accompaniment
CLES, 94, Choral with piano accompaniment and additional historical information
GREF, 40, d, Solo voice with piano accompaniment
GUL, 66, d, Text only
HAYMF, 30, d, Solo voice with piano accompaniment and additional historical information
HAYMS, 30, d, Solo voice with piano accompaniment and additional historical information
JOHJB, i, 65, d, Solo voice with piano accompaniment and additional historical information

LABC, 14, Solo voice with piano accompaniment
MCIB, 58, Melody and additional historical information
MIL3, 13, Solo voice with piano accompaniment
PETL, 82, d, Text only
PETL, 233, d, Text only
PETL, 284, d, Text only
SANH, 77, Uses Tonic Sol-fa notation
SIX, 16, Solo voice with piano accompaniment
TOBB, 14, Melody only
WORF, 41, Choral unaccompanied with additional historical information
WORJF, 73, d, Text only; Source includes additional historical information

Little David (2)
Little David play on your harp
Aspiration
Exodus 3:10; 1 Samuel 16:23*
ALTSH, 34, Solo voice with piano accompaniment
ALTSL, 34, Solo voice with piano accompaniment
BUR2H, 48, d, Solo voice with piano accompaniment
BUR2L, 48, d, Solo voice with piano accompaniment
DANF, 52, Melody only
DETD4, 10, d, Choral unaccompanied with additional historical information
DETR, 64, Choral unaccompanied with additional historical information
FENR, 139, Choral unaccompanied with additional historical information
HAWD, 28, Text only
HERB, 49, Text only
HERB, 50, Text only
JOHRA, 14, d, Solo voice with piano accompaniment
KENM, 160, d, Solo voice with piano accompaniment and additional historical information
LANC, 13, d, Melody, chord symbols, and additional historical information
MCIB, 172, d, Melody and additional historical information
NORS, 12, Melody and instrumental ensemble accompaniment
PETL, 233, d, Text only

SLA, 13, Choral arrangement
SPAG, 34, d, Solo voice with piano accompaniment and chord symbols
WALSH, 192, Solo voice with piano accompaniment
WALSL, 192, Solo voice with piano accompaniment

Little David (3)

Little David play on yo' harp
Aspiration
Exodus 3:10; 1 Samuel 16:23*
PETL, 399, d, Text only
SIMA, 9, d, Solo voice with piano accompaniment
WHIF, 81, d, Solo voice with piano accompaniment

Little David (4)

Hallelu
Aspiration
Exodus 3:10; 1 Samuel 16:23*
LIF, 211, Choral with piano accompaniment and additional historical information

Little Innocent Lamb

Little lamb little lamb little innocent lamb
Faith/Assurance
BECK, 7, Solo voice with piano accompaniment
HAY1H, 7, Solo voice with piano accompaniment
PETL, 134, d, Text only

Little Talk with Jesus

Brother pray brother pray
Faith/Assurance
BOAS, 15, Solo voice with piano accompaniment
HAWD, 62, Text only

Little Talk with Jesus Makes It Right

Little talk with Jesus makes it right
Faith/Assurance
JOHJB, ii, 74, d, Solo voice with piano accompaniment and additional historical information

PETL, 83, d, Text only

WORF, 24, d, Choral unaccompanied with additional historical information

Little Wheel Turning in My Heart

There's a little wheel turning in my heart

Praise

John 15:11*

CHET, 238, d, Text only

DANF, 50, d, Melody only

DETR, 168, d, Choral unaccompanied with additional historical information

FENC, 100, d, Choral unaccompanied with additional historical information

FENR, 100, d, Choral unaccompanied with additional historical information

FISS, 104, d, Solo voice with piano accompaniment and additional historical information

FIST, 18, d, Solo voice with piano accompaniment

GREF, 3, d, Solo voice with piano accompaniment

GUL, 24, d, Text only

HUTS, 85, d, Melody and additional historical information

LLOA, 146, d, Solo voice with piano accompaniment

PETL, 325, d, Text only

PITG, 91, d, Solo voice with piano accompaniment

SANH, 133, d, Uses Tonic Sol-fa notation

WIES, 195, d, Solo voice with piano accompaniment

Live A-Humble — see — Humble Yourself the Bell Done Ring

Live Humble (1)

Live a-humble humble yourselves de bell's a done a rung

Songs of Spiritual Journey

CLES, 108, Choral with piano accompaniment and additional historical information

DETR, 12, Choral unaccompanied with additional historical information

HAYMF, 106, d, Solo voice with piano accompaniment and additional historical information

HAYMS, 107, d, Solo voice with piano accompaniment and additional historical information

HERB, 51, Text only

PETL, 362, d, Text only

WORF, 4, Choral unaccompanied with additional historical information

WORJF, 54, d, Text only; Source includes additional historical information

WORJF, 74, d, Text only; Source includes additional historical information

Live Humble (2)

Ol' man Adam were de fus'man invented

   Songs of Spiritual Journey

      COLS, 91, d, Solo voice with piano accompaniment

Living Humble

Po' moanuh won't chew jus' believe

   Songs of Spiritual Journey

      PARS, 152, d, Melody only

Lonesome Valley (1)

I must walk this lonesome valley I must walk it for myself

   Songs of Spiritual Journey

      KINS, 25, d, Solo voice with piano accompaniment

      PETL, 21, d, Text only

Lonesome Valley (2)

My brother want to get religion

   Songs of Spiritual Journey

      ALLS, 5, Melody only

      BURS, 87, d, Solo voice with piano accompaniment

      FREC, 10, Solo voice with piano accompaniment

      KENM, 98, d, Solo voice with piano accompaniment and additional historical information

      PETL, 362, d, Text only

      PETL, 373, d, Text only

WORJF, 53, d, Text only; Source includes additional historical information

Lonesome Valley (3)
You got to walk that lonesome valley
Songs of Spiritual Journey
BLA, 7, d, Solo voice with piano accompaniment
CHET, 277, Text only
GRIN, 2, Melody only
KINS, 25, d, Solo voice with piano accompaniment
LOMJF, 444, d, Solo voice with piano accompaniment and additional historical information

Look at How They Done My Lord
Look-a how they done my Lord
Easter
BALS, 56, d, Choral unaccompanied with additional historical information
HERB, 52, Text only
JOHJB, ii, 168, d, Solo voice with piano accompaniment and additional historical information
PETL, 26, d, Text only

Look Away — see also — Some of These Mornings

Look Away in the Heaven (1)
Look away in-a-Heaven look away look away
Heaven
ANDW, 26, Choral arrangement
BOAS, 65, Solo voice with piano accompaniment
DITT, 54, Choral arrangement
PETL, 27, d, Text only

Look Away in the Heaven (2)
When I get to heav'n gwine to sing and shout cause there's no one there to turn me out
Heaven
SIX, 9, Solo voice with piano accompaniment

Look What a Wonder Jesus Done
Look what a wonder Jesus done
Jesus
BALS, 69, d, Choral unaccompanied with additional historical information
PETL, 326, d, Text only

Lord Abide with Me
Lord I need Thy saving arms about me
Prayer
BOAS, 61, Solo voice with piano accompaniment

Lord Answer My Prayer
Humm Lordy chained in Hell an' can't come out
Prayer
MCIB, 183, d, Melody and additional historical information
PETL, 138, d, Text only

Lord Bless the Name
I've got to go to judgment I don't know how soon
Admonition/Judgment
ODUN, 67, Text only; Source includes additional historical information

Lord Don't Move This Mountain
Lord don't move this mountain but give me strength
Aspiration
CLES, 173, Choral with piano accompaniment and additional historical information

Lord Have Mercy
Lord have mercy have mercy when I come to die Lord
Suffering
DETR, 236, Choral unaccompanied with additional historical information
HERB, 61, Text only
MCIB, 189, Melody and additional historical information
PETL, 34, d, Text only
RAIJ, 64, Solo voice with piano accompaniment

Lord Heal Him
> There's a sick man at the pool
>> Faith/Assurance
>>> KENMM, 25, d, Text only; Source includes additional historical information
>>> KENMM, 27, d, Melody only

Lord Help Me to Hold Out
> Lord help me to hold out
>> Faith/Assurance
>>> CLES, 194, Choral with piano accompaniment and additional historical information

Lord How Come Me Here
> Lord how come me here
>> Suffering
>>> CHET, 262, Text only
>>> HERB, 52, Text only
>>> OKS2, 18, Solo voice with piano accompaniment

Lord I Can Not Stay Here by Myself
> Lord I can not stay here by mase'f
>> Suffering
>>> MCIB, 178, d, Melody and additional historical information

Lord I Can't Keep from Crying
> Lord I just can't keep from cryin' some time
>> Suffering
>>> BONR, 138, d, Solo voice with piano accompaniment

Lord I Can't Stay Away — see — I Can't Stay Away

Lord I Can't Stay Here by Myself
> Lord I can't stay here by myself
>> Suffering
>>> CHET, 262, Text only

Lord I Can't Turn Back
> Lord I can't turn back Lord I can't turn just because I been born again

Rituals of Preparation for Renewal/Regeneration
LOYS, 26, d, Solo voice with piano accompaniment

Lord I Cannot Stay Here by Myself
Lord I cannot stay here by myself
Suffering
PETL, 27, d, Text only

Lord I Cannot Stay Here by Myself — see also — I Cannot Stay Here by Myself

Lord I Don't Feel Noways Tired — see — I Am Seeking for a City

Lord I Done Done
Lord I done done o Lord I done done
Faith/Assurance
FISS, 130, d, Solo voice with piano accompaniment and additional historical information
HERB, 25, Text only

Lord I Just Can't Keep from Crying
Lord I just can't keep from cryin' sometime
Suffering
TAYA, 48, d, Solo voice with piano accompaniment

Lord I Just Got Over
I have been tryin' a great long while
Deliverance
ODUN, 66, Text only; Source includes additional historical information

Lord I Want to Be a Christian
Lord I want to be a Christian
Aspiration
Ephesians 6:6; 1 John 3:18; Matthew 5:8*
AAH, 463, Choral with piano accompaniment and additional historical information
ANDW, 29, Choral arrangement

SIX, 23, Solo voice with piano accompaniment
SLA, 9, Choral arrangement
STIT, 37, d, Solo voice with piano accompaniment and additional historical information
WAL14H, 35, Solo voice with piano accompaniment
WAL15H, 35, Solo voice with piano accompaniment
WAL15L, 35, Solo voice with piano accompaniment
WALSH, 35, Solo voice with piano accompaniment
WALSL, 35, Solo voice with piano accompaniment
WORF, 17, Choral unaccompanied with additional historical information
WORJF, 131, d, Text only; Source includes additional historical information

Lord I Want to Be a Christian/Give Me Jesus

Lord I want to be a Christian in my heart
Aspiration
Ephesians 6:6; 1 John 3:18; Matthew 5:8*
OKS1, 45, Solo voice with piano accompaniment

Lord I Want Two Wings — see — Two Wings

Lord I Wish I Had Come

Lord I wish I had a-come
Suffering
Hebrews 12:25*
MARS, 196, d, Choral unaccompanied with additional historical information
PETL, 27, d, Text only
SANH, 79, Uses Tonic Sol-fa notation

Lord I'm Hungry

Lord I'm hungry
Suffering
CHET, 266, Text only
PETL, 35, d, Text only
WORJT, 7, Choral unaccompanied with additional historical information

Lord Is My Shepherd
    Lord the Lord the Lord is my shepherd
        Faith/Assurance
            PETL, 83, d, Text only
            WORJA, 223, Choral unaccompanied with additional historical information

Lord Is This Heaven
    Lord is this Heaven
        Heaven
            CHEA, 12, Solo voice with piano accompaniment
            MCIB, 174, d, Melody and additional historical information
            PETL, 234, d, Text only

Lord Keep Me from Sinking Down — see — Keep Me from Sinking Down

Lord Lord Lord
    Lord Lord Lord you've sure been good to me
        Praise
            ANDW, 24, Choral arrangement

Lord Make Me More Patient
    Lord make me more patient
        Songs of Spiritual Journey
            ALLS, 52, Melody only
            PETL, 363, d, Text only

Lord Make Us More Holy
    Lord make us more holy
         Deliverance
            SEV, 69, Choral with piano accompaniment and additional historical information

Lord Remember Me
    Death he is a little man
        Death
         Luke 23:40–43#
            ALLS, 12, Melody only
            PETL, 400, d, Text only

Lord These Bones of Mine
> Lord these bones of mine
>> Rituals of Preparation for Renewal/Regeneration
>>> BALS, 70, d, Choral unaccompanied with additional historical information
>>> PETL, 329, d, Text only

Lord Time Is Drawing Nigh
> Good-bye Mother
>> Death
>>> PARS, 185, d, Melody only

Lord Touch Me
> Lord I want you to touch me
>> Aspiration
>>> CLES, 199, Choral with piano accompaniment and additional historical information

Lord Until I Reach My Home
> Lord until I reach my home
>> Faith/Assurance
>>> CHET, 262, Text only
>>> DETD3, 32, Choral unaccompanied with additional historical information
>>> FENR, 171, Choral unaccompanied with additional historical information
>>> PETL, 134, d, Text only

Lord Write My Name
> Lord write my name
>> Songs of Spiritual Journey
>>> HALC, 49, Choral with piano accompaniment and additional historical information
>>> PETL, 401, d, Text only

Lord's Been Here
> Lord's been here and blessed my soul
>> Rituals of Preparation for Renewal/Regeneration
>>> HERB, 82, Text only
>>> PETL, 326, d, Text only

Lordy Lordy Lordy
Me 'n' my pahdner an' two'r three mo'
Work Songs
ODUN, 257, d, Text only; Source includes additional historical information

Lost Sheep — see — Done Found My Lost Sheep

Love and Serve the Lord — see — If You Love God Serve Him

Love Come Trickling Down
Ask an' a you shall be given
Praise
KENM, 119, d, Melody only

Love Come Twinkling Down
Love come twinkling down
Praise
WORJF, 65, d, Text only; Source includes additional historical information

Love Feast in Heaven
There's a love feast in Heaven
Heaven
DANF, 30, Melody only
MARS, 182, Choral unaccompanied with additional historical information
PETL, 84, d, Text only

Love King Jesus
Elder you say you love King Jesus
Jesus
MAR3, 309, Choral unaccompanied with additional historical information
WORJF, 69, d, Text only; Source includes additional historical information

Love King Jesus — see also — Elder You Say You Love King Jesus

Love the Lord
Well did you say that you love Jesus
Jesus
ODUN, 94, Text only; Source includes additional historical information

Low Down Chariot
Let-n me ride oh low down the chariot
Songs of Spiritual Journey
CALA, 23, Text only
LOMJO, 36, Melody only
LOMJO2, 36, Melody only

Made My Vow to the Lord — see — Done Made My Vow to the Lord

Make a Me Holy
Make a me holy I do love
Praise
MAR3, 290, Choral unaccompanied with additional historical information
MARS, 256, Choral unaccompanied with additional historical information

Man Goin' Round Taking Names — see — There's a Man Going Around Taking Names

Many Thousand Go
No more peck of corn for me no more auction block for me
Deliverance
ALLS, 48, Melody only
BARN, 162, d, Solo voice with piano accompaniment and additional historical information
BRYI, 53, d, Melody only
CHET, 263, Text only
CLES, 137, Choral with piano accompaniment and additional historical information
DETD1, 31, Choral unaccompanied with additional historical information

March Along

March Down to Jordan

March On (1)
March on and we shall gain the victory
Deliverance
NAA, 20, Melody and chord symbols
WORJF, 71, d, Text only; Source includes additional historical
information

March On (2)
Way over in de Egyp'lan'
Deliverance
GREF, 46, Solo voice with piano accompaniment
JOHHG, 38, Solo voice with piano accompaniment
JOHHH, 46, d, Solo voice with piano accompaniment
MARS, 166, Choral unaccompanied with additional historical
information
PETL, 135, d, Text only
PIKJ, 206, Choral unaccompanied with additional historical
information
SEWJC, 51, Choral unaccompanied with additional historical
information

Marching Up the Heavenly Road
Marching up the heavenly road
Heaven
PETL, 135, d, Text only

Mary and Martha
Mary and Martha's just gone along
Women
Luke 10:38–42*
ANDW, 2, d, Choral arrangement
CHET, 263, Text only
CLES, 162, Choral with piano accompaniment and additional
historical information
DETD1, 23, Choral unaccompanied with additional historical
information
HERB, 53, Text only
JOHJB, ii, 81, d, Solo voice with piano accompaniment and addi-
tional historical information

Luke 1:26–38; Matthew 1:18–25+
BALS, 5, d, Choral unaccompanied with additional historical information
BALS, 40, d, Choral unaccompanied with additional historical information
BALS, 41, d, Choral unaccompanied with additional historical information
BECK, 61, Solo voice with piano accompaniment
BRYW, 15, Melody only
BUCS, 14, Instrumental Ensemble accompaniment
BULA, 185, Solo voice with piano accompaniment
CALA, 21, Text only
CHET, 263, Text only
HAY1H, 61, Solo voice with piano accompaniment
HERB, 54, Text only
JOHHT, 46, d, Solo voice with piano accompaniment
JOHJB, ii, 124, d, Solo voice with piano accompaniment and additional historical information
PETL, 28, d, Text only
WAL14H, 38, Solo voice with piano accompaniment
WAL15H, 38, Solo voice with piano accompaniment
WAL15L, 38, Solo voice with piano accompaniment
WALSH, 38, Solo voice with piano accompaniment
WALSL, 38, Solo voice with piano accompaniment

Mary Had a Baby (2)
Mary had a baby O Lord
Christmas
Luke 1:26–38; Matthew 1:18–25+
CALA, 22, Text only

Mary Wept and Martha Moaned
Mary wept an'-a Martha moaned
Women
GRIN, 34, d, Melody only
GUL, 53, d, Text only
KENM, 135, d, Solo voice with piano accompaniment and additional historical information
PETL, 181, d, Text only

Mary Where Is Your Baby
Read in de gospel o' Mathayew
Christmas
KENM, 137, d, Solo voice with piano accompaniment and additional historical information

Mary Wore Three Links of Chain
Mary wo' three links of chain every link was Jesus' name
Songs of Spiritual Journey
LLOA, 147, Solo voice with piano accompaniment
LOMJF, 468, d, Solo voice with piano accompaniment and additional historical information

Mary's Baby Boy — see — Mary Had a Baby

Master Going to Sell Us — see — Mother Is Master Going to Sell Us Tomorrow

May Be the Last Time
I don't know I don't know I don't know
Death
DITT, 28, Choral arrangement
PARS, 166, d, Text only; Source includes additional historical information
PETL, 29, d, Text only

Meet Oh Lord
Meet oh Lord on the milk-white horse
Christmas
ALLS, 43, Melody only
PETL, 284, d, Text only

Meet You in the Morning — see — Shine Shine I'll Meet You in the Morning

Members Don't Get Weary
Members don't get weary
Faith/Assurance
JOHJB, ii, 155, d, Solo voice with piano accompaniment and additional historical information
PETL, 84, d, Text only

Moan Member Moan
Tell-a me who dat had a rod
Admonition/Judgment
LOMJA, 578, d, Melody only

Moanin' Dove — see — Sometimes I Feel Like a Moanin' Dove

Moaning
Trumpet sounds it in my soul
Deliverance
LOMJA, 579, d, Melody only

Moses Smote the Water
Moses smote the water
Deliverance
BALS, 86, d, Choral unaccompanied with additional historical
information
PETL, 181, d, Text only

Most Done Traveling — see — Almost Done Traveling

Mother Don't You Weep
When I'm gone o mother don't you weep
Admonition/Judgment
BLOR, 208, Text and chord symbols
BUR2H, 19, d, Solo voice with piano accompaniment
BUR2L, 19, d, Solo voice with piano accompaniment
BURS, 180, d, Solo voice with piano accompaniment
DANF, 22, Melody only
PETL, 91, d, Text only
WALSH, 158, d, Solo voice with piano accompaniment
WALSL, 158, Solo voice with piano accompaniment
WORF, 40, Choral unaccompanied with additional historical
information

Mother Is Master Going to Sell Us Tomorrow
Mother is massa gwine to sell us tomorrow

Suffering
    CHET, 263, Text only
    DETR, 230, d, Choral unaccompanied with additional historical information
    FENC, 86, d, Choral unaccompanied with additional historical information
    FENR, 86, d, Choral unaccompanied with additional historical information
    FISS, 92, d, Solo voice with piano accompaniment and additional historical information
    PETL, 21, d, Text only
    PETL, 28, d, Text only
    TAYA, 16, d, Solo voice with piano accompaniment

Motherless Child — see — Sometimes I Feel Like a Motherless Child

Motherless Children Have a Hard Time
Motherless children have a hard time
    Suffering
        DITT, 27, Choral arrangement
        GUL, 56, d, Text only
        PETL, 30, d, Text only

Mount Zion
On my journey now
    Songs of Spiritual Journey
        PETL, 364, d, Text only

Move Along
Let us move along move along
    Heaven
        MAR3, 260, Choral unaccompanied with additional historical information
        MARS, 226, Choral unaccompanied with additional historical information
        PETL, 182, d, Text only

Move Me
Move me move me move me to do Thy will

Aspiration
    CLES, 185, Choral with piano accompaniment and additional historical information

Move Members Move
Move members move Daniel got on my rough shed shoes
    Church
        COUN, 230, Melody only
        COUNS, 2, Solo voice with piano accompaniment and additional historical information
        JOHRS, 19, Solo voice with piano accompaniment

Move Out the Way and Let Me Shine
Moob out duh way en' lemme shine shine shine
    Praise
        GUL, 55, d, Text only

Move the Camping Ground
Duh preachuh gawt 'uh moob
    Faith/Assurance
        GUL, 54, d, Text only

Move Up the King's Highway
All up the way the host is tramping
    Songs of Spiritual Journey
        BOAS, 75, Solo voice with piano accompaniment

Murmering Word — see — He Never Said a Mumbling Word

My Army's Crossing Over
My brother take care of Satan
    Deliverance
        ALLS, 38, Melody only
        PETL, 182, d, Text only

My Body Rock Along Fever — see — My Body Rocked a Long Fever

My Body Rocked a Long Fever
Wait my brother better true believe

Suffering
ALLS, 32, Melody only
PETL, 30, d, Text only

My Brethren Don't Get Weary — see — Brothers Don't Get Weary

My Brother I Do Wonder
My brother I do wonder
Aspiration
DETD1, 18, Choral unaccompanied with additional historical information

My Brother's Died and Gone to Heaven
My brother's died and gone to Heaven
Death
FISS, 108, d, Solo voice with piano accompaniment and additional historical information
PETL, 236, d, Text only

My Faith Looks Up to Thee
My faith looks up to Thee
Faith/Assurance
CLES, 215, Choral with piano accompaniment and additional historical information
NAA, 34, Melody and chord symbols

My Father How Long
My Father how long poor sinner suffer here
Suffering
ALLS, 93, Melody only
PETL, 182, d, Text only
SILSP, 40, Solo voice with piano accompaniment

My Father Took a Light
My father took a light and went to Heaven
Songs of Spiritual Journey
FISS, 112, d, Solo voice with piano accompaniment and additional historical information
PETL, 400, d, Text only

My God He Is a Man of War
My God He is a man a man of war
Praise
GRIN, 28, Melody only
PETL, 85, d, Text only

My God Is a Rock
My God is a rock in a weary land
Praise
CHET, 264, Text only
PARS, 161, Text only; Source includes additional historical information
PETL, 85, d, Text only

My God Is So High
My God is so high yuh can't get over Him
Praise
BRUT, 4, d, Solo voice with piano accompaniment and additional historical information
CALA, 22, Text only
CHET, 263, d, Text only
CLES, 105, d, Choral with piano accompaniment and additional historical information
HAYMF, 82, d, Solo voice with piano accompaniment and additional historical information
HAYMS, 83, d, Solo voice with piano accompaniment and additional historical information
HERB, 54, Text only
JOHHG, 6, Solo voice with piano accompaniment
JOHHH, 14, d, Solo voice with piano accompaniment
PETL, 379, d, Text only

My Good Lord's Been Here
My good Lord's done been here
Rituals of Preparation for Renewal/Regeneration
Luke 18:37*
BLA5, 14, Solo voice with piano accompaniment
BOAS, 77, Solo voice with piano accompaniment
BRYW, 5, Melody only

My Head Wet with the Midnight Dew

My head wet with the midnight dew

Rituals of Preparation for Renewal/Regeneration

My Little Black Star

My baby is lak' a little black star

Songs of Spiritual Journey

My Little Soul

I don't care where you bury my body

Heaven

My Little Soul's Going to Shine
My little soul's going to shine shine
Faith/Assurance
ARMH, 173, d, Choral unaccompanied with additional historical information
DANF, 16, d, Melody only
SIX, 19, d, Solo voice with piano accompaniment
WORJF, 56, d, Text only; Source includes additional historical information

My Lord Delivered Daniel
My Lord delivered Daniel
Deliverance
Daniel 3:28, 6:1–24+
ARMH, 193, d, Choral unaccompanied with additional historical information
DETR, 65, Choral unaccompanied with additional historical information
FENC, 21, d, Choral unaccompanied with additional historical information
FENR, 21, Choral unaccompanied with additional historical information
HAWD, 120, Text only
MAR3, 308, d, Choral unaccompanied with additional historical information
SANH, 82, Uses Tonic Sol-fa notation

My Lord God Rocking in the Weary Land
Way out yondah in de ocean
Faith/Assurance
KENM, 40, d, Melody only

My Lord Is Riding All the Time
He sees all you do and hears all you say
Admonition/Judgment
FENC, 98, Choral unaccompanied with additional historical information

My Lord Says He's Going to Rain Down Fire
My Lord my Lord

My Lord What a Morning

SLA, 31, Choral arrangement
SPAG, 38, d, Solo voice with piano accompaniment and chord symbols
SPAG, 62, d, Solo voice with piano accompaniment and chord symbols
TRAH, 75, Melody, chord symbols, and piano accompaniment
UNI, 719, Melody only
WAL25H, 43, d, Solo voice with piano accompaniment
WAL25L, 43, Solo voice with piano accompaniment
WALSH, 196, d, Solo voice with piano accompaniment
WALSL, 196, d, Solo voice with piano accompaniment
WARE, 66, d, Solo voice with piano accompaniment and additional historical information
WHIF, 114, d, Solo voice with piano accompaniment

My Lord What a Mourning — see — My Lord What a Morning

My Lord What Shall I Do
What you goin' to do wen death comes creeping in
Admonition/Judgment
BOAS, 19, Solo voice with piano accompaniment
HAWD, 107, Text only
KENMM, 81, d, Solo voice with piano accompaniment and additional historical information
MCIB, 187, d, Melody and additional historical information
PETL, 89, d, Text only

My Lord What Should I Do — see — My Lord What Shall I Do

My Lord's Coming Again
My Lord's comin' again
Admonition/Judgment
ODUN, 74, d, Text only; Source includes additional historical information

My Lord's Going to Move This Wicked Race
My Lord's goin' move this wicked race
Faith/Assurance
HAWD, 95, Text only

PETL, 285, d, Text only

WORJA, 217, d, Choral unaccompanied with additional historical information

My Lord's Riding All the Time — see — My Lord's Writing All the Time

My Lord's Writing All the Time

He sees all you do and hears all you say

Admonition/Judgment

BOAS, 39, Solo voice with piano accompaniment

CHET, 264, d, Text only

DETR, 150, d, Choral unaccompanied with additional historical information

FENR, 98, d, Choral unaccompanied with additional historical information

GREF, 54, d, Solo voice with piano accompaniment

HAWD, 115, Text only

HERB, 56, Text only

JOHHG, 24, d, Solo voice with piano accompaniment

JOHHH, 32, d, Solo voice with piano accompaniment

JOHJB, i, 123, d, Solo voice with piano accompaniment and additional historical information

PETL, 285, d, Text only

My Lord's Writing Down Time

Goose quill's a scratchin' in de count book

Death

BURP, 6, d, Solo voice with piano accompaniment

My Loving Brother

My lovin' brother

Suffering

ANDW, 2, d, Choral arrangement

My Merlindy Brown

Light bugs glimmer down de lane

Suffering

BURP, 12, d, Solo voice with piano accompaniment

My Mind Stayed on Freedom
   I woke up this morning with my mind
      Faith/Assurance
         PETL, 86, d, Text only

My Mother Got a Letter
   Well my mother got a letter oh yes
      Admonition/Judgment
         ODUN, 120, Text only; Source includes additional historical
            information

My Mother's in Heaven
   My mother's in Heaven
      Heaven
         LOGR, 3, Melody only

My Name's Been Written Down
   How's you know written down
      Deliverance
         COUN, 244, Melody only

My Name's Written on High
   Hail hail I belong to the bloodwashed army
      Praise
         PETL, 237, d, Text only
         WORF, 13, Choral unaccompanied with additional historical
            information

My Ship Is on the Ocean
   My Father how long
      Deliverance
         JOHJB, ii, 150, d, Solo voice with piano accompaniment and
            additional historical information
         MARS, 165, Choral unaccompanied with additional historical
            information
         PETL, 183, d, Text only
         PIKJ, 205, Choral unaccompanied with additional historical
            information
         SANH, 84, Uses Tonic Sol-fa notation

My Soul's Been Anchored in the Lord (1)

My soul's been anchored in the Lord
Faith/Assurance
Acts 27:9–12; Psalm 27:5; Hebrews 6:19+
HERB, 57, d, Text only
PETL, 364, d, Text only
WORF, 43, Choral unaccompanied with additional historical information

My Soul's Been Anchored in the Lord (2)

In de Lord in de Lord my soul's been anchored in de Lord
Faith/Assurance
Acts 27:9–12; Psalm 27:5; Hebrews 6:19+
BLA5, 4, d, Solo voice with piano accompaniment
CALA, 28, Melody only
CHET, 264, d, Text only
CLES, 74, d, Choral with piano accompaniment and additional historical information
JOHJB, ii, 37, d, Solo voice with piano accompaniment and additional historical information
PETL, 401, d, Text only
PRI4, 79, d, Solo voice with piano accompaniment
TAYA, 83, d, Solo voice with piano accompaniment

My Soul's Determined

Ma little soul's determin'
Faith/Assurance
MCIB, 181, d, Melody and additional historical information
PETL, 136, d, Text only

My Soul's Going to Heaven

Goin' to weep goin' to mourn
Aspiration
ODUN, 101, d, Text only; Source includes additional historical information

My Time Is Come

Jesus was settin' at the last Passover

Admonition/Judgment

> BALS, 59, d, Choral unaccompanied with additional historical information
>
> PETL, 31, d, Text only

My Trouble Is Hard

I know a man that was here before Christ

> Suffering
>
> > ODUN, 130, Text only; Source includes additional historical information

My Way's Cloudy

Brothern my way my way's cloudy

> Suffering
>
> Leviticus 25:8–13; Matthew 24:27, 31*
>
> > BAYF, 34, d, Solo voice with piano accompaniment and chord symbols
> >
> > BURS, 172, d, Solo voice with piano accompaniment
> >
> > CHET, 265, Text only
> >
> > CHIA, 32, Melody only
> >
> > DETD1, 28, Choral unaccompanied with additional historical information
> >
> > DETR, 231, Choral unaccompanied with additional historical information
> >
> > FENC, 97, Choral unaccompanied with additional historical information
> >
> > FENR, 97, Choral unaccompanied with additional historical information
> >
> > FREC, 23, Solo voice with piano accompaniment
> >
> > HERB, 58, Text only
> >
> > JOHJB, i, 92, d, Solo voice with piano accompaniment and additional historical information
> >
> > MARS, 167, Choral unaccompanied with additional historical information
> >
> > PETL, 31, d, Text only
> >
> > PETL, 32, d, Text only
> >
> > PIKJ, 207, Choral unaccompanied with additional historical information

SANH, 85, Uses Tonic Sol-fa notation
SEWJC, 52, Choral unaccompanied with additional historical information
SILSP, 28, d, Solo voice with piano accompaniment
WALSH, 202, d, Solo voice with piano accompaniment
WALSL, 202, Solo voice with piano accompaniment

Negro Lullaby
Mammy's baby go ter sleep
Faith/Assurance
BURP, 14, d, Solo voice with piano accompaniment

Never a Man Speak like This Man
Look-a death look-a death
Jesus
KREA, 159, d, Choral with piano accompaniment and additional historical information

Never Leave Me Alone
Never leave me alone alone
Faith/Assurance
DITT, 26, Choral arrangement
PETL, 87, d, Text only

Never Me One
When my mother done gone
Suffering
BALS, 43, d, Choral unaccompanied with additional historical information
PETL, 184, d, Text only

Never Said a Mumbalin — see — He Never Said a Mumbling Word

Never Saw Such a Man
Never saw such a man before
Jesus
PETL, 87, d, Text only

New Born
Newborn oh my good Lord there in the manger lies the Savior
Christmas
BOAT, 93, d, Solo voice with piano accompaniment

New Born Again
I found free grace and dying love
Rituals of Preparation for Renewal/Regeneration
John 3:3^
AAH, 362, Choral with piano accompaniment and additional
historical information
BAP, 474, Choral with piano accompaniment and additional
historical information
BARO, 7, d, Melody only
FISS, 119, d, Solo voice with piano accompaniment and additional
historical information
PETL, 327, d, Text only

New Born Baby
Baby born in Bethlehem glory to the new born babe
Christmas
BOAT, 13, d, Solo voice with piano accompaniment
FISS, 24, d, Solo voice with piano accompaniment and additional
historical information
PETL, 87, d, Text only

New Burying Ground
My Lord good and kind take the little babe
Death
BARO, 35, d, Melody only

New Hiding Place
The rocks and the mountains shall all flee away
Heaven
BOAS, 47, Solo voice with piano accompaniment

Ninety-Nine and a Half Wouldn't Do
Oh you gawt'uh preach right to mek up a hundud

Faith/Assurance
GUL, 59, d, Text only

No Condemnation in My Soul

I feel all right no condemnation
Rituals of Preparation for Renewal/Regeneration
GRIN, 92, Melody only
PETL, 365, d, Text only

No Devil in Our Land

I'm so glad dere aint no devil in our lan'
Praise
MCIB, 129, d, Melody and additional historical information
PETL, 237, d, Text only

No Hiding Place — see also — There's No Hiding Place Down There

No Hiding Place

No hidin' place
Admonition/Judgment
HALU, 10, d, Solo voice with piano accompaniment
HAWD, 67, Text only
PARS, 151, d, Melody only

No I Ain't Ashamed

No I ain't ashame
Rituals of Preparation for Renewal/Regeneration
MCIB, 191, d, Melody and additional historical information
PETL, 328, d, Text only

No Liar Can Stand

Juniors ride aller roun' Gawd's alter
Admonition/Judgment
MCIB, 193, d, Melody and additional historical information
PETL, 286, d, Text only

No Man Can Hinder Me

Walk in kind Saviour

Faith/Assurance
>ALLS, 10, Melody only
>PETL, 137, d, Text only

No More Auction Block — see — Many Thousand Gone

No More My Dear Brother
No mo' my dear brother
>Songs of Spiritual Journey
>>BALS, 42, d, Choral unaccompanied with additional historical information
>>PETL, 365, d, Text only

No More Rain Fall to Wet You
No more rain fall for wet you
>Death
>>ALLS, 46, Melody only
>>CHET, 265, Text only
>>PETL, 237, d, Text only

Noah Hoist the Window
Norah hist the windah let the dove come in
>Work Songs
>Genesis 6:14–22+
>>GUL, 61, d, Text only
>>HUTS, 57, d, Melody and additional historical information
>>PARS, 134, d, Melody only

Noah Noah
Noah Noah who built this ark
>Work Songs
>Genesis 6:14–22+
>>COUN, 246, Melody only
>>GUL, 62, d, Text only
>>GUL, 63, d, Text only
>>SIX, 54, Solo voice with piano accompaniment

Nobody Knows the Trouble I Feel

Nobody knows the trouble I feel
Suffering
PETL, 32, d, Text only

Nobody Knows the Trouble I See (1)

Nobody knows the trouble I see
Suffering
Revelation 2:2, 9; 1 Thessalonians 5:25*
BAYF, 22, d, Solo voice with piano accompaniment and chord symbols
BRYW, 45, Melody only
CHAT, 65, Solo voice with piano accompaniment
CLES, 170, Choral with piano accompaniment and additional historical information
DANF, 4, Melody only
FISS, 124, d, Solo voice with piano accompaniment and additional historical information
GAIF, 211, Solo voice with piano accompaniment
HAWD, 23, Text only
HERB, 58, Text only
KREA, 164, Choral with piano accompaniment and additional historical information
LOGR, 32, Melody only
PETL, 33, d, Text only
SKEG, 22, d, Solo voice with piano accompaniment and chord symbols
SPAG, 39, d, Solo voice with piano accompaniment and chord symbols
UNI, 520, Melody only
WHIF, 9, d, Solo voice with piano accompaniment
WORJF, 57, d, Text only; Source includes additional historical information

Nobody Knows the Trouble I See (2)

Nobody knows the trouble I see Lord brothers will you pray for me
Suffering
Revelation 2:2, 9; 1 Thessalonians 5:25*
CALA, 29, Melody only

CLES, 171, Choral with piano accompaniment and additional historical information on the spiritual

DETD3, 31, Choral unaccompanied with additional historical information

FIST, 13, Solo voice with piano accompaniment

HERB, 59, Text only

JOHJB, ii, 34, d, Solo voice with piano accompaniment and additional historical information

LIF, 172, Choral with piano accompaniment and additional historical information

MARS, 125, Choral unaccompanied with additional historical information

PIKJ, 165, Choral unaccompanied with additional historical information

SAAT, 4, d, Solo voice with piano accompaniment

SANH, 86, Uses Tonic Sol-fa notation

SEWJ, 5, Choral arrangement

SEWJC, 9, Choral unaccompanied with additional historical information

WORJF, 50, d, Text only; Source includes additional historical information

Nobody Knows the Trouble I've Had
Nobody knows the trouble I've had
Suffering
ALLS, 55, Melody only
FREC, 30, Solo voice with piano accompaniment
LLOA, 137, d, Solo voice with piano accompaniment
SLA, 1, Melody only

Nobody Knows the Trouble I've Seen
Nobody knows the trouble I've seen nobody knows but Jesus
Suffering
Revelation 2:2, 9; 1 Thessalonians 5:25*
ALTRH, 40, d, Solo voice with piano accompaniment
ALTRL, 40, d, Solo voice with piano accompaniment
ALTSH, 50, Solo voice with piano accompaniment
ALTSL, 50, Solo voice with piano accompaniment
ANDW, 31, Choral arrangement

MIL3, 31, Solo voice with piano accompaniment
PETL, 33, d, Text only
SILSP, 32, Solo voice with piano accompaniment
SIX, 31, d, Solo voice with piano accompaniment
SNYS, 10, d, Solo voice with piano accompaniment
WALSH, 199, Solo voice with piano accompaniment
WALSL, 199, Solo voice with piano accompaniment
WARE, 68, d, Solo voice with piano accompaniment and additional
    historical information
WIES, 197, d, Solo voice with piano accompaniment

Nobody Knows Who I Am

Nobody knows who I am
  Admonition/Judgment
    PETL, 34, d, Text only
    WORF, 39, Choral unaccompanied with additional historical
      information

None but the Righteous

None but the righteous shall see God come Thou fount of every blessing
  Praise
    BOAS, 8, Solo voice with piano accompaniment
    HAWD, 68, Text only

Not Weary Yet

Me no weary yet
  Faith/Assurance
    ALLS, 12, Melody only
    PETL, 137, d, Text only

Now Is the Needy Time

Now is the needy time
  Deliverance
    BOAS, 16, Solo voice with piano accompaniment
    HAWD, 72, Text only

Now Let Me Fly

Way down yonder in de middle o' de fiel' angel workin' at de chariot
wheel

Aspiration
CHIA, 36, Melody only
JOHRA, 41, Solo voice with piano accompaniment

Now We Take This Feeble Body
Now we take this feeble body
Death
1 Corinthians 15:55; Philippians 3:20–21*
DETS, 14, Solo voice with piano accompaniment
MAR3, 253, Choral unaccompanied with additional historical information
MARS, 219, Choral unaccompanied with additional historical information
PETL, 34, d, Text only
SANH, 88, Uses Tonic Sol-fa notation
WORJF, 59, d, Text only; Source includes additional historical information

Number Me One
Nummer me one
Admonition/Judgment
PARS, 188, d, Melody only

O Adam Where Are You — see — What a Trying Time

Oh Daniel
You call yourself a church member
Admonition/Judgment
Daniel 6:20–21+
ALLS, 94, Melody only
CHET, 266, Text only
PETL, 183, d, Text only

Oh Fix Me
Oh oh fix me oh oh fix me
Rituals of Preparation for Renewal/Regeneration
CHET, 267, Text only

Oh Freedom

Oh freedom over me and before I'd be a slave I'd be buried in my grave and go home to my Lord and be free

Deliverance

Galatians 4:26; John 8:36; Luke 14:18*

SLA, 38, Choral arrangement
WARE, 70, d, Solo voice with piano accompaniment and additional historical information

Oh Glory

Oh glory oh glory there is enough room in paradise
Heaven
HERB, 60, Text only
JOHHH, 108, d, Solo voice with piano accompaniment
OKS2, 52, Solo voice with piano accompaniment
PETL, 88, d, Text only

Oh Graveyard

Oh graveyard oh graveyard
Death
JOHHT, 64, d, Solo voice with piano accompaniment

Oh Holy Lord

Oh Holy Lord done with the sin and sorrow
Praise
Isaiah 6:3, 7*
BOAS, 38, Solo voice with piano accompaniment
HAWD, 147, Text only
JOHRS, 12, Solo voice with piano accompaniment
MARS, 157, Choral unaccompanied with additional historical information
PETL, 238, d, Text only
PIKJ, 197, Melody only
SANH, 95, Uses Tonic Sol-fa notation
SEWJC, 43, Melody only

Oh Holy Savior

Oh Holy Savior
Deliverance
DETD4, 32, Choral unaccompanied with additional historical information

Oh Jerusalem

Oh Jerusalem oh my Lord

Songs of Spiritual Journey
  DETR, 190, Choral unaccompanied with additional historical
    information
  FENR, 111, Choral unaccompanied with additional historical
    information
  PETL, 366, d, Text only

Oh Lawd How Long — see — Before This Time Another Year

Oh Lord What Harm I Done
  I gone tuh duh winduh fuh tuh look out
    Suffering
      GUL, 64, d, Text only
      HUTS, 59, d, Melody and additional historical information

Oh Mary
  Oh Mary what you gonna name that pretty little baby
    Christmas
      AFR, 30, Choral arrangement

Oh Mary Oh Martha
  Oh Mary oh Martha go tell my disciples
    Aspiration
      GRIN, 14, d, Melody only
      PETL, 89, d, Text only

Oh Redeemed Redeemed
  Redeem redeem been washed in the blood of the Lamb
    Rituals of Preparation for Renewal/Regeneration
    Revelation 7:14*
      BRUO, 5, d, Solo voice with piano accompaniment
      GREF, 62, d, Solo voice with piano accompaniment
      HALC, 52, d, Choral with piano accompaniment and additional
        historical information
      MARS, 128, Choral unaccompanied with additional historical
        information
      PETL, 330, d, Text only

PETL, 403, d, Text only
PIKJ, 168, Choral unaccompanied with additional historical information
SAAT2, 10, d, Solo voice with piano accompaniment
SANH, 103, Uses Tonic Sol-fa notation
SEWJ, 8, Choral arrangement
SEWJC, 31, Choral unaccompanied with additional historical information

Oh Sinner

Oh sinner yo' bed's too short
Admonition/Judgment
GRIN, 44, Melody only
PETL, 288, d, Text only

Oh the Robe

Oh de robe de robe my Lord
Death
PARS, 180, d, Text only; Source includes additional historical information

Oh the Sunshine

Oh the sunshine
Praise
ODUN, 67, Text only; Source includes additional historical information

Oh Yes (1)

Oh yes oh yes
Faith/Assurance
ARMH, 186, d, Choral unaccompanied with additional historical information
DETR, 210, Choral unaccompanied with additional historical information
FENC, 14, Choral unaccompanied with additional historical information
FENR, 14, Choral unaccompanied with additional historical information
PETL, 240, d, Text only

Oh Yes (2)

I come this night to sing and pray
Faith/Assurance
BAYF, 48, d, Solo voice with piano accompaniment and chord symbols
FREC, 40, d, Solo voice with piano accompaniment
JOHJB, ii, 105, d, Solo voice with piano accompaniment and additional historical information
MAR3, 246, Choral unaccompanied with additional historical information
MARS, 212, Choral unaccompanied with additional historical information
MCLS, 46, d, Solo voice with piano accompaniment
PETL, 241, d, Text only
PETL, 402, d, Text only
SILSP, 38, d, Solo voice with piano accompaniment

Oh Yes (3)

I'm a-tellin' yo' mah bredren a mortal fac'
Faith/Assurance
DANF, 53, Melody only

Oh! Look-a Death — see — Never a Man Speak like This Man

Old Ark Is Moving Along (1)

Ol'ark's a-moverin'
Work Songs
ABBE, 12, d, Solo voice with piano accompaniment
ANDW, 32, d, Choral arrangement
CHET, 238, d, Text only
CLAC, 16, d, Solo voice with piano accompaniment
CLES, 113, d, Choral with piano accompaniment and additional historical information
JOHH, 28, d, Solo voice with piano accompaniment
JOHHG, 20, d, Solo voice with piano accompaniment
JOHJB, ii, 25, d, Solo voice with piano accompaniment and additional historical information
LOMAF, 475, d, Melody, chord symbols, and additional historical information

MAR3, 310, Choral unaccompanied with additional historical information

PETL, 368, d, Text only

SIX, 41, d, Solo voice with piano accompaniment

SLA, 18, Choral arrangement

TOBB, 18, d, Melody only

WORF, 19, d, Choral unaccompanied with additional historical information

WORJF, 73, d, Text only; Source includes additional historical information

Old Ark Is Moving Along (2)

Just wait a little while

Work Songs

ARMH, 249, d, Choral unaccompanied with additional historical information

DETD2, 24, d, Choral unaccompanied with additional historical information

DETR, 58, d, Choral unaccompanied with additional historical information

FENC, 77, d, Choral unaccompanied with additional historical information

FENR, 77, d, Choral unaccompanied with additional historical information

PETL, 90, d, Text only

Old Churchyard

O come come with me to the old churchyard

Deliverance

MCKF, 8, Solo voice with piano accompaniment

Old Egypt (1)

Keep uh runnin' (keep on running)

Admonition/Judgment

HUTS, 61, d, Melody and additional historical information

Old Egypt (2)

Leaduh don' let yo' elduh condemn yuh

Admonition/Judgment

HUTS, 63, d, Melody and additional historical information

Old Man Devil Gotta Go Some
>Broken-hearted world broken-hearted children
>>Satan
>>>CHAT, 94, d, Solo voice with piano accompaniment

Old Satan
>Old Satan is one busy ole man
>>Satan
>>>PETL, 241, d, Text only

Old Sheep Done Know the Road
>Old sheep done know the road
>>Rituals of Preparation for Renewal/Regeneration
>>>ARMH, 198, d, Choral unaccompanied with additional historical information
>>>CHET, 278, Text only
>>>DETR, 4, d, Choral unaccompanied with additional historical information
>>>FENC, 26, d, Choral unaccompanied with additional historical information
>>>FENR, 26, d, Choral unaccompanied with additional historical information
>>>JOHJB, ii, 160, d, Solo voice with piano accompaniment and additional historical information
>>>PETL, 328, d, Text only

Old Ship Maria
>'Tis the ole ship Maria
>>Deliverance
>>>BALS, 34, d, Choral unaccompanied with additional historical information
>>>PETL, 186, d, Text only

Old Ship of Zion (1)
>What ship is that a-sailing hallelujah
>>Deliverance
>>>HERB, 61, Text only
>>>MARS, 152, Choral unaccompanied with additional historical information
>>>PETL, 185, d, Text only

      PETL, 186, d, Text only

      PIKJ, 192, Choral unaccompanied with additional historical information

      SEWJC, 35, Choral unaccompanied with additional historical information

Old Ship of Zion (2)

Come along come along and let's go home

  Deliverance

      ALLS, 102, Melody only

      BARO, 23, d, Melody only

      CLES, 131, d, Choral with piano accompaniment and additional historical information on the spiritual

      CLES, 189, Choral with piano accompaniment and additional historical information on the spiritual

      DETD2, 29, d, Choral unaccompanied with additional historical information

      FENC, 85, d, Choral unaccompanied with additional historical information

      FENR, 85, d, Choral unaccompanied with additional historical information

      SIX, 32, Solo voice with piano accompaniment

      UNI, 345, d, Melody only

Old Ship of Zion (3)

This ole ship is a reelin' an' a rockin'

  Deliverance

      ODUN, 117, d, Text only; Source includes additional historical information

      PETL, 186, d, Text only

Old Ship of Zion (4)

Ole ship o' Zion ole ship o' Zion

  Deliverance

      KENMM, 126, d, Text only; Source includes additional historical information

Old Time Religion

Gimme that old time religion gimme that old time religion it's good enough for me

Church
Psalm 22:4*

APPA, 164, Solo voice with piano accompaniment
BLOR, 211, Text and chord symbols
BOAS, 2, Solo voice with piano accompaniment
BRYI, 12, d, Melody only
CALA, 35, Melody only
CHET, 268, d, Text only
CHIA, 12, Melody only
CLES, 89, d, Choral with piano accompaniment and additional historical information
CREO, 5, d, Solo voice with piano accompaniment
DETR, 200, d, Choral unaccompanied with additional historical information
FRAS, 24, Solo voice with piano accompaniment
GUL, 32, d, Text only
HAWD, 35, Text only
HERB, 20, d, Text only
JOHJB, i, 76, d, Solo voice with piano accompaniment and additional historical information
JOHRA, 50, d, Solo voice with piano accompaniment
KENMM, 15, d, Melody only
LOYS, 69, d, Solo voice with piano accompaniment
LUEB, 30, d, Melody, chord symbols, and piano accompaniment
MARS, 158, Choral unaccompanied with additional historical information
MIL3, 41, Solo voice with piano accompaniment
NAA, 22, Melody and chord symbols
NEW, 151, Choral with piano accompaniment and additional historical information
ODUN, 142, d, Text only; Source includes additional historical information
PETL, 62, d, Text only
PETL, 101, d, Text only
PIKJ, 198, Choral unaccompanied with additional historical information
SAAT2, 3, d, Solo voice with piano accompaniment
SANH, 112, Uses Tonic Sol-fa notation
SEWJC, 41, Choral unaccompanied with additional historical information

SLA, 11, Choral arrangement
SNYS, 54, d, Solo voice with piano accompaniment
SPAG, 17, d, Solo voice with piano accompaniment and chord symbols
WIES, 203, d, Solo voice with piano accompaniment
WORJF, 65, d, Text only; Source includes additional historical information

Old Zion's Children Marching Along
Old Zion's children marching along
Songs of Spiritual Journey
PETL, 368, d, Text only

On Calvary — see — Calvary

On Canaan Shore
Sister Cath'rine hold your light sister Cath'rine hold your light
Songs of Spiritual Journey
DANF, 41, Melody only

On My Journey
On mah journey now Mount Zion
Faith/Assurance
Psalm 125:1; Mark 1:10; John 1:51; Acts 7:56+
CALA, 36, d, Melody only
CHET, 269, d, Text only
CLES, 157, d, Choral with piano accompaniment and additional historical information

On My Knees — see — Communion

On the Banks of Jordan
It's cool down there on the banks of Jordan
Heaven
PITG, 97, Solo voice with piano accompaniment

On the Lamb
Onnuh yuh mudduh fuh duh good 'e hab done
Faith/Assurance
GUL, 65, d, Text only

On the Other Side of Jordan — see — Going to Roll in My Jesus' Arms

On to Glory
Come my sisters bretheren too come an' jine dis heab'nly crew
Praise
ALLS, 66, Melody only
JOHRR, 105, d, Solo voice with piano accompaniment and additional historical information
PETL, 242, d, Text only

One More River — see — Noah's Ark

One More River to Cross
Wasn't that a wide river
Songs of Spiritual Journey
APPA, 177, Solo voice with piano accompaniment
HAWD, 108, Text only
SPAG, 43, d, Solo voice with piano accompaniment and chord symbols

One of These Days
One'a these days I'm a gonna walk on the streets of glory
Death
PARS, 167, d, Text only; Source includes additional historical information
SIX, 48, d, Solo voice with piano accompaniment

Only a Look
Only a look at Jesus oh so bowed down with care
Admonition/Judgment
CLES, 197, Choral with piano accompaniment and additional historical information

Onward Christian Soldiers
Onward Christian soldiers
Faith/Assurance
NAA, 28, Melody and chord symbols

Open Door
O brethren all that mourn and weep just lay your burden down

Heaven
DANF, 23, Melody only

Open the Window Noah

Open the window Noah
Work Songs
Genesis 6:14–22+
BRYA, 40, Melody, chord symbols, and additional historical information
BUCS, 12, Instrumental Ensemble accompaniment
CHET, 269, Text only
PETL, 329, d, Text only

Other World Is Not Like This

I was walking along the other day
Admonition/Judgment
ODUN, 123, d, Text only; Source includes additional historical information

Our Lord Healed the Sick

Our Lord heal' de sick gave sight to de blin'
Faith/Assurance
DANF, 57, d, Melody only

Over My Head

Over my head I hear music in the air
Heaven
BLOR, 211, Text and chord symbols
BRUT, 8, d, Solo voice with piano accompaniment and additional historical information
CALA, 37, Melody only
CHET, 269, Text only
CLES, 167, Choral with piano accompaniment and additional historical information
NEW, 488, Choral with piano accompaniment and additional historical information
WHII, 52, d, Solo voice with piano accompaniment

Over the Crossing
Bending knees a-aching body racked with pain
Suffering
ALLS, 72, d, Melody only
HERB, 64, Text only
PETL, 91, d, Text only

Over Yonder
I got a sister over yonder
Songs of Spiritual Journey
JOHHT, 38, d, Solo voice with piano accompaniment

Paul and Silas — see — All Night Long

Peter Go Ring Them Bells
Peter go ring dem bells Peter go ring dem bells I heard f'om Heav'n today
Heaven
Psalms 99:1–9, 149:1–9; Mark 9:1–13; Luke 9:27–36; Ephesians
1:11–23;
2 Peter 1:16–21+
ARMH, 174, d, Choral unaccompanied with additional historical
information
BAYF, 28, d, Solo voice with piano accompaniment and chord
symbols
BELT, 9, d, Uses Tonic Sol-fa notation
BONR, 172, d, Solo voice with piano accompaniment
BRYA, 28, Melody, chord symbols, and additional historical
information
BURC1, 21, d, Solo voice with piano accompaniment
BURS, 198, d, Solo voice with piano accompaniment
CHAT, 68, d, Solo voice with piano accompaniment
CHET, 269, d, Text only
CHIA, 37, Melody only
CLES, 97, Choral with piano accompaniment and additional
historical information
DETR, 204, d, Choral unaccompanied with additional historical
information

FENC, 2, d, Choral unaccompanied with additional historical information

FENR, 2, d, Choral unaccompanied with additional historical information

FRAS, 66, Solo voice with piano accompaniment

FREC, 8, d, Solo voice with piano accompaniment

HAWD, 128, Text only

HELC, 34, d, Solo voice with piano accompaniment

HERB, 65, Text only

JOHJB, i, 137, d, Solo voice with piano accompaniment and additional historical information

JOHRA, 30, d, Solo voice with piano accompaniment

MAR3, 270, Choral unaccompanied with additional historical information

MARS, 236, Choral unaccompanied with additional historical information

MIL3, 9, Solo voice with piano accompaniment

PETL, 243, d, Text only

SANH, 100, Uses Tonic Sol-fa notation

SILSP, 10, d, Solo voice with piano accompaniment

SIX, 44, d, Solo voice with piano accompaniment

SNYS, 52, d, Solo voice with piano accompaniment

SPAG, 40, d, Solo voice with piano accompaniment and chord symbols

SPAG, 56, d, Solo voice with piano accompaniment and chord symbols

STIT, 73, d, Solo voice with piano accompaniment and additional historical information

WHIF, 28, d, Solo voice with piano accompaniment

WIES, 207, d, Solo voice with piano accompaniment

WORJF, 46, d, Text only; Source includes additional historical information

Peter on the Sea

Peter Peter Peter on the sea

Faith/Assurance

Daniel 6:16; Jonah 1:17; Matthew 14:29–30, 24:31+

BARO, 40, d, Melody only

DETR, 68, Choral unaccompanied with additional historical information

FENC, 88, Choral unaccompanied with additional historical information

FENR, 88, Choral unaccompanied with additional historical information

GREF, 88, Solo voice with piano accompaniment

HAWD, 27, Text only

JOHRA, 48, d, Solo voice with piano accompaniment

JOHRR, 83, d, Solo voice with piano accompaniment and additional historical information

PETL, 139, d, Text only

RAIJ, 72, Solo voice with piano accompaniment

WHIF, 89, d, Solo voice with piano accompaniment

Pharaoh's Army

If you want your souls converted you'd better be a-praying
Deliverance
DANF, 28, Melody only

Pick and Shovel Song

Run here mama run here mama
Work Songs
ODUN, 255, Text only; Source includes additional historical information

Pilgrim's Song

I'm just a poor wayfarin' stranger a travelin' through this world of woe
Deliverance
CALA, 28, Text only
CHET, 254, Text only
DETR, 191, Choral unaccompanied with additional historical information
FENR, 126, Choral unaccompanied with additional historical information
HAG3, 178, Solo voice with piano accompaniment
LIF, 19, Choral with piano accompaniment and additional historical information

LOMJF, 438, d, Solo voice with piano accompaniment and additional historical information
LOYS, 77, d, Solo voice with piano accompaniment
ODUN, 137, Text only; Source includes additional historical information
PETL, 140, d, Text only
SLA, 4, Choral arrangement
TRAH, 73, Melody, chord symbols, and piano accompaniment
WAR1, 42, Solo voice with piano accompaniment

Plenty Good Room (1)

God got plenty o' room way in the Kingdom so many weeks and days have passed

Heaven

John 14:2^

ALLS, 106, Melody only
HAY1H, 3, Solo voice with piano accompaniment
PETL, 64, d, Text only

Plenty Good Room (2)

Plenty good room in my Father's Kingdom plenty good room my Lord's done just what He said

Heaven

John 14:2^

AAH, 352, Choral with piano accompaniment and additional historical information
BECK, 3, Solo voice with piano accompaniment
BOAT, 102, d, Solo voice with piano accompaniment
CALA, 23, Text only
CHET, 238, d, Text only
CHIA, 38, Melody only
CLES, 99, Choral with piano accompaniment and additional historical information
HAYMF, 64, d, Solo voice with piano accompaniment and additional historical information
HAYMS, 64, d, Solo voice with piano accompaniment and additional historical information
HERB, 65, Text only
HERB, 66, Text only

PETL, 92, d, Text only
PETL, 403, d, Text only
WORF, 10, Choral unaccompanied with additional historical information

Poor Heathens Are Dying
Poor heathens are dyin'
Rituals of Preparation for Renewal/Regeneration
BALS, 15, d, Choral unaccompanied with additional information
PETL, 330, d, Text only

Poor Little Jesus
Po' li'l Jesus hail Lawd child o' Mary
Jesus
GREF, 10, d, Solo voice with piano accompaniment
HERB, 63, d, Text only
KENM, 78, d, Solo voice with piano accompaniment and additional historical information
LOMJF, 446, d, Solo voice with piano accompaniment and additional historical information
PETL, 35, d, Text only

Poor Me — see — Trouble Will Bury Me Down

Poor Moaner You Shall Be Free
Fo' de Lawd gwine take my stan'
Deliverance
LOGR, 12, d, Melody only

Poor Mourner (1)
Charley went out huntin' on a moonshiney night
Suffering
NILS, 6, d, Solo voice with piano accompaniment and additional historical information

Poor Mourner (2)
Get out de population an' raise yo' voices high
Suffering
DANF, 35, Melody only

Poor Mourner's Got a Home At Last

Poor mourner's got a home at last no harm no harm no harm tell brudder 'Lijah

Death

DETD1, 22, Choral unaccompanied with additional historical information

HERB, 67, Text only

JOHHT, 56, d, Solo voice with piano accompaniment

JOHJB, ii, 78, d, Solo voice with piano accompaniment and additional historical information

OWEN, 7, d, Solo voice with piano accompaniment

PATN, 69, d, Solo voice with piano accompaniment

PETL, 92, d, Text only

Poor Pilgrim (1)

I am a poor wayfaring stranger

Suffering

DETR, 169, Melody only

Poor Pilgrim (2)

I am a poor pilgrim of sorrow I'm in this wide world alone

Suffering

CHIA, 39, Melody only

HAYMF, 77, d, Solo voice with piano accompaniment and additional historical information

HAYMS, 77, d, Solo voice with piano accompaniment and additional historical information

TRAH, 71, Melody, chord symbols, and piano accompaniment

Poor Rosy

Poor Rosy poor gal

Suffering

ALLS, 7, Melody only

Poor Sinner

Poor sinner now is your time

Death

Acts 26:18; Ecclesiastics 12:1–2; Genesis 2:7*

SANH, 102, Uses Tonic Sol-fa notation

Poor Sinner Fare You Well
I ain't got time to tarry
Admonition/Judgment
MCIB, 194, d, Melody and additional historical information
PETL, 290, d, Text only

Poor Sinner Man
My mother 'n' yo' mother both daid an' gone
Suffering
ODUN, 88, d, Text only; Source includes additional historical information

Poor Wayfaring Stranger — see — Pilgrim's Song

Praise Chant
From Heaven
Deliverance
PETL, 187, d, Text only

Praise Member
Praise member praise God
Praise
ALLS, 4, Melody only

Praise the Lamb
Got glory an' honor praise Jesus
Praise
MCIB, 202, d, Melody and additional historical information
PETL, 244, d, Text only

Prancing Horses
Brother an' a hey hey ma Lord who's dat comin'
Jesus
MCIB, 204, d, Melody and additional historical information
PETL, 244, d, Text only

Pray All Night
Pray on brothers pray all night
Prayer
LOGR, 20, Melody only

Pray All the Members

Pray all the member

Prayer

ALLS, 35, Melody only

PETL, 140, d, Text only

Pray On

Pray on pray on

Prayer

ALLS, 97, Melody only

BARO, 14, d, Melody only

PETL, 330, d, Text only

Pray on the Way

I promised my Lord I would deny Him not

Prayer

DETD4, 12, Choral unaccompanied with additional historical information

Prayer Is the Key of Heaven

Prayer is the key of Heaven

Prayer

James 5:15–16*

CHET, 269, Text only

DETR, 171, d, Choral unaccompanied with additional historical information

FENR, 146, d, Choral unaccompanied with additional historical information

JOHHT, 54, d, Solo voice with piano accompaniment

PETL, 368, d, Text only

SANH, 119, Uses Tonic Sol-fa notation

Praying in the Land

Praying in de lan'

Prayer

HALC, 17, d, Choral with piano accompaniment and additional historical information

PETL, 369, d, Text only

Praying Is the Key to the Kingdom
Pray is the key to the Kingdom
 Prayer
  BALS, 73, d, Melody only
  PETL, 369, d, Text only

Prepare Me One Body
Prepare me
 Songs of Spiritual Journey
  HAYMF, 96, d, Solo voice with piano accompaniment and additional historical information
  HAYMS, 96, d, Solo voice with piano accompaniment and additional historical information
  PETL, 403, d, Text only
  SEWJC, 49, Choral unaccompanied with additional historical information

Prepare Us
Prepare me prepare me Lord prepare me when death shall shake this frame
 Songs of Spiritual Journey
  MARS, 164, Choral unaccompanied with additional historical information
  PETL, 370, d, Text only
  PIKJ, 204, Choral unaccompanied with additional historical information
  SAAT2, 17, d, Solo voice with piano accompaniment

Pretty Little Baby
Virgin Mary had a little baby
 Jesus
  BLOR, 211, Text and chord symbols

Promise Land
Oh Uh gawt uh manshum up on high w'ut en'(t) mek wid han'
 Songs of Spiritual Journey
  GUL, 67, d, Text only
  HUTS, 65, d, Melody and additional historical information

Pure Religion
Lord you must have dat pure religion
Admonition/Judgment
MCIB, 206, Melody and additional historical information
PETL, 291, d, Text only

Put John on the Island
Hail hail put John on the island
Admonition/Judgment
DETR, 160, d, Choral unaccompanied with additional historical information
FENR, 122, d, Choral unaccompanied with additional historical information
PETL, 187, d, Text only

Rain Fall and Wet Becca Lawton
Rain fall and wet Becca Lawton
Suffering
ALLS, 21, Melody only
PETL, 37, d, Text only

Raise the Iron
Brother Rabbit Brother Bear
Work Songs
ODUN, 262, Text only; Source includes additional historical information

Rally All Around the Fountain Lord
Oh rally aw(l) roun'(g) duh founting Lawd
Praise
GUL, 68, d, Text only

Reborn Again
Rebawn again rebawn again if you want to get to Heaven got to reborn again
Rituals of Preparation for Renewal/Regeneration
GUL, 69, d, Text only
HUTS, 67, d, Melody and additional historical information

Reign Master Jesus

Reign oh reign oh reign my Saviour
Aspiration
DETR, 49, d, Choral unaccompanied with additional historical information
FENR, 175, d, Choral unaccompanied with additional historical information
MAR3, 287, Choral unaccompanied with additional historical information
MARS, 253, Choral unaccompanied with additional historical information
PETL, 187, d, Text only

Reign My Savior

Reign my saviour reign Master Jesus
Aspiration
John 5:14; Revelation 11:15*
SANH, 104, Uses Tonic Sol-fa notation

Reign Oh Reign

Reign oh reign oh reign my Savior
Aspiration
MARS, 169, Choral unaccompanied with additional historical information
MCIB, 152, d, Melody and additional historical information
PETL, 179, d, Text only
PETL, 245, d, Text only
PIKJ, 209, Melody only
SEWJC, 55, Melody only
WORJF, 72, d, Text only; Source includes additional historical information

Religion Is a Fortune

Religion is a fortune I raly do believe
Faith/Assurance
ARMH, 189, d, Choral unaccompanied with additional historical information
DANF, 38, Melody only

DETR, 201, Choral unaccompanied with additional historical information

FENC, 17, Choral unaccompanied with additional historical information

FENR, 17, Choral unaccompanied with additional historical information

JOHHT, 72, d, Solo voice with piano accompaniment

JOHJB, ii, 53, d, Solo voice with piano accompaniment and additional historical information

PETL, 92, d, Text only

WORF, 14, Choral unaccompanied with additional historical information

WORJF, 48, d, Text only; Source includes additional historical information

Religion So Sweet
Walk Jordan long road
Praise
ALLS, 13, Melody only
CHET, 270, Text only
LOMJA, 582, d, Melody only
PETL, 93, d, Text only

Religion That My Lord Gave Me
Religion that my Lord gave me
Faith/Assurance
PETL, 93, d, Text only

Remember Me
Do Lord remember me
Admonition/Judgment
Luke 23:40–43#
AAH, 434, Choral with piano accompaniment and additional historical information
PETL, 291, d, Text only

Remember the Dying Lamb
Go Mary go stay Martha stay

Faith/Assurance
    MCIB, 208, d, Melody and additional historical information
    PETL, 245, d, Text only

Remon
Mo parle Remon
  Faith/Assurance
    ALLS, 110, Melody only

Restitution
Restitution it's a great great doctrine
  Admonition/Judgment
    CHAT, 99, Solo voice with piano accompaniment

Resurrection Morn
Run Mary run hallelu hallelu
  Praise
    ALLS, 54, Melody only
    PETL, 246, d, Text only

Ride On
Ride on ride on
  Heaven
  Revelation 19:11–16*
    DETR, 194, Choral unaccompanied with additional historical information
    FENR, 120, Choral unaccompanied with additional historical information
    PETL, 246, d, Text only

Ride On Conquering King
I've been tempted
  Heaven
    DITT, 44, Choral arrangement
    PARS, 182, Text only; Source includes additional historical information
    PETL, 246, d, Text only

Ride On Jesus

Ride on ride on ride on Jesus ride on conquering King
Heaven
Revelation 19:11–16*
>BALS, 92, d, Melody only
>DETR, 148, Choral unaccompanied with additional historical information
>JOHHT, 8, d, Solo voice with piano accompaniment
>KINS, 29, d, Solo voice with piano accompaniment

Ride On King Jesus (1)

Ride on King Jesus no man can a-hinder me
Jesus
Psalm 45:4^
>AAH, 225, Choral with piano accompaniment and additional historical information
>BALF, 9, Solo voice with cello accompaniment
>BAYF, 24, d, Solo voice with piano accompaniment and chord symbols
>BURS, 147, d, Solo voice with piano accompaniment
>CALA, 38, Melody only
>CHAT, 111, Solo voice with piano accompaniment
>CHET, 270, Text only
>CLES, 77, Choral with piano accompaniment and additional historical information
>FISS, 138, d, Solo voice with piano accompaniment and additional historical information
>FIST, 22, Solo voice with piano accompaniment
>HERB, 68, Text only
>HERB, 69, Text only
>JOHHH, 113, d, Solo voice with piano accompaniment
>JOHHH, 118, d, Solo voice with piano accompaniment
>JOHHH, 123, d, Solo voice with piano accompaniment
>LIF, 97, Choral with piano accompaniment and additional historical information
>MARS, 168, Choral unaccompanied with additional historical information
>PETL, 141, d, Text only
>PIKJ, 208, Melody only

SANH, 120, Uses Tonic Sol-fa notation
SEWJC, 54, Melody only
SNYS, 40, d, Solo voice with cello accompaniment
WARE, 74, d, Solo voice with piano accompaniment and additional historical information

Ride On King Jesus (2)
Ride on King Jesus ride conquering King I want to go to Heaven in the morning
Jesus
Psalm 45:4^
BOAT, 107, d, Solo voice with piano accompaniment
OKS2, 40, Solo voice with piano accompaniment
PETL, 247, d, Text only

Ride On Moses
I've been traveling all day ride on Moses
Deliverance
JOHJB, i, 70, d, Solo voice with piano accompaniment and additional historical information
PETL, 404, d, Text only
SPAG, 46, d, Solo voice with piano accompaniment and chord symbols

Ride the Chariot
Ride the chariot in the morning Lord
Songs of Spiritual Journey
ALTRH, 6, Solo voice with piano accompaniment
ALTRL, 6, Solo voice with piano accompaniment
HERB, 69, Text only
PETL, 405, d, Text only

Ride Up in the Chariot — see — Going to Ride Up in the Chariot

Ring Jerusalem
Jerusalem ma happy home
Rituals of Preparation for Renewal/Regeneration
MCIB, 210, Melody and additional historical information
PETL, 331, d, Text only

Ring the Bells
Ring the bells all God's children
Faith/Assurance
DITT, 40, Choral arrangement
PETL, 93, d, Text only

Rise and Shine (1)
Brethren rise and shine and give God the glory
Praise
Isaiah 60:1; Leviticus 25:8–13*
HAWD, 119, Text only
HERB, 70, Text only
MAR3, 251, Choral unaccompanied with additional historical information
MARS, 217, Choral unaccompanied with additional historical information
SANH, 91, Uses Tonic Sol-fa notation

Rise and Shine (2)
Oh de Lo'd says to Noah it's gwine be a little floody floody
Praise
Isaiah 60:1; Leviticus 25:8–13*
COLS, 86, d, Solo voice with piano accompaniment

Rise and Shine (3)
Rise and shine and give God the glory
Praise
Isaiah 60:1; Leviticus 25:8–13*
ARMH, 212, d, Choral unaccompanied with additional historical information
BOAT, 112, d, Solo voice with piano accompaniment
CHET, 271, d, Text only
CLES, 79, d, Choral with piano accompaniment and additional historical information
DANF, 17, Melody only
DETD1, 26, Choral unaccompanied with additional historical information
DETR, 198, d, Choral unaccompanied with additional historical information

Rise Mourners Rise

Rise Shine for Thy Light Is Coming

WORJF, 49, d, Text only; Source includes additional historical information

Rise Up Shepherd and Follow

There's a star in the east on Christmas morn

Christmas

Matthew 2:1–12; Luke 2:8–20#

AAH, 212, d, Choral with piano accompaniment and additional historical information

AFR, 33, Choral arrangement

ALTSH, 57, Solo voice with piano accompaniment

ALTSL, 57, Solo voice with piano accompaniment

ANDW, 41, d, Melody only

BALS, 91, d, Melody only

BENF, 13, Solo voice with piano accompaniment

BLOR, 211, Text and chord symbols

BONR, 176, d, Solo voice with piano accompaniment

BRYI, 43, d, Melody only

CALA, 24, d, Text only

CHET, 271, Text only

DANF, 12, d, Melody only

DETR, iv, d, Choral unaccompanied with additional historical information

FENR, 173, d, Choral unaccompanied with additional historical information

HERB, 71, Text only

JACL, 31, Choral with piano accompaniment and additional historical information

JOHJB, ii, 66, d, Solo voice with piano accompaniment and additional historical information

LIF, 24, Choral with piano accompaniment and additional historical information

LOMAF, 481, Melody, chord symbols, and additional historical information

PETL, 188, d, Text only

SEV, 138, Choral with piano accompaniment and additional historical information

SIX, 27, Solo voice with piano accompaniment

SLA, 15, d, Melody only

Road Is Rugged but I Must Go
Road is rugged but I must go
Songs of Spiritual Journey
DITT, 32, Choral arrangement
PETL, 141, d, Text only

Road to Heaven
Lie on me lie on all lie on everybody
Heaven
LOGR, 19, Melody only

Rock Chariot
Rock chariot I told you to rock judgment goin'
Admonition/Judgment
COUN, 227, Melody only
COUNS, 9, Solo voice with piano accompaniment and additional
historical information

Rock Mount Sinai
Rock Mount Sinai in de mawnin
Faith/Assurance
1 Samuel 16:19; 17: 15, 34, 49–51+
HALC, 68, Melody only
KENM, 46, d, Solo voice with piano accompaniment and additional historical information
PETL, 248, d, Text only

Rock My Soul (1)
Rock oh my soul in the bosom of Abraham
Faith/Assurance
ALLS, 73, d, Melody only
BLOR, 212, d, Text and chord symbols
FRAS, 73, Solo voice with piano accompaniment
HERB, 71, d, Text only
HERB, 72, d, Text only
JOHRR, 60, d, Solo voice with piano accompaniment and additional historical information
LANC, 5, d, Melody, chord symbols, and additional historical information

LIES, 52, d, Solo voice with piano accompaniment

LUEB, 96, Melody, chord symbols, and piano accompaniment

MCIB, 196, d, Melody and additional historical information

PETL, 406, d, Text only

SHEH, 24, Melody and chord symbols

SKEG, 28, d, Solo voice with piano accompaniment and chord symbols

SLA, 6, d, Choral arrangement

SPAG, 48, d, Solo voice with piano accompaniment and chord symbols

Rock My Soul (2)

Rocka my soul
>> Faith/Assurance
>>> CHET, 271, d, Text only
>>> PETL, 94, d, Text only

Rock of Ages

My loving brother
>> Faith/Assurance
>>> PETL, 94, d, Text only

Rock of Jubilee

Rock o jubilee
>> Songs of Spiritual Journey
>>> ALLS, 25, d, Melody only
>>> PETL, 406, d, Text only

Rocking Jerusalem

Mary oh Martha oh Mary ring them bells
>> Praise
>>> BRYW, 35, Melody only
>>> CALA, 39, d, Melody only
>>> CLES, 103, d, Choral with piano accompaniment and additional historical information
>>> LIF, 17, d, Choral with piano accompaniment and additional historical information
>>> PETL, 248, d, Text only

WORJA, 226, d, Choral unaccompanied with additional historical information

Rocks and the Mountains

Rocks and the mountains shall flee away

Songs of Spiritual Journey

Revelation 6:14–17*

ANDW, 44, Melody only

BRYA, 36, Melody, chord symbols, and additional historical information

DETR, 161, Choral unaccompanied with additional historical information

MARS, 141, Choral unaccompanied with additional historical information

PETL, 248, d, Text only

PIKJ, 181, Choral unaccompanied with additional historical information

SANH, 111, Uses Tonic Sol-fa notation

SEWJC, 24, Choral unaccompanied with additional historical information

Rocks Don't Fall on Me

Rocks don't fall on me

Admonition/Judgment

BUR2H, 58, d, Solo voice with piano accompaniment

BUR2L, 58, d, Solo voice with piano accompaniment

BURS, 55, d, Solo voice with piano accompaniment

HAWD, 59, Text only

HERB, 63, Text only

JOHJB, i, 164, d, Solo voice with piano accompaniment and additional historical information

JOHRA, 32, Solo voice with piano accompaniment

PETL, 290, d, Text only

WALSH, 206, d, Solo voice with piano accompaniment

WALSL, 206, Solo voice with piano accompaniment

WORF, 30, d, Choral unaccompanied with additional historical information

WORJF, 58, d, Text only; Source includes additional historical information

Roll and Rock

Roll an' rock can't you come along
Faith/Assurance
MCIB, 222, d, Melody and additional historical information
PETL, 94, d, Text only

Roll Away That Stone

Roll away that stone brother and let Lord Jesus out
Jesus
CHAT, 116, Solo voice with piano accompaniment

Roll Him Out Again

Devil was a busy ole man
Satan
BALS, 30, d, Choral unaccompanied with additional historical information
PETL, 332, d, Text only

Roll Jordan

Sister Mary 'ought to been there
Deliverance
LOGR, 18, Melody only

Roll Jordan Roll (1)

Roll Jordan roll I want to go to Heaven when I die to hear old Jordan roll
Aspiration
Joshua 3:15*
ANDM, 81, d, Solo voice with piano accompaniment
ANDW, 39, Melody only
BALS, 77, d, Choral unaccompanied with additional historical information
BRYW, 37, Melody only
CHAT, 70, Solo voice with piano accompaniment
CHET, 271, Text only
CLES, 117, Choral with piano accompaniment and additional historical information

SLA, 23, Choral arrangement
SNYS, 23, d, Solo voice with piano accompaniment
SPAG, 49, d, Solo voice with piano accompaniment and chord symbols
WIES, 196, Solo voice with piano accompaniment

Roll Jordan Roll (2)
My brother sitting on the tree of life
Aspiration
Joshua 3:15*
ALLS, 1, Melody only
PETL, 370, d, Text only

Roll Jordan Roll (3)
Here He comes the Judge severe
Aspiration
Joshua 3:15*
LOMAF, 458, Melody, chord symbols, and additional historical information

Roll On
Roll on roll on sweet moments roll on
Faith/Assurance
PETL, 95, d, Text only
WORF, 5, Choral unaccompanied with additional historical information

Roll the Old Chariot Along
Roll the old chariot along
Songs of Spiritual Journey
DETR, 192, d, Choral unaccompanied with additional historical information
FENR, 106, d, Choral unaccompanied with additional historical information
HALC, 22, d, Choral with piano accompaniment and additional historical information
HAWD, 144, Text only
JOHJB, i, 110, d, Solo voice with piano accompaniment and additional historical information
PETL, 370, d, Text only

Rolling in Jesus' Arms
I'm a-rolling in Jesus' arms
Faith/Assurance
CHET, 272, Text only
MCIB, 224, d, Melody and additional historical information
PETL, 95, d, Text only

Room Enough
Brothers don't stay away
Heaven
BOAS, 53, Solo voice with piano accompaniment
MARS, 127, Choral unaccompanied with additional historical information
PETL, 95, d, Text only
PETL, 194, d, Text only
PIKJ, 167, Choral unaccompanied with additional historical information
SAAT2, 12, d, Solo voice with piano accompaniment
SEWJ, 7, Choral arrangement
SEWJC, 30, Choral unaccompanied with additional historical information

Room Enough in the Heaven
There's room enough in the Heaven
Heaven
BALS, 85, d, Choral unaccompanied with additional historical information
PETL, 407, d, Text only

Rough and Rolling Sea
Farewell farewell to my only child
Suffering
FENC, 90, Choral unaccompanied with additional historical information
FENR, 90, Choral unaccompanied with additional historical information
PETL, 37, d, Text only

Round About the Mountain
Round about de mountain 'round about de mountain my God's a-rulin'

Faith/Assurance
MCLS, 50, d, Solo voice with piano accompaniment
PETL, 96, d, Text only

Round the Glory Manger
Dey turn 'way Mary an'a Joseph
Jesus
AFR, 34, d, Choral with piano accompaniment

Rule Death in His Arms
When God commanded Michael in the morning to stretch at dividing line
Death
BARO, 22, d, Melody only

Run Here Jeremiah
Run here Jeremiah ho ma Lord
Admonition/Judgment
MCIB, 220, Melody and additional historical information
PETL, 142, d, Text only

Run Mary Run
Run Mary run I know de udder worl' is not like dis'
Women
ARMH, 188, d, Choral unaccompanied with additional historical information
CHET, 272, Text only
DANF, 47, Melody only
DETR, 18, Choral unaccompanied with additional historical information
FENC, 16, Choral unaccompanied with additional historical information
FENR, 16, Choral unaccompanied with additional historical information
JOHJB, ii, 166, d, Solo voice with piano accompaniment and additional historical information
PETL, 142, d, Text only

Run Moaner Run

Run mo'ner run Heaven is a shinin'
Faith/Assurance
MCIB, 213, d, Melody and additional historical information
PETL, 249, d, Text only

Run Mona Run

Run Mona run Heaven is ashouting
Rituals of Preparation for Renewal/Regeneration
RAIJ, 70, Solo voice with piano accompaniment

Run Mourner Run

There's singing here
Rituals of Preparation for Renewal/Regeneration
HERB, 73, Text only
PETL, 332, d, Text only

Run Sinner Run

Run sinner run
Admonition/Judgment
BONR, 178, d, Solo voice with piano accompaniment
JOHHG, 11, Solo voice with piano accompaniment
JOHHH, 19, d, Solo voice with piano accompaniment

Run to Jesus

Run to Jesus shun the danger
Admonition/Judgment
CHET, 272, Text only
DETD3, 17, Choral unaccompanied with additional historical information
DETR, 15, Melody only
FISS, 142, d, Solo voice with piano accompaniment and additional historical information
MARS, 188, Choral unaccompanied with additional historical information
PETL, 143, d, Text only

Run to My Lord
Christians what yer gwinter do when de Lord soun' His trumpet
Songs of Spiritual Journey
JOHRR, 64, d, Solo voice with piano accompaniment and additional historical information

Run to the City of Refuge — see — You Better Run to the City of Refuge

Running for My Life
I'm running for my life
Suffering
FOUS, 16, Solo voice with piano accompaniment

Sabbath Has No End (1)
Going to walk about Zion I really do believe
Songs of Spiritual Journey
ALLS, 69, Melody only
BARO, 37, d, Melody only
PETL, 371, d, Text only

Sabbath Has No End (2)
In the River uv Jurdun
Songs of Spiritual Journey
PARS, 172, Melody only

Sail Oh Believer
Sail oh believer sail
Faith/Assurance
ALLS, 24, Melody only
PETL, 188, d, Text only

Sailing Over Yonder
We are sailin' over yonder on de udder side de sho
Faith/Assurance
FISS, 148, d, Solo voice with piano accompaniment and additional historical information
MCIB, 215, Melody and additional historical information
PETL, 96, d, Text only

Same Train

I am talkin' 'bout the same train carry my mother same train
Deliverance
> BALS, 9, d, Choral unaccompanied with additional historical information
> CARS, 15, Solo voice with piano accompaniment
> DITT, 53, Choral arrangement
> JOHJB, ii, 60, d, Solo voice with piano accompaniment and additional historical information
> ODUN, 112, Text only; Source includes additional historical information
> PETL, 188, d, Text only

Samson

Delilah was a woman fine and fair
Deliverance
Judges 14:3, 5–9, 15:4–16, 16:4–30+
> LOMAF, 478, Melody, chord symbols, and additional historical information
> LOMJO, 6, Melody only
> LOMJO2, 6, Melody only

Samson's Wife Sat on His Knees

I knows I's a witness for my Lord
Songs of Spiritual Journey
Genesis 5:25; Judges 16:6, 17+
> LOGR, 24, d, Melody only

Samuel's Sister

Sam-yul sistuh come uh screamin' en' uh hollerin'
Death
> GUL, 71, d, Text only
> HUTS, 69, d, Melody and additional historical information

Satan's a Liar

Satan's a liar an' a conju'h too
Faith/Assurance
> COLS, 82, Solo voice with piano accompaniment

Satan's Camp Fire
   Fire my Savior fire
      Admonition/Judgment
         ALLS, 27, d, Melody only
         CHET, 272, Text only
         PETL, 292, d, Text only

Satisfied
   Rich folks worries' 'bout trouble
      Work Songs
         ODUN, 249, Text only; Source includes additional historical
            information

Save Me Jesus Save Me Now
   I'm goin' to climb up Jacob's ladder
      Deliverance
         BALS, 60, d, Choral unaccompanied with additional historical
            information
         PETL, 189, d, Text only

Save Me Lord Save Me
   I called to my Father
      Deliverance
         DETD2, 18, Choral unaccompanied with additional historical
            information
         MARS, 161, Choral unaccompanied with additional historical
            information
         PETL, 189, d, Text only
         PIKJ, 201, Choral unaccompanied with additional historical
            information
         SAAT2, 15, d, Solo voice with piano accompaniment
         SEWJC, 46, Choral unaccompanied with additional historical
            information

Save Me Now Save Me
   Yo' save muh brudduh save me now
      Deliverance
         BALS, 39, d, Choral unaccompanied with additional historical
            information

Scandalize My Name
I met my sister the other day I give her my right hand
Suffering
BULA, 157, Solo voice with piano accompaniment
CHET, 273, Text only
CLES, 159, Choral with piano accompaniment and additional historical information
HALC, 65, Choral with piano accompaniment and additional historical information
JOHHT, 12, d, Solo voice with piano accompaniment
PETL, 37, d, Text only
RAGS, 27, Solo voice with piano accompaniment

Sea Is Going to Deliver Up Dry Bones
Sea gwine deliver up dry bones
Admonition/Judgment
BALS, 31, d, Melody only
PETL, 332, d, Text only

See Me Here My Leader
Sim-me yuh muh leaduh
Prayer
HUTS, 73, d, Melody and additional historical information

See the Signs of Judgment
See the signs of the judgment
Admonition/Judgment
PETL, 292, d, Text only
SIX, 26, d, Solo voice with piano accompaniment
WORJA, 225, Choral unaccompanied with additional historical information

Seek and Ye Shall Find
Seek and ye shall find knock and de door shall be opened
Faith/Assurance
BLOR, 212, d, Text and chord symbols
DETR, 20, Choral unaccompanied with additional historical information

Send One Angel Down

Send Them Angels Down

Separating Line

Serving My God

Shall I Die

Shepherd Shepherd
Shepherd shepherd where'd you lose your sheep
Suffering
PETL, 38, d, Text only

Shine for Jesus
When the clouds are hanging low shine and you know not where to go shine
Faith/Assurance
BOAS, 35, Solo voice with piano accompaniment

Shine like a Star in the Morning
Shine shine shine
Praise
JONF, 271, Melody only

Shine on Me (1)
I heard the voice of Jesus say "Come unto me and rest"
Faith/Assurance
Psalm 31:16^
AAH, 527, Choral with piano accompaniment and additional historical information
CHET, 273, Text only

Shine on Me (2)
Plunged in a gulf of dark despair
Faith/Assurance
Psalm 31:16^
SIX, 29, Solo voice with piano accompaniment

Shine Shine
I don't care where you bury my body
Aspiration
MAR3, 254, Choral unaccompanied with additional historical information
MARS, 220, Choral unaccompanied with additional historical information
PETL, 250, d, Text only

Shine Shine I'll Meet You in the Morning
Shine shine I'll meet you in the morning
Aspiration
GLAS, 20, Melody and chord symbols
MARS, 151, Choral unaccompanied with additional historical information
PETL, 236, d, Text only
PIKJ, 191, Melody only
SEWJC, 37, Melody only

Shock Along John
Shock along John shock along
Work Songs
ALLS, 67, Melody only

Shoot dat Buffey — see — Trip to Raleigh

Shout All Over God's — see — Going to Shout All Over God's Heaven

Shout Away
Shout oh shout oh shout away
Praise
ALLS, 71, Melody only

Shout for Joy
Lord shout for joy
Praise
CHET, 273, Text only
PETL, 251, d, Text only

Shout Jerusalem
Shout Jerusalem preach Jerusalem in de mornin'
Praise
MCIB, 228, Melody and additional historical information
PETL, 251, d, Text only

Shout Jubilee
My Lawd call me I mus' go (My lord calls me I must go)

Songs of Spiritual Journey
HUTS, 71, d, Melody and additional historical information

Shout on Children
Shout on children you never die
Praise
ALLS, 60, Melody only
PETL, 96, d, Text only

Show Me the Way (1)
Brother have you come to show me the way
Songs of Spiritual Journey
MARS, 191, Choral unaccompanied with additional historical information
PETL, 333, d, Text only

Show Me the Way (2)
My good Lord show me the way
Songs of Spiritual Journey
GREF, 70, d, Solo voice with piano accompaniment
JOHJB, ii, 133, d, Solo voice with piano accompaniment and additional historical information
PETL, 184, d, Text only
PETL, 334, d, Text only
SIX, 60, Solo voice with piano accompaniment
WORF, 22, Choral unaccompanied with additional historical information

Signs of the Judgment — see — See the Signs of Judgment

Sin Sick Soul
Brother George is going to glory
Admonition/Judgment
ALLS, 49, Melody only
PETL, 292, d, Text only

Sing Ho That I Had the Wings of a Dove
Sing a ho that I had the wings of a dove

Songs of Spiritual Journey
>FISS, 151, d, Solo voice with piano accompaniment and additional historical information
>GREF, 6, d, Solo voice with piano accompaniment
>PETL, 407, d, Text only
>WORF, 16, d, Choral unaccompanied with additional historical information

Sing till the Power of the Lord Comes Down
I'm gonna sing till the power of the Lord comes down
>Songs of Spiritual Journey
>>CHET, 274, Text only
>>SILS, 26, Solo voice with piano accompaniment and additional historical information

Singing on the Old Church Ground
We're singing singing tonight
>Death
>>HALC, 19, d, Choral with piano accompaniment and additional historical information on the spiritual
>>PETL, 97, d, Text only

Singing with a Sword in My Hand
Singing with a sword in my hand
>Praise
>>CHET, 273, d, Text only
>>GUIU, 46, d, Solo voice with piano accompaniment
>>HAWD, 42, Text only
>>HERB, 74, Text only
>>JOHJB, i, 86, d, Solo voice with piano accompaniment and additional historical information
>>LUEB, 100, d, Melody, chord symbols, and piano accompaniment
>>PETL, 143, d, Text only

Sinking Down
They whipped Him up the hill
>Easter
>>PETL, 15, d, Text only

Sinner Die

Sinner die sinner die

Admonition/Judgment

ODUN, 75, Text only; Source includes additional historical information

Sinner Man

Sinner man where you gonna run to

Admonition/Judgment

BLOR, 212, Text and chord symbols

BUCS, 28, Instrumental Ensemble accompaniment

LUEB, 9, d, Melody, chord symbols, and piano accompaniment

MARS, 176, Choral unaccompanied with additional historical information

PETL, 367, d, Text only

PIKJ, 216, Choral unaccompanied with additional historical information

SEWJC, 61, Choral unaccompanied with additional historical information

Sinner Man So Hard to Believe

Ain't dat a pity Lord ain't dat a shame

Suffering

Luke 16:20–26+

JOHHT, 48, d, Solo voice with piano accompaniment

Sinner Now Is the Time for to Pray

Sinner now is de time for to pray

Admonition/Judgment

KENMM, 19, d, Melody only

Sinner Please Don't Let This Harvest Pass

Sinner please doan let dis harves' pass

Admonition/Judgment

BONF, 38, d, Solo voice with piano accompaniment and additional historical information

BONF, 42, d, Solo voice with piano accompaniment and additional historical information

Sinner What Are You Doing Down There?

Sinnuh w'ah yuh doin' down deh
Admonition/Judgment

Sinner Why Would You Die on That Day

W'en yuh yeah duh trumpet blowin' on da' day on da' day
Death

Sinner Won't Die No More

Lamb done been here and died

Sister Mary Had But One Child
   Sister Mary had-a but one child
      Women
         CHET, 274, d, Text only
         HAYMF, 98, d, Solo voice with piano accompaniment and additional historical information
         HAYMS, 98, d, Solo voice with piano accompaniment and additional historical information
         HERB, 75, Text only
         PETL, 38, d, Text only

Sit Down
   Set down set down set down got to heav'n and I can't set down
      Heaven
         PATN, 79, d, Solo voice with piano accompaniment

Sit Down Servant
   Sit down servant sit down I can't sit down
      Death
         BECK, 15, Solo voice with piano accompaniment
         BOAS, 20, Solo voice with piano accompaniment
         BONR, 120, d, Solo voice with piano accompaniment
         CALA, 25, Text only
         CHET, 274, Text only
         CLAC, 20, d, Solo voice with piano accompaniment
         CLES, 160, Choral with piano accompaniment and additional historical information
         GUL, 72, d, Text only
         HAWD, 74, Text only
         HAY1H, 15, Solo voice with piano accompaniment
         HERB, 76, Text only
         LOMJA, 584, Melody only
         LOMJF, 454, d, Solo voice with piano accompaniment and additional historical information
         MCIS, 6, Solo voice with piano accompaniment
         PETL, 97, d, Text only
         PETL, 251, d, Text only

Sitting Down Beside the Lamb
New Jerusalem new Jerusalem
Admonition/Judgment
LOGR, 6, d, Melody only
PETL, 144, d, Text only

Sitting Down by the Side of the Lamb
Way down yonder on Jordan's stream I hear them crying
Admonition/Judgment
MAR3, 304, Choral unaccompanied with additional historical information

Sitting Down Side of My Jesus
Lamb sitting down side ob my Jesus
Faith/Assurance
HALC, 59, d, Melody only
PETL, 98, d, Text only

Slavery's Chain
Slav'ry chain done broke at las'
Deliverance
CALA, 40, Melody only
CHET, 274, Text only
DETR, 112, d, Melody only
PETL, 252, d, Text only

So Glad I'm Here
So glad I'm here Lord so glad I'm here in Jesus' name
Praise
1 Chronicles 29:13^
AAH, 305, Choral with piano accompaniment and additional historical information

So I Can Write My Name
My blessed Lord gimme the lil' book now Daniel
Songs of Spiritual Journey
JESM, 60, d, Solo voice with piano accompaniment and additional historical information

So Sad
Got to go to the judgment my myself
Admonition/Judgment
HALC, 61, Melody only
PETL, 293, d, Text only

Social Band
Bright angels on the water
Heaven
ALLS, 105, Melody only
PETL, 39, d, Text only

Soldier for Jesus
I'm a soldier for Jesus
Faith/Assurance
BARO, 9, d, Melody only
BARO, 27, d, Melody only
DEF, 24, Solo voice with piano accompaniment and additional historical information

Solid Rock
My hope is built on nothing less than Jesus' blood
Faith/Assurance
NAA, 35, Melody and chord symbols

Some Come Cripple — see — Hail the Crown

Some Day
Beams of Heaven as I go through this wilderness
Faith/Assurance
CLES, 207, Choral with piano accompaniment and additional historical information

Some of These Days — see also — One of These Days

Some of These Days (1)
I'm gonna tell God how you treat me
Admonition/Judgment
GRIN, 20, d, Melody only
PETL, 293, d, Text only

Some of These Days (2)

I'm go'n'ter set down at de welcome table I'm going down to the River of Jordan

Aspiration

CHET, 275, d, Text only

JOHHG, 17, d, Solo voice with piano accompaniment

JOHHH, 25, d, Solo voice with piano accompaniment

Some of These Days (3)

I'm a gonna walk on the streets of glory

Aspiration

SIX, 48, d, Solo voice with piano accompaniment

Some of These Mornings

Going to see my mother some o' dese mornin's

Faith/Assurance

ARMH, 190, d, Choral unaccompanied with additional historical information

DETR, 46, Choral unaccompanied with additional historical information

FENC, 18, d, Choral unaccompanied with additional historical information

FENR, 18, d, Choral unaccompanied with additional historical information

JOHRS, 22, d, Solo voice with piano accompaniment

MAR3, 284, Choral unaccompanied with additional historical information

PETL, 98, d, Text only

WORJF, 47, d, Text only; source includes additional historical information

Some Valiant Soldier

Lord I want some valiant soldier

Suffering

ALLS, 50, Melody only

Some Will Love You and Some Will Hate You

Some will love you and some will hate you

Songs of Spiritual Journey

BALS, 68, d, Melody only

PETL, 372, d, Text only

Somebody Got Lost in the Storm
Somebody got lost in the storm
Suffering
FISS, 154, d, Solo voice with piano accompaniment and additional historical information
JOHRR, 76, d, Solo voice with piano accompaniment and additional historical information
PETL, 39, d, Text only

Somebody's Buried in the Graveyard
Somebody's buried in the graveyard
Death
PETL, 190, d, Text only
WORF, 8, Choral unaccompanied with additional historical information
WORJF, 34, d, Text only; Source includes additional historical information
WORJF, 60, d, Text only; Source includes additional historical information

Somebody's Calling My Name — see — Hush Somebody's Calling My Name

Somebody's in You It Must Be Jesus
Somebawdy een yu(n)h it mus' be Jedus
Jesus
GUL, 79, d, Text only
HUTS, 81, d, Melody and additional historical information

Somebody's Knocking at Your Door
Somebody's knockin' at your door o sinner why don't you answer
Admonition/Judgment
Revelation 3:20^
AAH, 348, d, Choral with piano accompaniment and additional historical information
ANDW, 34, d, Choral arrangement
BAP, 480, Choral with piano accompaniment and additional historical information
BOAS, 87, Solo voice with piano accompaniment

WHIF, 65, d, Solo voice with piano accompaniment
WIES, 201, Solo voice with piano accompaniment

Sometimes I Feel Like a Moanin' Dove

Sometimes I-uh-fell like a moanin' dove
Suffering
Psalm 88+

CLES, 155, Choral with piano accompaniment and additional historical information
DANF, 7, Melody only
GRIN, 72, Melody only
PETL, 40, d, Text only

Sometimes I Feel Like a Motherless Child

Sometimes I feel like a motherless child
Suffering
Psalm 88+

AASB, 12, d, Solo voice with piano accompaniment
AASM, 18, d, Solo voice with piano accompaniment
AASS, 18, d, Solo voice with piano accompaniment
AAST, 12, d, Solo voice with piano accompaniment
ALTAH, 50, Solo voice with piano accompaniment
ALTAL, 50, Solo voice with piano accompaniment
APPA, 178, Solo voice with piano accompaniment
BARN, 124, d, Solo voice with piano accompaniment and additional historical information
BARO, 18, d, Melody only
BAYF, 18, d, Solo voice with piano accompaniment and chord symbols
BOYE, 54, Solo voice with piano accompaniment
BROS, 6, d, Solo voice with piano accompaniment
BRYI, 21, d, Melody only
BUR2H, 68, d, Solo voice with piano accompaniment
BUR2L, 68, d, Solo voice with piano accompaniment
BURA, 26, d, Solo voice with piano accompaniment
BURS, 64, d, Solo voice with piano accompaniment
CALA, 42, Melody only
CHET, 275, Text only

Sometimes I Feel Like I Wanna Go Home

Sometimes I feel like I wanna go home
Suffering

Sometimes My Trouble Makes Me Tremble — see — Were You There

Somewhere Around a Throne

Goodbye I'm goin' home
Faith/Assurance

Soon and Very Soon

Soon and very soon we are going to see the King
Deliverance

Soon I Will Be Done

Soon we will be done with the troubles of the world
Death

Isaiah 35:10; Revelation 21:4*

    CALA, 25, d, Text only

    CHET, 276, d, Text only

    CLES, 158, d, Choral with piano accompaniment and additional historical information

    DETR, 234, Choral unaccompanied with additional historical information

    HERB, 77, Text only

    HERB, 78, d, Text only

    LOMAF, 472, Melody, chord symbols, and additional historical information

    NAA, 43, Melody and chord symbols

    NEW, 492, d, Choral with piano accompaniment and additional historical information

    PETL, 98, d, Text only

    PETL, 408, d, Text only

    SANH, 123, Uses Tonic Sol-fa notation

    WORJF, 56, d, Text only; Source includes additional historical information

Soon in the Morning (1)

I'm goin' up home soon in de morning

    Songs of Spiritual Journey

        BARO, 6, d, Melody only

Soon in the Morning (2)

So soon in the mornin' when the clouds roll away I'll never go astray

    Songs of Spiritual Journey

        RAIJ, 77, d, Solo voice with piano accompaniment

Soon One Morning

Soon one mornin' death comes a-creepin' in my room

    Death

        GRIN, 8, d, Melody only

        HAWD, 47, Text only

        LOMJF, 450, d, Solo voice with piano accompaniment and additional historical information

        LOMJO, 30, d, Melody only

        LOMJO2, 30, d, Melody only

    PATN, 20, d, Solo voice with piano accompaniment
    PETL, 41, d, Text only

Soon We Will Be Done — see — Soon I Will Be Done

Soon Will I Be Done — see — Soon I Will Be Done

Sorry to Tell
  Sorry to tell you
    Suffering
      HALC, 61, Melody only
      PETL, 41, d, Text only

Spirit of the Lord Done Fell on Me
  John hallelujah oh John spirit of the Lord done fell on me
    Deliverance
      JESM, 10, d, Solo voice with piano accompaniment and additional
        historical information

Stand by Me
  When the storm of life is raging
    Faith/Assurance
      FISS, 166, d, Solo voice with piano accompaniment and additional
        historical information
      FOUS, 24, Solo voice with piano accompaniment
      HAWD, 15, Text only
      PETL, 144, d, Text only

Stand on a Sea of Glass
  Dis union sing dis union
    Songs of Spiritual Journey
      BARO, 28, d, Melody only

Stand Steady
  Stan' steady bretheren
    Faith/Assurance
      JESM, 30, d, Solo voice with piano accompaniment and additional
        historical information

Stand Still Jordan (1)
Stand still Jordan Lord I can't stand still
Heaven
BURA, 18, d, Solo voice with piano accompaniment
BURS, 34, d, Solo voice with piano accompaniment
HERB, 78, Text only
JOHHT, 62, d, Solo voice with piano accompaniment
JOHJB, i, 82, d, Solo voice with piano accompaniment and additional historical information
PETL, 145, d, Text only

Stand Still Jordan (2)
Who yuh gawt een He(b)'m ho yuh gawt een He(b)'m
Heaven
GUL, 93, d, Text only

Stand the Storm
Stand the storm it won't be long
Faith/Assurance
DETR, 189, Choral unaccompanied with additional historical information
PETL, 146, d, Text only

Stand Up like Soldiers
God is sweeping this world today
Admonition/Judgment
KENMM, 32, d, Text only; Source includes additional historical information

Stand Up Stand Up for Jesus
Stand up stand up for Jesus
Faith/Assurance
NAA, 36, Melody and chord symbols

Standing in the Need of Prayer
Not my brother nor my sister but it's me oh Lord
Prayer

James 5:13; Psalm 5:2*

Standing on the Sea of Glass

Stars Begin to Fall

Stars Begin to Fall — see also — Stars in the Elements

Stars in the Elements

> FENC, 84, Choral unaccompanied with additional historical information
>
> FENR, 84, Choral unaccompanied with additional historical information
>
> FENR, 103, d, Choral unaccompanied with additional historical information
>
> PETL, 294, d, Text only

Stay in the Field

Stay in the field 'til de war is ended

    Admonition/Judgment

> BARO, 27, d, Melody only
>
> DETR, 22, d, Choral unaccompanied with additional historical information
>
> FENC, 103, Choral unaccompanied with additional historical information
>
> PETL, 146, d, Text only
>
> WORJF, 71, d, Text only; Source includes additional historical information

Steady Jesus Is Listening

Steady Jesus is listening

    Rituals of Preparation for Renewal/Regeneration

> BONR, 186, d, Solo voice with piano accompaniment
>
> PETL, 334, d, Text only

Steal Away

Steal away steal away to Jesus

    Death

    Exodus 33:22; Hebrews 10:19–21; Isaiah 40:31; Psalm 31; Zechariah 1:3+

> AAH, 546, Choral with piano accompaniment and additional historical information
>
> ANDW, 22, Melody only
>
> APPA, 179, Solo voice with piano accompaniment
>
> BAYF, 20, d, Solo voice with piano accompaniment and chord symbols
>
> BELT, 5, Uses Tonic Sol-fa notation

JOHHH, 128, d, Solo voice with piano accompaniment

JOHJB, i, 114, d, Solo voice with piano accompaniment and additional historical information

JOHRA, 16, Solo voice with piano accompaniment

JORS, 24, d, Text only

LIF, 103, Choral with piano accompaniment and additional historical information

LUEB, 95, Melody, chord symbols, and piano accompaniment

MACS, 44, Melody only

MARS, 147, Choral unaccompanied with additional historical information

MIL3, 26, Solo voice with piano accompaniment

NEW, 505, d, Choral with piano accompaniment and additional historical information

ODUN, 139, Text only; Source includes additional historical information

OKS1, 63, Solo voice with piano accompaniment

PETL, 191, d, Text only

PIKJ, 187, Choral unaccompanied with additional historical information

RAGS, 12, Solo voice with piano accompaniment

RUTF, 10, Solo voice with piano accompaniment

SANH, 124, Uses Tonic Sol-fa notation

SEWJ, 28, Choral arrangement

SEWJC, 28, Choral unaccompanied with additional historical information

SILSP, 22, Solo voice with piano accompaniment

SKEG, 34, d, Solo voice with piano accompaniment and chord symbols

SLA, 32, Choral arrangement

SNYS, 17, d, Solo voice with piano accompaniment

SPAG, 52, d, Solo voice with piano accompaniment and chord symbols

UNI, 704, Melody only

WAL14H, 43, Solo voice with piano accompaniment

WAL15H, 43, Solo voice with piano accompaniment

WAL15L, 43, Solo voice with piano accompaniment

WALSH, 222, Solo voice with piano accompaniment

WALSL, 222, Solo voice with piano accompaniment

WARE, 84, d, Solo voice with piano accompaniment and additional historical information

WHIF, 46, d, Solo voice with piano accompaniment

WIES, 208, Solo voice with piano accompaniment

WORF, 20, Choral unaccompanied with additional historical information

WORJF, 89, d, Text only; Source includes additional historical information

Steal Away and Pray

Steal away and pray

Prayer

Exodus 33:22; Hebrews 10:19–21; Isaiah 40:31; Psalm 31; Zechariah 1:3+

HAWD, 93, Text only

PETL, 146, d, Text only

Steal Away to Heaven

Nobody knows the trouble I've seen

Heaven

HAY1L, 17, Solo voice with piano accompaniment

Steal Away to My Father's Kingdom

Steal away steal away

Deliverance

GRIN, 78, d, Melody only

PETL, 191, d, Text only

Steamboat Song

Captain where are you bound for

Songs of Spiritual Journey

FISS, 172, d, Solo voice with piano accompaniment and additional historical information

Story of Noah

Now didn't ole Norah build himself an ark

Work Songs

Genesis 6:14, 7:8–9+
> NILS, 4, d, Solo voice with piano accompaniment and additional historical information

Study War No More — see — I Ain't Going to Study War No More

Sun Don't Set in the Mornin'
Sun don't set in the morning
Prayer
> ALTAH, 53, Solo voice with piano accompaniment
> ALTAL, 53, Solo voice with piano accompaniment
> DANF, 21, d, Melody only
> DETR, 23, d, Choral unaccompanied with additional historical information
> FENR, 130, d, Choral unaccompanied with additional historical information
> JONF, 77, d, Melody only
> PETL, 408, d, Text only

Sun Mows Down
Hurry mourner hurry mourner
Death
> PETL, 99, d, Text only
> WORJA, 229, Choral unaccompanied with additional historical information

Sun Shine into My Soul
Sun shine sun shine sun shine into my soul
Songs of Spiritual Journey
> HALC, 73, Melody only
> PETL, 408, d, Text only

Sun Will Never Go Down
Sun will never go down go down
Praise
> COUN, 238, Melody only

Sunday Morning Band (1)
What kin' o' ban' you goin' t' join

Praise
>> MCIB, 230, d, Melody and additional historical information
>> PETL, 252, d, Text only

Sunday Morning Band (2)
> What band that Sunday morning
>> Praise
>>> PETL, 253, d, Text only

Sunshine into My Soul — see — Sun Shine into My Soul

Surely God Is Able
> Surely surely He's able to carry you thro'
>> Faith/Assurance
>>> CLES, 193, Choral with piano accompaniment and additional historical information

Surely He Died on Calvary — see — Calvary

Sweet Canaan
> Land I am bound for
>> Aspiration
>>> ARMH, 234, d, Choral unaccompanied with additional historical information
>>> DETR, 188, Choral unaccompanied with additional historical information
>>> FENC, 62, Choral unaccompanied with additional historical information
>>> FENR, 62, Choral unaccompanied with additional historical information
>>> MAR3, 277, Choral unaccompanied with additional historical information
>>> MARS, 243, Choral unaccompanied with additional historical information
>>> PETL, 192, d, Text only

Sweet Heaven
> Heaven sweet Heaven oh Lord I want to go to Heaven

Heaven
> BARO, 10, d, Melody only
> HERB, 30, d, Text only
> HERB, 79, Text only
> MCIB, 237, d, Melody and additional historical information
> PETL, 409, d, Text only

Sweet Heaven Is a Handsome Place
Sweet Heaven is a handsome place
> Heaven
> > LOGR, 17, Melody only

Sweet Home
Sweet home
> Heaven
> > BRUS, 42, d, Solo voice with piano accompaniment
> > HERB, 80, Text only
> > PETL, 41, d, Text only

Sweet Jesus
Sweet Jesus sweet Jesus
> Jesus
> > CHET, 276, Text only
> > WHAG, 5, Solo voice with piano accompaniment

Sweet Turtle Dove
Sweet turtle dove she sing-a so sweet
> Admonition/Judgment
> > ARMH, 240, d, Choral unaccompanied with additional historical information
> > DETR, 164, Choral unaccompanied with additional historical information
> > FENC, 68, d, Choral unaccompanied with additional historical information
> > FENR, 68, Choral unaccompanied with additional historical information
> > FENR, 68, d, Choral unaccompanied with additional historical information
> > PETL, 294, d, Text only

Sweet Water Rolling
Sweet water rollin'
Rituals of Preparation for Renewal/Regeneration
BALS, 49, d, Melody only
PETL, 335, d, Text only

Sweetest Sound I Ever Heard
Sweetest sound I ever heard
Death
BULA, 55, Solo voice with piano accompaniment
CARS, 33, Solo voice with piano accompaniment

Swing Down Chariot
Swing down chariot and let me ride
Deliverance
PETL, 192, d, Text only

Swing Low Chariot
Swing low chariot low in the eas' let God's people
Death
DETR, 100, Choral unaccompanied with additional historical information
FENR, 68, Choral unaccompanied with additional historical information
PETL, 192, d, Text only

Swing Low Sweet Chariot (1)
Swing low sweet chariot comin' for to carry me home
Deliverance
2 Kings 2:1–12; Psalm 68:17*
AAH, 539, Choral with piano accompaniment and additional historical information
ANDW, 38, d, Choral arrangement
APPA, 182, Solo voice with piano accompaniment
BAYF, 8, d, Solo voice with piano accompaniment and chord symbols
BELT, 3, Uses Tonic Sol-fa notation
BLOR, 212, Text and chord symbols
BOAS, 28, Solo voice with piano accompaniment

WIES, 202, Solo voice with piano accompaniment

WORF, 21, Choral unaccompanied with additional historical information

WORJF, 59, d, Text only; Source includes additional historical information

WORJF, 121, d, Text only; Source includes additional historical information

Swing Low Sweet Chariot (2)

Swing low sweet chariot I don't want you to leave me behind
Deliverance
2 Kings 2:1–12; Psalm 68:17*

ARMH, 179, d, Choral unaccompanied with additional historical information

DETR, 101, Choral unaccompanied with additional historical information

DETR, v, Choral unaccompanied with additional historical information

FENC, 7, Choral unaccompanied with additional historical information

FENR, 7, Choral unaccompanied with additional historical information

HERB, 81, Text only

PETL, 42, d, Text only

PETL, 170, d, Text only

SANH, 44, Uses Tonic Sol-fa notation

Swing Low Sweet Chariot (3)

Swing low oh swing low
Deliverance
2 Kings 2:1–12; Psalm 68:17*

PARS, 154, Melody only

Take Me to the Water

Take me to the water to be baptized
Rituals of Preparation for Renewal/Regeneration
Acts 8:36^

AAH, 675, Choral with piano accompaniment and additional historical information

CALA, 43, Melody only

CHET, 277, Text only

JACL, 99, Choral with piano accompaniment and additional historical information

LIF, 134, Choral with piano accompaniment and additional historical information

PATN, 87, d, Solo voice with piano accompaniment

WARE, 91, d, Solo voice with piano accompaniment and additional historical information

Take My Mother Home

I think I heard him say while He was dy'in on de cross

Jesus

BELS, 129, d, Solo voice with piano accompaniment

JOHHH, 139, d, Solo voice with piano accompaniment

LOGR, 4, Melody only

Takes a Little Bit of Man to Rock Dan

Takes a little bit of man to rock Dan

Songs of Spiritual Journey

HALC, 24, d, Choral with piano accompaniment and additional historical information

PETL, 372, d, Text only

Talk About a Child That Do Love Jesus

Talk about a chil' that do love Jesus

Jesus

BLA5, 2, Solo voice with piano accompaniment

BULA, 187, Solo voice with piano accompaniment

Talk About Me

Yes I know you goin' talk 'bout me

Admonition/Judgment

ODUN, 84, Text only; Source includes additional historical information

Tall Angel at the Bar (1)

Doan you want to go to Heaven

Admonition/Judgment

JESM, 70, d, Solo voice with piano accompaniment and additional historical information

Tall Angel at the Bar (2)
Who dat comin tall angel at de bar
Admonition/Judgment
HALC, 46, d, Melody only
KENM, 7, d, Melody only
PETL, 294, d, Text only

Tell All the World John
Tell all the world John
Prayer
PETL, 99, d, Text only
WORF, 34, Choral unaccompanied with additional historical
information

Tell Brother Elijah
Sinnah ain you tired of sinnin'
Deliverance
BARO, 5, d, Melody only

Tell It
Father Abraham sitting down side-a the Holy Lamb
Heaven
HALC, 26, Choral with piano accompaniment and additional
historical information
PETL, 99, d, Text only

Tell Jesus
Tell Jesus done done all I can
Songs of Spiritual Journey
Matthew 14:12*
FENR, 129, Choral unaccompanied with additional historical
information
JOHRS, 7, d, Solo voice with piano accompaniment
PETL, 373, d, Text only
SANH, 126, Uses Tonic Sol-fa notation

Tell John Don't Call the Roll
Tell John don' call duh roll 'tell I git dere oh

Songs of Spiritual Journey
    HUTS, 83, d, Melody and additional historical information
    JOHRS, 14, Solo voice with piano accompaniment

Tell Me Brother
Tell me brudder Jonas an' tell me true
    Praise
        GREF, 80, d, Solo voice with piano accompaniment

Tell My Jesus Morning
In the morning when I rise
    Jesus
        ALLS, 15, Melody only
        PETL, 253, d, Text only

Tell Them I'm Gone
When you miss me from 'round the fireside
    Deliverance
        GRIN, 6, d, Melody only
        PETL, 193, d, Text only

Ten Virgins — see — There Were Ten Virgins

Thank God I'm in the Field
Lord I neber knowed de battle was so hard
    Faith/Assurance
        HALC, 15, d, Choral with piano accompaniment and additional
          historical information
        PETL, 409, d, Text only

Thank God I'm on My Way to Heaven
You may talk about me just as much as you please
    Heaven
        PETL, 253, d, Text only

Thank You Lord
Thank you Lord I just want to thank you Lord
    Praise

Psalm 108:3^
AAH, 531, Choral with piano accompaniment and additional
historical information

That Lonesome Stream
When you look way across dat lonesome stream
Suffering
LOMJA, 602, d, Melody only

That Lonesome Valley — see — Lonesome Valley

That Sabbath Has No End
I went down in the valley
Admonition/Judgment
ODUN, 63, d, Text only; Source includes additional historical
information

That Same Train
That same train's going to be back tomorrow
Deliverance
MCIB, 79, d, Melody and additional historical information
PETL, 194, d, Text only

That Suits Me
Come on el-duh let's go 'roun de wall
Songs of Spiritual Journey
HALC, 63, d, Choral with piano accompaniment and additional
historical information
JOHHT, 26, d, Solo voice with piano accompaniment
KENM, 129, d, Solo voice with piano accompaniment and addi-
tional historical information
PARS, 137, Melody only
PETL, 374, d, Text only

That Sun Going Down
Dat sun gwine down
Admonition/Judgment
HALC, 38, d, Choral with piano accompaniment and additional
historical information
PETL, 290, d, Text only

The Church Is Moving On
Moving along the church is moving along
Church
BOAS, 84, Solo voice with piano accompaniment

The Crucified — see — Were You There

The Crucifixion — see — Were You There

The Golden Street
Soon we gwine walk oh Lawd soon we gwine walk oh Lawd
Rituals of Preparation for Renewal/Regeneration
GUL, 20, d, Text only

The Gospel Train
The gospel train's a-comin'
Deliverance
SKEG, 2, d, Solo voice with piano accompaniment and chord symbols

The Lord's Prayer
Our Father which art in Heaven hallowed a-be Thy name
Prayer
CHAT, 84, Solo voice with piano accompaniment
HAWD, 156, Text only
MARS, 222, Choral unaccompanied with additional historical information
MAR3, 256, Choral unaccompanied with additional historical information

The Ten Virgins — see — There Were Ten Virgins

Them Bones
Dem bones dem bones dem bones
Deliverance
LOMJO, 23, d, Melody only
LOMJO2, 23, d, Melody only

Them Charming Bells
Come along my brothers come along

Heaven
BARO, 15, d, Melody only

Then My Little Soul's Going to Shine — see — I'm Going to Join the Great Association

There Are Angels Hovering Around
There are angels hov'rin' 'roun' there are angels hov'rin' 'roun'
Christmas
BRUO, 14, d, Solo voice with piano accompaniment and additional historical information

There Is a Balm in Gilead — see — Balm in Gilead

There Is a Light Shining
There is a light shining in the Heavens for us
Heaven
BOAS, 63, Solo voice with piano accompaniment

There Is a Mighty Shouting
Dis day Lord dere is a mighty shoutin' in de Hebbe
Heaven
MCIB, 225, d, Melody and additional historical information
PETL, 254, d, Text only

There Is Rest for the Weary Traveler
There is rest for the weary traveler
Faith/Assurance
BALS, 31, d, Choral unaccompanied with additional historical information
PETL, 100, d, Text only

There Were Ten Virgins
There were ten virgins when the bridegroom came
Aspiration
Matthew 25:1–13*
DETR, 72, Choral unaccompanied with additional historical information

FENC, 90, Choral unaccompanied with additional historical information

FENR, 90, Choral unaccompanied with additional historical information

GREF, 78, d, Solo voice with piano accompaniment

MARS, 159, Choral unaccompanied with additional historical information

PETL, 295, d, Text only

PIKJ, 199, Choral unaccompanied with additional historical information

SAAT2, 13, d, Solo voice with piano accompaniment

SANH, 37, d, Uses Tonic Sol-fa notation

SEWJC, 44, Choral unaccompanied with additional historical information

There's a Great Camp Meeting — see — Walk Together Children

There's a Handwriting on the Wall
There's a handwriting on the wall
Admonition/Judgment
Daniel 5:5, 12, 24–28+
BALS, 29, d, Choral unaccompanied with additional historical information
JOHJB, ii, 161, d, Solo voice with piano accompaniment and additional historical information
PETL, 295, d, Text only

There's a Heavenly Home Up Yonder
There's a heavenly home up yonder
Heaven
SANH, 131, Uses Tonic Sol-fa notation

There's a Light in the Valley
Dey's a light een duh walley fuh me
Songs of Spiritual Journey
GUL, 13, d, Text only

There's a Little Wheel — see — Little Wheel Turning in My Heart

There's a Man Going Around Taking Names

There's a man going around taking names

Death

BRON, 12, d, Solo voice with piano accompaniment

FISS, 28, d, Solo voice with piano accompaniment and additional historical information

KENMM, 100, d, Solo voice with piano accompaniment and additional historical information

LOMJA, 591, d, Melody only

LOYS, 80, d, Solo voice with piano accompaniment

PETL, 42, d, Text only

RAGS, 19, d, Solo voice with piano accompaniment

RAIJ, 66, d, Solo voice with piano accompaniment

WHIF, 58, d, Solo voice with piano accompaniment

There's a Meeting Here Tonight (1)

I take my text in Matthew

Church

ALLS, 9, Melody only

JOHRS, 17, d, Solo voice with piano accompaniment

PETL, 100, d, Text only

There's a Meeting Here Tonight (2)

Get you ready there's a meeting here tonight

Church

ANDW, 16, d, Choral arrangement

CHET, 279, Text only

CLES, 91, Choral with piano accompaniment and additional historical information

DETD1, 11, Choral unaccompanied with additional historical information

DETR, 182, d, Choral unaccompanied with additional historical information

FISS, 16, d, Solo voice with piano accompaniment and additional historical information

GREF, 76, d, Solo voice with piano accompaniment

HERB, 83, Text only

MARS, 184, Choral unaccompanied with additional historical information

PETL, 147, d, Text only

Prayer
>> PETL, 42, d, Text only
>> WORJA, 222, Choral unaccompanied with additional historical information

These Are All My Father's Children
> These all my Father's children
> Jesus
>> ALLS, 101, Melody only
>> MCIB, 88, d, Melody and additional historical information
>> PETL, 147, d, Text only
>> PETL, 254, d, Text only
>> SEWJC, 54, Melody only

These Are My Father's Children
> These are my Father's children
> Songs of Spiritual Journey
>> PETL, 374, d, Text only
>> PIKJ, 208, Melody only
>> SANH, 133, Uses Tonic Sol-fa notation

These Bones Going to Rise Again
> Lawd He thought He'd make a man
> Admonition/Judgment
> Genesis 2:7–9, 16–25, 3:1–24+
>> BARO, 32, d, Melody only
>> CHET, 238, d, Text only
>> COLS, 88, d, Solo voice with piano accompaniment
>> JOHRR, 40, d, Solo voice with piano accompaniment and additional historical information
>> LOMAF, 476, d, Melody, chord symbols, and additional historical information
>> LOMJA, 597, d, Melody only
>> MAR3, 300, Choral unaccompanied with additional historical information

These Dry Bones of Mine
> What kind of shoes is dem you wear

WORF, 44, Choral unaccompanied with additional historical information

WORJF, 75, d, Text only; Source includes additional historical information

This Is the Healing Water

This is de healin' water water
Rituals of Preparation for Renewal/Regeneration
JOHHT, 52, d, Solo voice with piano accompaniment

This Is the Man

This is the Man who made this earth
Jesus
DITT, 36, Choral arrangement
PETL, 100, d, Text only

This Is the Trouble of the World

I ask Father Georgy for religion
Church
ALLS, 99, Melody only
PETL, 43, d, Text only

This Is the Way I Pray

This is the way I pray in my home
Prayer
PETL, 335, d, Text only

This Little Light of Mine

This little light of mine I'm gonna let it shine
Praise
Matthew 5:14–16^
AAH, 549, Choral with piano accompaniment and additional historical information
BONR, 188, d, Solo voice with piano accompaniment
BOY3M, 90, Solo voice with piano accompaniment
BRYA, 16, Melody, chord symbols, and additional historical information
CALA, 44, Melody only

This May Be My Last Time

This may be my las' time

Death

This Old Time Religion — see — Old Time Religion

This Old World's a Hell to Me
Dear brother don't you leave
Suffering
ODUN, 116, d, Text only; Source includes additional historical information

This Old World's Rolling
Well the ole worl' is a rollin' rollin' rollin'
Admonition/Judgment
ODUN, 118, d, Text only; Source includes additional historical information

This Train
This train is bound for glory this train
Deliverance
HERB, 85, Text only
JORS, 34, d, Text only
LOMAF, 484, Melody, chord symbols, and additional historical information
LOMJA, 593, Melody only
LUEB, 110, Melody, chord symbols, and piano accompaniment
PETL, 194, d, Text only
SKEG, 36, d, Solo voice with piano accompaniment and chord symbols
TRAH, 78, Melody, chord symbols, and piano accompaniment

This Train Is Bound For Glory — see — This Train

This World Is Not My Home
This world is not my home
Heaven
BARO, 9, d, Melody only
SPAG, 54, d, Solo voice with piano accompaniment and chord symbols
SKEG, 38, d, Solo voice with piano accompaniment and chord symbols

Three Long Nights and Three Long Days
Three long nights and three long days
Songs of Spiritual Journey
BALS, 47, d, Choral unaccompanied with additional historical information
PETL, 254, d, Text only

Till I Get There
Don't strike dem golden harps till I get there
Heaven
SIX, 22, Solo voice with piano accompaniment

Time Ain't Long
The time ain't long there's a star in the east
Death
BOAS, 7, Solo voice with piano accompaniment

Time for Praying
Time for praying won't be long
Prayer
CLES, 133, Choral with piano accompaniment and additional historical information

Time Is Drawing Nigh
See the signs of the Judgment yes
Admonition/Judgment
GRIN, 54, d, Melody only
PETL, 296, d, Text only

'Tis Jordan's River
'Tis Jordan's river and I must go 'cross
Songs of Spiritual Journey
1 Corinthians 15:22; Deuteronomy 9:1*
MAR3, 248, Choral unaccompanied with additional historical information
MARS, 214, Choral unaccompanied with additional historical information
PETL, 410, d, Text only
SANH, 134, d, Uses Tonic Sol-fa notation

'Tis Me O Lord — see — Standing in the Need of Prayer

'Tis the Old Ship of Zion — see — Old Ship of Zion

To Be Baptized — see — Take Me to the Water

To See God's Bleeding Lamb — see — Want to Go to Heaven When I Die

Toll the Bell Angel
Wen I lay my body down aye Lawd in de graveyahd
Death
KENM, 150, d, Solo voice with piano accompaniment and additional historical information
PETL, 255, d, Text only

Tomorrow You May Die
Sinner today you better repent
Admonition/Judgment
FISS, 178, d, Solo voice with piano accompaniment and additional historical information
PETL, 298, d, Text only

Tone the Bell Easy
When you hear dat Ise a-dyin'
Death
LOMJA, 605, d, Melody only

Too Late
Too late too late sinner
Admonition/Judgment
BALS, 32, d, Choral unaccompanied with additional historical information
GUL, 9, d, Text only
JOHJB, ii, 102, d, Solo voice with piano accompaniment and additional historical information
PETL, 298, d, Text only

Towe the Bell — see — Toll the Bell

Trip to Raleigh
Now I went down to Raleigh
Songs of Spiritual Journey
NILS, 10, d, Solo voice with piano accompaniment and additional
historical information

Trouble
Trouble trouble all Ah see
Faith/Assurance
CHAT, 124, Solo voice with piano accompaniment

Trouble Done Bore Me Down
Lord oh Lord
Suffering
MCIB, 238, d, Melody and additional historical information
PETL, 44, d, Text only

Trouble of the World
I want to be my Father's children
Suffering
ALLS, 8, Melody only
PETL, 45, d, Text only

Trouble Will Bury Me Down
I'm sometimes up I'm sometimes down
Suffering
BARO, 24, d, Melody only
HERB, 66, Text only
PETL, 36, d, Text only
SLA, 3, Choral arrangement
WHIF, 42, d, Solo voice with piano accompaniment

Trouble's Going to Weigh Me Down
Trouble's going to weigh me down
Suffering
FISS, 182, d, Solo voice with piano accompaniment and additional
historical information
PETL, 46, d, Text only

Troubled in Mind
Now I'm troubled in mind
Suffering
BARO, 24, d, Melody only

Troubles Was Hard
Tell yuh 'bout a man wat live befo' Chris'
Suffering
Genesis, 3:6, 16–19; Revelation 21:4–8; I Samuel 17:49–50, 19:10–12+
KENM, 82, d, Solo voice with piano accompaniment and additional historical information

True Religion
Well you must have that true religion
Admonition/Judgment
ODUN, 83, Text only; Source includes additional historical information

Trying to Cross the Red Sea
Didn't old Pharaoh get lost
Faith/Assurance
PETL, 255, d, Text only

Trying to Get Home
Lord I'm bearin' heavy burdens
Suffering
CARS, 42, d, Solo voice with piano accompaniment
CLES, 130, d, Choral with piano accompaniment and additional historical information
HERB, 86, Text only
PETL, 148, d, Text only
WHAG, 18, d, Solo voice with piano accompaniment
WHII, 42, d, Solo voice with piano accompaniment

Turn Back Pharaoh's Army
Goin' to write to massa Jesus to send some valiant soldiers to turn back Pharaoh's army
Deliverance

Exodus 2:23, 14:21–22, 27–28+

MARS, 132, Choral unaccompanied with additional historical information

PETL, 148, d, Text only

SEWJ, 10, Choral arrangement

SEWJC, 10, Choral unaccompanied with additional historical information

SEWJC, 172, Choral unaccompanied with additional historical information

SIX, 33, Solo voice with piano accompaniment

Turn Sinner

Turn sinner turn while yo' maker axer yo' to turn

Songs of Spiritual Journey

MCIB, 232, Melody and additional historical information

PETL, 375, d, Text only

Turn Sinner Turn

Turn sinner turn today

Songs of Spiritual Journey

ALLS, 36, Melody only

PETL, 375, d, Text only

'Twas on One Sunday Morning

It was on one Sunday morning

Easter

Luke 16:1–6, 24:2–4, 12; Matthew 28:2+

AFR, 31, Choral with piano accompaniment

PETL, 195, d, Text only

Two Wings

I want two wings to veil my face

Prayer

Revelation 12:14; 1 Thessalonians 4:1, 6+

GRIN, 80, d, Melody only

HAWD, 80, Text only

HAYMF, 41, d, Solo voice with piano accompaniment and additional historical information

HAYMS, 41, d, Solo voice with piano accompaniment and additional historical information
HERB, 87, Text only
JOHRR, 31, d, Solo voice with piano accompaniment and additional historical information
KENM, 121, d, Solo voice with piano accompaniment and additional historical information
MCIB, 233, Melody and additional historical information
NORS, 18, Melody and instrumental ensemble accompaniment
PETL, 101, d, Text only
PETL, 196, d, Text only
PETL, 399, d, Text only

Under the Rail
Under the rail under the tie
Work Songs
ODUN, 260, Text only; Source includes additional historical information

Until I Found the Lord
Lord I cried I cried
Suffering
CLES, 177, Choral with piano accompaniment and additional historical information

Until I Reach My Home
Until I reach my home
Aspiration
HALC, 39, d, Choral with piano accompaniment and additional historical information
HAWD, 57, Text only
HERB, 87, Text only
JOHJB, i, 177, d, Solo voice with piano accompaniment and additional historical information
PETL, 149, d, Text only

Up on the Mountain
Way up on the mountain Lord

Wait a Little While

Wait Mr Mackright

Wake Up Children

Wake Up Jacob

Wake Up Jonah
Wake up Jonah you are the man
Faith/Assurance
Jonah 1:5–6+
COUN, 223, Melody only
COUNS, 7, Solo voice with piano accompaniment and additional historical information
LANC, 19, Melody, chord symbols, and additional historical information

Walk About Elders
Walk about elders Jesus a listenin'
Faith/Assurance
GRIN, 46, Melody only
PETL, 102, d, Text only

Walk God's Heavenly Road
March along oh Canaan land
Faith/Assurance
MCIB, 244, d, Melody and additional historical information
PETL, 103, d, Text only

Walk in Jerusalem Just like John — see also — I Want to Be Ready

Walk in Jerusalem Just like John (1)
Last Sunday morning last Sunday morning
Deliverance
DITT, 50, Choral arrangement
HAWD, 37, Text only
HERB, 88, Text only
PETL, 196, d, Text only

Walk in Jerusalem Just like John (2)
I want to be ready
Aspiration
BARO, 35, d, Melody only
FREC, 32, Solo voice with piano accompaniment
GREF, 74, Solo voice with piano accompaniment
GUL, 86, d, Text only

> JOHJB, ii, 58, d, Solo voice with piano accompaniment and additional historical information
> MIL3, 46, Solo voice with piano accompaniment
> PETL, 256, d, Text only
> SIX, 57, Solo voice with piano accompaniment
> SKEG, 40, d, Solo voice with piano accompaniment and chord symbols
> SPAG, 57, d, Solo voice with piano accompaniment and chord symbols

Walk in Jerusalem Just like John (3)
When I come to die I want t' be ready
Aspiration
MCIB, 147, d, Melody and additional historical information
PETL, 397, d, Text only

Walk in Jerusalem Just like John (4)
Jerusalem Lawd
Aspiration
BALS, 46, d, Choral unaccompanied with additional historical information

Walk Mary Down the Lane
Three long nights and three long days
Songs of Spiritual Journey
JOHJB, ii, 147, d, Solo voice with piano accompaniment and additional historical information
PETL, 149, d, Text only

Walk Through the Valley
We shall walk through the valley and the shadow of death
Faith/Assurance
WORJF, 55, d, Text only; Source includes additional historical information

Walk Through the Valley in Peace
We will walk thro' the valley in peace
Faith/Assurance
BARO, 7, d, Melody only

Walk Together Children

Walk together children don't you get weary

Faith/Assurance

3 John 4^

AAH, 541, Choral with piano accompaniment and additional historical information

ARMH, 222, d, Choral unaccompanied with additional historical information

BOAS, 74, Solo voice with piano accompaniment

BRYW, 28, Melody only

CALA, 28, Text only

CHET, 281, d, Text only

CLES, 156, Choral with piano accompaniment and additional historical information

DETR, 26, d, Choral unaccompanied with additional historical information

FENC, 50, d, Choral unaccompanied with additional historical information

FENR, 50, d, Choral unaccompanied with additional historical information

FISS, 188, d, Solo voice with piano accompaniment and additional historical information

HAWD, 45, Text only

HERB, 1, Text only

HERB, 89, Text only

HOGDH, 36, d, Solo voice with piano accompaniment and additional historical information

HOGDL, 36, d, Solo voice with piano accompaniment and additional historical information

JOHJB, ii, 180, d, Solo voice with piano accompaniment and additional historical information

MARS, 246, d, Choral unaccompanied with additional historical information

MIL3, 23, Solo voice with piano accompaniment

NAA, 4, Melody and chord symbols

PETL, 66, d, Text only

PETL, 197, d, Text only

STIT, 45, d, Solo voice with piano accompaniment and additional historical information

WORJF, 45, d, Text only; Source includes additional historical information

Walk with Me — see — I Want Jesus to Walk with Me

Walk You in the Light
Walk you in de light
Faith/Assurance
Ephesians 6:4; Exodus 15:20; John 12:35; Romans 5:8*
ARMH, 238, d, Choral unaccompanied with additional historical information
DETR, 24, d, Choral unaccompanied with additional historical information
FENC, 66, d, Choral unaccompanied with additional historical information
FENR, 66, d, Choral unaccompanied with additional historical information
PETL, 103, d, Text only
SANH, 135, Uses Tonic Sol-fa notation

Walking in God's Commandments
Hallelujah my God walking God's commandments
Rituals of Preparation for Renewal/Regeneration
HALC, 71, Melody only
PETL, 335, d, Text only

Walking in the Light
Let yo' light shine all over the world
Faith/Assurance
DETR, 116, d, Choral unaccompanied with additional historical information
FENC, 102, d, Choral unaccompanied with additional historical information
FENR, 102, d, Choral unaccompanied with additional historical information
ODUN, 137, d, Text only; Source includes additional historical information
PETL, 336, d, Text only

Want to Go to Heaven When I Die

Wasn't That a Mighty Day

Wasn't That a Wide River

    DETR, 98, d, Choral unaccompanied with additional historical information

    FENC, 22, d, Choral unaccompanied with additional historical information

    FENR, 22, d, Choral unaccompanied with additional historical information

    HERB, 89, Text only

    JOHJB, i, 152, d, Solo voice with piano accompaniment and additional historical information

    MARS, 200, Choral unaccompanied with additional historical information

    MIL3, 16, Solo voice with piano accompaniment

    PETL, 185, d, Text only

    SANH, 113, Uses Tonic Sol-fa notation

    SNYS, 36, d, Solo voice with piano accompaniment

    WIES, 205, Solo voice with piano accompaniment

    WORJF, 47, d, Text only; source includes additional historical information

Wasn't That a Witness for My Lord

Wasn that a witness fo' my Lord

    Rituals of Preparation for Renewal/Regeneration

    Genesis 2:2, 22, 3:2–3, 16; Judges 13:24, 14:15–17, 16:17–18+

        HALC, 72, Melody only

        PETL, 376, d, Text only

Wasn't That a Wonder

Wasn' that a wonder in the Heaven

    Heaven

        PARS, 139, d, Melody only

Wasn't That Hard Trials

Wasn't that hard trials great tribulation

    Suffering

        KENMM, 63, d, Solo voice with piano accompaniment and additional historical information

Watch and Pray — see — Mother Is Master Going to Sell Us Tomorrow

Watch the Stars
Watch the stars see how they run
Songs of Spiritual Journey
BALS, 58, d, Choral unaccompanied with additional historical
information
PETL, 402, d, Text only

Watching the Sky
Oh watch the sun see how it runs the sun goes down and another
day is done
Faith/Assurance
PITG, 86, Solo voice with piano accompaniment

Way By and By
Way bye and bye way bye and bye
Heaven
BALS, 49, d, Choral unaccompanied with additional historical
information
COUN, 253, Melody only
PETL, 104, d, Text only

Way Bye and Bye — see — Way By and By

Way Down in Hell
It's always midnight way down in Hell
Suffering
MCIB, 241, Melody and additional historical information
PETL, 46, d, Text only

Way in the Heaven By and By
Way in the Heaven by and by
Heaven
DITT, 23, d, Choral arrangement
PETL, 103, d, Text only

**Way Over in de Promise' Land — see — Wonder Where Is Good Old
Daniel**

Way Over in the Egypt Land
    Way over in the Egypt land you shall gain the victory
        Songs of Spiritual Journey
        Acts 2:4, 14; Mark 1:16–18; Matthew 4:18–20+
            SANH, 136, Uses Tonic Sol-fa notation

Way Over Jordan
    Way over Jordan
        Songs of Spiritual Journey
            MARS, 202, d, Choral unaccompanied with additional historical information
            PETL, 411, d, Text only

Way Up on the Mountain
    Way up on the mountain Lord
        Deliverance
            HALC, 34, d, Melody only
            JOHJB, i, 64, d, Solo voice with piano accompaniment and additional historical information
            PETL, 411, d, Text only

Wayfaring Stranger — see — Pilgrim's Song

We Are Almost Home (1)
    We are almost home
        Faith/Assurance
            DETR, 89, Choral unaccompanied with additional historical information
            MARS, 204, Choral unaccompanied with additional historical information
            PETL, 151, d, Text only
            SANH, 137, Uses Tonic Sol-fa notation

We Are Almost Home (2)
    Come along muh sistuh come along
        Faith/Assurance
             GUL, 88, d, Text only

We Are Building on a Rock
We are building on a rock
Faith/Assurance
CHET, 281, Text only
DETD2, 27, Choral unaccompanied with additional historical information
DETR, 115, Choral unaccompanied with additional historical information
FENR, 123, Choral unaccompanied with additional historical information
PETL, 105, d, Text only

We Are Climbing Jacob's Ladder — see — Jacob's Ladder

We Are Climbing the Hills of Zion
We are climbing the hills of Zion
Aspiration
Psalm 24:3*
MARS, 200, Choral unaccompanied with additional historical information
PETL, 150, d, Text only
SANH, 139, Uses Tonic Sol-fa notation

We Are Traveling to the Grave
Traveling traveling we are traveling
Death
DETD3, 25, Choral unaccompanied with additional historical information

We Are Walking Down the Valley
We are walkin' down the valley our Savior so low
Faith/Assurance
KENMM, 56, d, Melody only

We Are Walking in the Light — see — Walking in the Light

We Need More Reapers — see — Work's Being Done

We Shall Walk Through the Valley
We will march through the valley in peace
Songs of Spiritual Journey
ALLS, 73, Melody only
ANDW, 36, Melody only
BAP, 501, Choral with piano accompaniment and additional historical information
BOAS, 55, Solo voice with piano accompaniment
MARS, 194, Choral unaccompanied with additional historical information
NEW, 533, Choral with piano accompaniment and additional historical information
PETL, 377, d, Text only

We Will March Through the Valley — see — We Shall Walk Through the Valley

We'll Die in the Field
What do you say seekers
Death
MAR3, 173, Choral unaccompanied with additional historical information
MARS, 139, Choral unaccompanied with additional historical information
PETL, 150, d, Text only
SEWJ, 21, Choral arrangement
SEWJC, 21, Choral unaccompanied with additional historical information

We'll March Down Jordan
We'll march down Jerden hallelu
Songs of Spiritual Journey
MCIB, 243, d, Melody and additional historical information
PETL, 377, d, Text only

We'll Overtake the Army
We'll overtake the army
Faith/Assurance
Ephesians 6:10–13; Exodus 15:3*
MARS, 203, Choral unaccompanied with additional historical information

PETL, 151, d, Text only
SANH, 140, Uses Tonic Sol-fa notation

We'll Stand the Storm
Stand the storm
Faith/Assurance
CHET, 282, Text only
MARS, 154, Choral unaccompanied with additional historical information
PETL, 105, d, Text only
PIKJ, 194, Choral unaccompanied with additional historical information
SAAT2, 25, d, Solo voice with piano accompaniment
SEWJC, 39, Choral unaccompanied with additional historical information

We'll Wait 'til Jesus Comes
We'll wait till Jesus comes down by the river
Songs of Spiritual Journey
Acts 16:13; Revelation 19:6*
SANH, 115, Uses Tonic Sol-fa notation

We're Almost Home — see — We Are Almost Home

We're Some of the Praying People
We're some of the praying people
Prayer
BARO, 16, d, Melody only

We've Come a Long Way Lord
We've come a long way Lord a mighty long way
Songs of Spiritual Journey
CHET, 282, Text only

We've Come This Far by Faith
We've come this far by faith
Faith/Assurance
CLES, 192, Choral with piano accompaniment and additional historical information

Welcome to the Undying Lamb
    Ev'rybody bids you welcome welcome welcome
        Rituals of Preparation for Renewal/Regeneration
            BRUO, 10, d, Solo voice with piano accompaniment and additional historical information

Well She Ask Me in the Parlor
    Well she ask me whuk in de parlor whuk
        Work Songs
            ODUN, 258, d, Text only; Source includes additional historical information

Were You There
    Were you there when they crucified my Lord
        Easter
        Acts 2:23–24^
            AAH, 254, Choral with piano accompaniment and additional historical information
            ALBGH, 9, Solo voice with piano accompaniment
            ALBGL, 9, Solo voice with piano accompaniment
            ANDW, 43, Choral arrangement
            BALS, 88, d, Melody only
            BAP, 108, Choral with piano accompaniment and additional historical information
            BARO, 40, d, Melody only
            BAYF, 14, d, Solo voice with piano accompaniment and chord symbols
            BELT, 18, Uses Tonic Sol-fa notation
            BLOR, 212, Text and chord symbols
            BOAS, 25, Solo voice with piano accompaniment
            BOCH, 287, Choral with piano accompaniment and additional historical information
            BRYW, 39, Melody only
            BURA, 40, d, Solo voice with piano accompaniment
            BURS, 46, d, Solo voice with piano accompaniment
            CALA, 48, Melody only
            CHAT, 87, Solo voice with piano accompaniment
            CHET, 282, Text only

What a Beautiful City

What Is the Matter With the Mourners — see — Jubilee

What Kind of Shoes You Going to Wear
What kind of shoes you going to wear
Aspiration
DETS, 2, Solo voice with piano accompaniment
GREF, 82, d, Solo voice with piano accompaniment
HAWD, 103, d, Text only
JOHHH, 144, d, Solo voice with piano accompaniment
MACS, 42, d, Melody only
MAR3, 202, Choral unaccompanied with additional historical information
MARS, 168, Choral unaccompanied with additional historical information
SIX, 43, Solo voice with piano accompaniment

What Month Was Jesus Born In
What month was Jesus born in
Christmas
AFR, 42, Melody only
COUN, 245, Melody only

What Shall I Do
I'm so glad trouble don't last always
Faith/Assurance
PETL, 257, d, Text only

What Shall I Render
What shall I render into God for all His mercies
Aspiration
CLES, 190, Choral with piano accompaniment and additional historical information

What You Going to Do
Sinner what you goin' to do
Admonition/Judgment
LOGR, 1, d, Melody only
ODUN, 77, d, Text only; Source includes additional historical information

What You Going to Do When the Lamp Burns Down
    Poor sinner now is your time
        Admonition/Judgment
            CHET, 282, d, Text only
            DETD2, 30, Choral unaccompanied with additional historical
                information
            DETR, 140, d, Choral unaccompanied with additional historical
                information
            FENR, 136, d, Choral unaccompanied with additional historical
                information
            HALC, 28, d, Choral with piano accompaniment and additional
                historical information on the spiritual
            HERB, 91, d, Text only
            JOHJB, i, 170, d, Solo voice with piano accompaniment and
                additional historical information
            PETL, 299, d, Text only
            PETL, 378, d, Text only

What You Going to Name That Pretty Little Baby
    Mary what you going to name the pretty little baby
        Jesus
            BOAT, 133, d, Solo voice with piano accompaniment
            BRUO, 17, d, Solo voice with piano accompaniment and additional
                historical information
            PETL, 257, d, Text only

Wheel in a Wheel
    Wheel in a wheel oh my Lord
        Faith/Assurance
        Ezekiel 1:15–21, 10:10*
            BALS, 2, d, Choral unaccompanied with additional historical
                information
            DANF, 15, Melody only
            DETR, 184, Choral unaccompanied with additional historical
                information
            DITT, 42, d, Choral arrangement
            FENR, 110, Choral unaccompanied with additional historical
                information
            PETL, 11, d, Text only

Deliverance
SIX, 37, Solo voice with piano accompaniment

When Moses Smote the Water
When Moses smote the water de chillun all crossed over
Deliverance
GLAS, 22, Melody and chord symbols
JESM, 54, d, Solo voice with piano accompaniment and additional
historical information
MARS, 175, Choral unaccompanied with additional historical
information
PETL, 198, d, Text only
PIKJ, 215, Choral unaccompanied with additional historical
information
SEWJC, 60, Choral unaccompanied with additional historical
information

When My Blood Runs Chilly and Cold
When a my blood runs chilly an' col' I've got to go
Death
LOMJA, 610, d, Melody only
LOMJF, 452, d, Solo voice with piano accompaniment and addi-
tional historical information

When My Lord Calls Me I Must Go
I'm goin' to cross that ocean by mysel'
Faith/Assurance
GUL, 58, d, Text only
PARS, 157, Text only; Source includes additional historical
information

When Shall I Get There
There's a heavenly home up yonder
Heaven
MARS, 183, Choral unaccompanied with additional historical
information
PETL, 151, d, Text only

When the Bridegroom Comes
I hope you'll all be ready when the Bridegroom comes
Faith/Assurance
DANF, 58, Melody only

When the Chariot Comes
Who will drive the chariot when she comes
Death
BARO, 44, d, Melody only

When the Devil Comes Around
Dat day when you'se weary fightin' wiv sin
Death
BURP, 8, d, Solo voice with piano accompaniment

When the General Roll Is Called — see — General Roll Call

When the Lord Called Moses
When the Lord called Moses
Aspirations
Exodus 3:4+
FISS, 200, d, Solo voice with piano accompaniment and additional historical information
PETL, 378, d, Text only

When the Lord Shall Appear — see — Children We All Shall Be Free

When the Saints Go Marching In
When the saints go marching in
Aspiration
Jude 14–15^
AAH, 595, Choral with piano accompaniment and additional historical information
APPA, 184, Solo voice with piano accompaniment
BLOR, 212, Text and chord symbols
BOAS, 33, Solo voice with piano accompaniment
BRYA, 21, Melody, chord symbols, and additional historical information

BRYI, 3, d, Melody only
BUCS, 20, Instrumental Ensemble accompaniment
CALA, 29, Text only
FRAS, 70, Solo voice with piano accompaniment
GUIU, 76, Solo voice with piano accompaniment
GUL, 90, d, Text only
HAWD, 76, Text only
HERB, 92, Text only
HERB, 93, Text only
JOHHG, 4, d, Solo voice with piano accompaniment
JOHHH, 12, d, Solo voice with piano accompaniment
LLOA, 148, Solo voice with piano accompaniment
LOMAF, 454, Melody, chord symbols, and additional historical information
LUEB, 88, Melody, chord symbols, and piano accompaniment
PETL, 259, d, Text only
RUTF, 44, Solo voice with piano accompaniment
SHEH, 38, Melody and chord symbols
SKEG, 45, d, Solo voice with piano accompaniment and chord symbols
SPAG, 61, d, Solo voice with piano accompaniment and chord symbols

When the Stars Begin to Fall — see — My Lord What a Morning

When the Train Comes Along
Well I may be sick an' cannot rise
Death
BALS, 12, d, Choral unaccompanied with additional historical information
DITT, 4, Choral arrangement
ODUN, 111, d, Text only; Source includes additional historical information
PETL, 199, d, Text only
PETL, 412, d, Text only

When We Do Meet Again
When we do meet again

Faith/Assurance
    PETL, 107, d, Text only

When You Feel Like Moaning
When you feel like moanin' it ain't nothin' but
    Suffering
        COUN, 238, Melody only
        COUNS, 13, Solo voice with piano accompaniment and additional
           historical information

When You Hear My Coffin Sound
When you hear my coffin sound
    Death
        DITT, 41, Choral arrangement
        PETL, 49, d, Text only

Where Do You Think I Found My Soul
Where do you think I found my soul
    Rituals of Preparation for Renewal/Regeneration
    Luke 15:3–10*
        SANH, 146, Uses Tonic Sol-fa notation

Where Is Mary Gone
Where is Mary gone
    Women
        LOGR, 2, Melody only

Where Shall I Be (1)
Where shall I be when the first trumpet sounds
    Admonition/Judgment
        BRYW, 47, Melody only
        CHET, 283, d, Text only
        DETR, 173, d, Choral unaccompanied with additional historical
           information
        FENR, 172, d, Choral unaccompanied with additional historical
           information
        HALC, 8, d, Choral with piano accompaniment and additional
           historical information

Who Shall Deliver Poor Me (1)
Paul an' Silas laid in jail all night long
Deliverance
KENMM, 116, d, Solo voice with piano accompaniment and additional historical information

Who Shall Deliver Poor Me (2)
Jacob rassled with the angels all night long
Deliverance
RAIJ, 68, Solo voice with piano accompaniment

Who Will Join the Union
Hallelujah oh hallelujah
Deliverance
ARMH, 220, d, Choral unaccompanied with additional historical information
DETR, 142, d, Choral unaccompanied with additional historical information
FENC, 48, d, Choral unaccompanied with additional historical information
FENR, 48, d, Choral unaccompanied with additional historical information
PETL, 200, d, Text only

Who You Got in Heaven
Who you got een Heben (Who you got in Heaven?)
Heaven
HUTS, 95, d, Melody and additional historical information

Who'll Be a Witness for My Lord — see — Witness

Who's Been Here
Who's been here since I've been gone
Faith/Assurance
BRON, 6, d, Solo voice with piano accompaniment

Who's Going to Close My Dying Eyes
I don' wan' be buried in de stawm

Death
    KENM, 69, d, Solo voice with piano accompaniment and additional historical information
    PETL, 49, d, Text only

Who's That Coming Over Yonder
Who dat coming ober yonder hallelujah
    Deliverance
        BRYA, 12, d, Melody, chord symbols, and additional historical information
        HALC, 20, d, Choral with piano accompaniment and additional historical information
        JOHJB, i, 104, d, Solo voice with piano accompaniment and additional historical information
        PETL, 243, d, Text only

Who's That Yonder
Who's that yonder dressed in red
    Jesus
        BARO, 45, d, Melody only
        JESM, 6, d, Solo voice with piano accompaniment and additional historical information
        JONF, 4, Melody only

Why Don't You Come Along
Hey why don't you come along
    Rituals of Preparation for Renewal/Regeneration
        MCIB, 242, d, Melody and additional historical information
        PETL, 338, d, Text only

Why Don't You Deliver Me
Ma Lord 'liver Daniel
    Deliverance
        MCIB, 248, d, Melody and additional historical information
        PETL, 200, d, Text only

Why Don't You Let God's People Go
Phar'oh Why don't you let Gawd's people go

Deliverance
Exodus 3:4–5, 5:1+
  MCIB, 250, d, Melody and additional historical information
  PETL, 201, d, Text only

Why He's the Lord of Lords — see — He Is the Lord of Lords

Wide Deep Troubled Water
I know a wide river aint no Mississippi
  Rituals of Preparation for Renewal/Regeneration
    NILS, 13, d, Solo voice with piano accompaniment and additional historical information

Wide River — see — Wasn't That a Wide River

Will The Lighthouse Shine on Me
Shine on me I wonder if the lighthouse will shine on me
  Heaven
    BOAS, 49, Solo voice with piano accompaniment

Winter
Winter oh the winter
  Suffering
    ALLS, 78, Melody only
    PETL, 201, d, Text only

Winter Will Soon Be Over
Winter winter the winter winter will soon be over children
  Faith/Assurance
    ARMH, 244, d, Choral unaccompanied with additional historical information
    BARO, 14, d, Melody only
    DETD2, 32, Choral unaccompanied with additional historical information
    FENC, 72, d, Choral unaccompanied with additional historical information
    FENR, 72, d, Choral unaccompanied with additional historical information

Wish I Was in Heaven Setting Down
    I wish I was in Heaven sittin' down sittin' down
        Heaven
            CHET, 283, Text only
            GRIN, 74, d, Melody only
            PETL, 412, d, Text only
            PETL, 413, d, Text only

Witness (1)
    My soul is a witness for my Lord
        Rituals of Preparation for Renewal/Regeneration
        Genesis 5:27; Judges 16:17–19, 28–30; Proverbs 14:25+
            BECK, 52, Solo voice with piano accompaniment
            BOAS, 34, Solo voice with piano accompaniment
            CALA, 31, Text only
            CHAT, 62, Solo voice with piano accompaniment
            CHET, 283, Text only
            HAWD, 24, Text only
            HAWD, 40, Text only
            HAY1H, 52, Solo voice with piano accompaniment
            HAYMF, 47, d, Solo voice with piano accompaniment and additional historical information
            HAYMS, 47, d, Solo voice with piano accompaniment and additional historical information
            HERB, 94, Text only
            JOHHG, 22, Solo voice with piano accompaniment
            JOHHH, 30, d, Solo voice with piano accompaniment
            JOHJB, i, 130, d, Solo voice with piano accompaniment and additional historical information
            PETL, 107, d, Text only
            PETL, 108, d, Text only
            SIX, 11, Solo voice with piano accompaniment
            WHIF, 68, d, Solo voice with piano accompaniment

Witness (2)
    Oh Lord what manner of man is this
        Rituals of Preparation for Renewal/Regeneration

Genesis 5:27; Judges 16:17–19, 28–30; Proverbs 14:25+
    HERB, 95, Text only
    JOHHH, 147, d, Solo voice with piano accompaniment
    JOHHH, 154, d, Solo voice with piano accompaniment

Witness (3)
Read in Genesis you understand
    Rituals of Preparation for Renewal/Regeneration
        HERB, 95, Text only
        ODUN, 132, Text only; Source includes additional historical
            information

Woe Be unto You
Woe be unto you
    Admonition/Judgment
        LOMJA, 604, Melody only

Woke Up This Morning
I woke up dis mornin' wid mah min' an' it was stayed
    Faith/Assurance
        CALA, 32, d, Text only
        CHET, 284, d, Text only
        CLES, 146, d, Choral with piano accompaniment and additional
            historical information

Woman at the Well
When Jesus met the woman at the well oh
    Women
        BLOR, 212, Text and chord symbols
        COUN, 252, Melody only

Won't You Sit Down
Won't you sit down Lord I can't sit down
    Heaven
        BOY3S, 68, Solo voice with piano accompaniment
        BRYA, 41, Melody, chord symbols, and additional historical
            information
        LUEB, 90, Melody, chord symbols, and piano accompaniment

Wonder Where Is Good Old Daniel

Wonder where is good ole Daniel

   Heaven

   Daniel 3:23, 6:16; John 20:27–28+

      CHET, 284, Text only

      COLS, 84, d, Solo voice with piano accompaniment

      DANF, 33, d, Melody only

      DETR, 73, Choral unaccompanied with additional historical information

      FENR, 107, d, Choral unaccompanied with additional historical information

      JONF, 145, Melody only

      PETL, 108, d, Text only

      WHIF, 78, d, Solo voice with piano accompaniment

Wonder Where Is My Brother Gone

Wonder where is my brother gone

   Suffering

      COUN, 228, Melody only

      COUNS, 46, Solo voice with piano accompaniment and additional historical information

Wonderful Counselor

Oh who do you call the Wonderful Counselor

   Praise

   Isaiah 9:6^

      AAH, 210, Choral with piano accompaniment and additional historical information

Wondrous Love

What wondrous love is this oh my soul

   Praise

      LOMJF, 440, d, Solo voice with piano accompaniment and additional historical information

Work's Being Done

We need more reapers in the harvest field

   Work Songs

John 4:34–38; Luke 10:1–2; Mark 6:12; Matthew 9:37–38+
> MAR3, 294, Choral unaccompanied with additional historical information
> MARS, 260, Choral unaccompanied with additional historical information
> SANH, 141, Uses Tonic Sol-fa notation

Working on the Building
If I wus a sinner man tell you what I'd do
Admonition/Judgment
> ODUN, 72, d, Text only; Source includes additional historical information

Workmen's Jingles
Sister Mary Aunt Jane
Work Songs
> ODUN, 251, Text only; Source includes additional historical information

Wrestle On Jacob
I held my brother with a trembling hand I would not let him go
Faith/Assurance
> ALLS, 4, Melody only
> BAYF, 36, d, Solo voice with piano accompaniment and chord symbols
> FREC, 45, Solo voice with piano accompaniment
> PETL, 152, d, Text only
> SILSP, 52, Solo voice with piano accompaniment

Wrestling Jacob (1)
All night wrastlin' Jacob's all night all night
Faith/Assurance
Genesis 32:22–32*
> BALS, 62, d, Choral unaccompanied with additional historical information
> DETR, 70, d, Choral unaccompanied with additional historical information
> PETL, 152, d, Text only

Wrestling Jacob (2)

Wrestling Jacob let me go
Faith/Assurance
Genesis 32:22–32*
BALS, 86, d, Choral unaccompanied with additional historical information
CHET, 270, d, Text only
FENR, 131, d, Choral unaccompanied with additional historical information
PETL, 153, d, Text only
SANH, 148, Uses Tonic Sol-fa notation

Wrestling Jacob (3)

Wrastling Jacob Day is a breaking
Faith/Assurance
Genesis 32:22–32*
BALS, 87, d, Melody only
HALC, 41, d, Choral with piano accompaniment and additional historical information
MARS, 180, Choral unaccompanied with additional historical information

Wretched Man That I Am

Wretched man that I am
Suffering
PETL, 36, d, Text only
WORJF, 53, d, Text only; Source includes additional historical information

Wring My Hands and Cry — see — Sometimes I Feel Like a Moanin' Dove

Yes God Is Real

There are some things I may not know
Faith/Assurance
CLES, 201, Choral with piano accompaniment and additional historical information

Yes He Did

He took my feet from the miry clay yes He did
Jesus
SIX, 12, Solo voice with piano accompaniment

Yes I'm Going Up

Yes I'm going up
Heaven
LOGR, 5, d, Melody only
WORJF, 66, d, Text only; Source includes additional historical
information

Yes My Lord

Gonna get to Heaven oh yes
Heaven
ALTRH, 22, Solo voice with piano accompaniment
ALTRL, 22, Solo voice with piano accompaniment

Yes Oh Yes Wait 'til I Get on My Robe — see — Oh Yes

Yes Yonder Comes My Lord

Yes yonder comes my Lord
Admonition/Judgment
DETR, 219, Choral unaccompanied with additional historical
information
FENR, 112, Choral unaccompanied with additional historical
information
PETL, 289, d, Text only

Yonder Comes Sister Mary

Yonder come sister Mary
Women
FISS, 208, d, Solo voice with piano accompaniment and additional
historical information
PETL, 260, d, Text only

You Better Get Religion Sinner Man

You better git religion sinner man

Admonition/Judgment
>> KENMM, 141, d, Solo voice with piano accompaniment and additional historical information

You Better Get Your Ticket
Well you better git yo' ticket
> Deliverance
>> ODUN, 112, d, Text only; Source includes additional historical information

You Better Run
God sent Jonah to de Ninevah land
> Admonition/Judgment
>> SIX, 17, Solo voice with piano accompaniment

You Better Run to the City of Refuge (1)
Read 'bout Samson from his birth he was de stronges' man on earth
> Admonition/Judgment
>> JOHRR, 90, d, Solo voice with piano accompaniment and additional historical information

You Better Run to the City of Refuge (2)
You better run you better run
> Admonition/Judgment
>> BALS, 44, d, Choral unaccompanied with additional historical information
>> HERB, 96, d, Text only
>> PETL, 301, d, Text only

You Can Dig My Grave
You can dig my grave with a silver spade
> Death
>> GUL, 73, d, Text only
>> TOBB, 38, Melody only

You Can Tell the World
You can tell the world about this

Praise

    BONF, 46, d, Solo voice with piano accompaniment and additional historical information

    BONF, 52, d, Solo voice with piano accompaniment and additional historical information

    BONF, 58, d, Solo voice with piano accompaniment and additional historical information

    BONF, 64, d, Solo voice with piano accompaniment and additional historical information

    BONR, 142, d, Solo voice with piano accompaniment

    CALA, 12, Text only

    HERB, 96, Text only

You Can't Cross Here

Where you going sinner

Deliverance

    BARO, 32, d, Melody only

    GUL, 10, d, Text only

You Can't Find a New Hiding Place

You can't find a new hiding place

Admonition/Judgment

    BALS, 35, d, Melody only

    PETL, 301, d, Text only

You Can't Hide

You cya(n)' hide you cya(n)' hide

Suffering

    GUL, 94, d, Text only

    HUTS, 97, d, Melody and additional historical information

You Can't Stay Away

Sister you can't stay away

Admonition/Judgment

    ODUN, 117, Text only; Source includes additional historical information

You Go I'll Go with You (1)

You go I'll go with you

Rituals of Preparation for Renewal/Regeneration
BALS, 81, d, Choral unaccompanied with additional historical information
DITT, 46, Choral arrangement
HERB, 97, Text only
JOHJB, ii, 44, d, Solo voice with piano accompaniment and additional historical information
PETL, 339, d, Text only

You Go I'll Go with You (2)
Lord when I go and tell them what you say
Faith/Assurance
PETL, 108, d, Text only

You Going to Reap Just What You Sow
You're going to reap just what you sow
Admonition/Judgment
CHET, 284, d, Text only
DETD2, 28, Choral unaccompanied with additional historical information
DETR, 28, d, Choral unaccompanied with additional historical information

You Got a Right
You got a right I got a right we all got a right
Faith/Assurance
BRYI, 47, d, Melody only
CHET, 284, Text only
HALC, 40, Choral with piano accompaniment and additional historical information
HERB, 97, Text only
JOHJB, i, 183, d, Solo voice with piano accompaniment and additional historical information
PETL, 153, d, Text only

You Got a Robe
You got a robe I got a robe
Heaven
ODUN, 97, Text only; Source includes additional historical information

You Got to Die
You jes' es well live in union you got to die
Death
GREF, 14, Solo voice with piano accompaniment
JOHRS, 15, Solo voice with piano accompaniment

You Got to Walk That Lonesome Valley — see — Lonesome Valley

You Hear the Lambs Crying — see — Hear the Lambs Crying

You May Bury Me in the East
You may bury me in the east
Faith/Assurance
BRYI, 9, d, Melody only
BUR2H, 86, d, Solo voice with piano accompaniment
BUR2L, 86, d, Solo voice with piano accompaniment
BURS, 137, d, Solo voice with piano accompaniment
DANF, 44, Melody only
DETS, 6, Solo voice with piano accompaniment
FISS, 82, d, Solo voice with piano accompaniment and additional historical information
HAYMF, 63, d, Solo voice with piano accompaniment and additional historical information
HAYMS, 63, d, Solo voice with piano accompaniment and additional historical information
HERB, 38, d, Text only
JOHJB, i, 181, d, Solo voice with piano accompaniment and additional historical information
KINS, 25, d, Melody only
MARS, 136, Choral unaccompanied with additional historical information
OWEN, 5, Solo voice with piano accompaniment
PETL, 109, d, Text only
PETL, 302, d, Text only
PIKJ, 176, Choral unaccompanied with additional historical information
SEWJ, 15, Melody only
SEWJC, 15, Choral unaccompanied with additional historical information

You Shall Reap
You shall reap just what you sow
Admonition/Judgment
BRYI, 35, d, Melody only
HERB, 99, d, Text only
PETL, 303, d, Text only

You Won't Find a Man Like Jesus
Like Jesus like Jesus and you won't find a man like Jesus
Jesus
CARS, 46, Solo voice with piano accompaniment
PRI4, 171, Solo voice with piano accompaniment
WORF, 23, Choral unaccompanied with additional historical
information

You'd Better Mind (1)
You'd better mind how you talk
Admonition/Judgment
CLES, 125, d, Choral with piano accompaniment and additional
historical information
HAWD, 129, Text only
PETL, 302, d, Text only

You'd Better Mind (2)
You'd better min' you got to give an account
Admonition/Judgment
CALA, 32, d, Text only
GUL, 92, d, Text only
JOHHH, 22, d, Solo voice with piano accompaniment
JOHRR, 88, d, Solo voice with piano accompaniment and addi-
tional historical information
MCIS, 18, d, Solo voice with piano accompaniment

You'd Better Run
You better run run run
Admonition/Judgment
BALS, 45, d, Choral unaccompanied with additional historical
information
PETL, 153, d, Text only
PETL, 302, d, Text only

You're My Brother So Give Me Your Hand
It makes no difference what church you may belong to
Songs of Spiritual Journey
PETL, 380, d, Text only

You're Tired Child
Sit down sister sit down I know you're tired
Songs of Spiritual Journey
HAYMF, 58, d, Solo voice with piano accompaniment and additional historical information
HAYMS, 58, d, Solo voice with piano accompaniment and additional historical information
PETL, 109, d, Text only

Young Lamb Mus' Fin' de Way — see — Old Sheep Done Know the Road

Your Low-Down Ways
Your low down ways
Admonition/Judgment
HERB, 98, Text only
PETL, 303, d, Text only

Your Sins Are Going to Find You Out
You can run a long time
Admonition/Judgment
GRIN, 52, d, Melody only
PETL, 300, d, Text only

Zion
Don't you be like the foolish virgin
Deliverance
Matthew 25:1–10+
PARS, 158, Text only; Source includes additional historical information

Zion Hallelujah
Zion halleluiah
Praise
MCIB, 199, Melody and additional historical information
PETL, 241, d, Text only

Zion Weep Low

Zion weep a-low

Praise

ARMH, 232, d, Choral unaccompanied with additional historical information

DETR, 196, d, Choral unaccompanied with additional historical information

FENC, 60, d, Choral unaccompanied with additional historical information

PETL, 261, d, Text only

Zion's Children

Zion's children comin along

Heaven

Psalm 149:2*

GLAS, 24, Melody and chord symbols

PETL, 154, d, Text only

PIKJ, 196, Melody only

SANH, 118, Uses Tonic Sol-fa notation

SEWJC, 42, Melody only

Dialect Title Index

-A-

Angel's Waitin' at de Tomb — see — Angel's Waiting at the Tomb
Angels Are Watchin' obuh Me — see — Angels Watching Over Me
Angels in Heab'n Gwineter Write My Name — see — Angels in Heaven
    Going to Write My Name
Arkangel — see — Archangel
At de Jedgement Bar — see — At the Judgment Bar
Aye Lawd Don't Leave Me — see — Aye Lord Don't Leave Me
Aye Lord Time Is Drawin' Nigh — see — Lord Time Is Drawing Nigh

-B-

Baby Bethlehem — see — New Born Baby
Babylon's Fallin' — see — Babylon's Falling
Band o' Gideon — see — Band of Gideon
Band ob Music — see — Band of Music
Baptizin' — see — Baptizing
Bear de Burden — see — Bear Your Burden
Been A-List'nin' — see — I've Been Listening All Night Long
Been A-Listening All the Night Long — see — I've Been Listening All
    Night Long
Been in the Storm — see — I've Been in the Storm So Long
Been Wash in de Blood ob de Lamb — see — Been Washed in the Blood
Bell Da Ring — see — Bell Done Rung
Bell Dun Ring — see — Bell Done Ring
Belshazza' Had a Feas' — see — Belshazzah Had a Feast
Bin A-Listenin' — see — I've Been Listening All Night Long
Black-Bird an' de Crow — see — Black Bird and the Crow
Bles' My Soul an' Gone — see — Bless My Soul and Gone
Blin' Man Lying at de Pool — see — Blind Man Lying at the Pool
Blin' Man Stood on de Road an' Cried — see — Blind Man Stood on
    the Road and Cried
Blin' Man Stood on de Way an' Cried — see — Blind Man Stood on the
    Road and Cried
Blow Gab'l — see — Blow Gabriel
Blow Gable Blow — see — Blow Gabriel
Blow Yo' Gospel Trumpet — see — Blow Your Gospel Trumpet
Boun' fer Canaan Lan' — see — Bound for Canaan Land
Bran' een dun Fo'head — see — Branded in the Forehead

-C-

-D-

Don't Yo' Hear de Lam's A-Cryin' — see — Hear the Lamb's Crying
Don't You View Dat Ship A-Come A-Sailin' — see — Don't You View That Ship Come Sailing
Don't You Wish Were in Hebben — see — Don't You Wish You Were in Heaven
Don't Yuh Min' W'at duh Debble Do — see — Don't You Mind What the Devil Do
Doncher Let Nobody Turn You Roun' — see — Don't You Let Nobody Turn You Around
Done Carry de Key an' Gone Home — see — Too Late
Done Foun' My Los' Sheep — see — Done Found My Lost Sheep
Done Made My Vow to de Lord — see — Done Made My Vow to the Lord
Down by de Ribbeh Side — see — Down by the Riverside
Down een duh Walley on Muh Prayin' Knee — see — Down in the Valley on My Praying Knees
Draw Lebble — see — Draw Level
Drinkeen' duh Wine — see — Drinking of the Wine
Dry Bones Goin' t' Rise Ag'in — see — Dry Bones Going to Rise
Duh Golding Ribbuh — see — Don't You Grieve After Me
Duh Golding Street — see — The Golden Street
Dun Found de Way At Las' — see — Done Found the Way At Last
Dust an' Ashes — see — Dust and Ashes
Dry Bones Dry Bones Goin' Rise Dry Bones Goin' t' Rise Again Dry Bones Going to Rise — see — Dry Bones Going to Rise

-E-

'E Rose 'E Rose — see — He Rose from the Dead
Early in de Mornin' — see — Early in the Morning
Eb'rybody Wants to Know Jis How I Die — see — Everybody Wants to Know Just How I Die
Eb'rybawdy Who Is Libbin' Gawt'uh Die — see — Everybody Who Is Living (Has) Got to Die
Ebery Time I Feels de Spirit — see — Every Time I Feel the Spirit
Een Dat Low Lan' — see — In That Low Land
Een Muh Haa't — see — Little Wheel Turning in My Heart
Een Muh Time ob Dyin' — see — In My Time of Dying
Ef de Lord Calls You — see — If the Lord Calls You

-F-

-G-

Git On Bo'd Lit'l' Children — see — Get On Board Little Children

Git On Board Little Chillen — see — Get On Board Little Children

Git On Board O' Ship o' Zion — see — Get On Board Old Ship of Zion

Git on de Boat Little Chillun — see — Get on the Boat Little Children

Git on the Evening Train — see — Get on the Evening Train

Git Yo' Ticket — see — Get Your Ticket

Give-a Way Jordan — see — Give Way Jordan

Give-er Me Jesus W'en I Die — see — Give Me Jesus When I Die

Give-er Me Jesus — see — Give Me Jesus

Glory an' Honor — see — Glory and Honor

Glory Hallelujah to de New—Born King — see — Glory Hallelujah to the New-Born King

Glory Hallelujah! — see — John Brown's Body

Go 'Lija — see — Go Elijah

Go and I Go wid You — see — Go and I Go with You

Go Down in de Lonesome Valley — see — Lonesome Valley

Go Mary an' Toll de Bell — see — Go Mary and Toll the Bell

Go Tell In on de Mountain — see — Go Tell It on the Mountain

God He's Gwine to Set Dis World on Fire — see — God's Going to Set This World on Fire

God Told Hezekiah — see — Little Black Train Is Coming

God's A-Gwineter Trouble de Water — see — Wade in the Water

God's Goin' to Straighten Them — see — God's Going to Straighten Them

God's Goin' Wake Up the Dead— see — God's Going to Wake Up the Dead

Goin' Away to See-er Ma Lord — see — Going Away to See My Lord

Goin' Down to Jordan — see — Going Down to Jordan

Goin' Home — see — I'm Going Home

Goin' Over on de Uddah Side of Jordan — see — Going Over on the Other Side of Jordan

Goin' to Heaven Anyhow — see — I'm Going Up to Heaven Anyhow

Goin' to Outshine the Sun — see — Going to Outshine the Sun

Goin' to See My Mother — see — Some of These Mornings

Goin' to Set Down and Rest Awhile — see — Going to Set Down and Rest Awhile

Goin' Up Yonder — see — Going Up

Goin' to Shout All Over God's Heab'n — see — Going to Shout All Over God's Heaven

Good By City o' Babylon — see — Good Bye City of Babylon

Good Lord Dun Been Here — see — Good Lord Done Been Here

-H-

Hail John's Army Ben' Down an' Die — see — Hail John's Army Bend Down and Died

Halleluiah to de Lamb — see — Halleluiah to the Lamb

Hallulujah to de Lam' — see — On to Glory

Han' Me Down — see — Hand Me Down My Silver Trumpet

Han' Me Down Muh Silbuh Trumpit — see — Hand Me Down My Silver Trumpet

Handwritin' on de Wall — see — There's a Handwriting on the Wall

Hangin' Over Hell — see — Hanging Over Hell

Have You Got Good R'ligion Cert'n'y Lord — see — Certainly Lord

He Ain't Comin' Here to Die No Mo' — see — Jesus Ain't Coming Here to Die No More

He Arose — see — Jews Killed Poor Jesus

He Day Belieb' — see — He Does Believe

He Never Said a Mambalin' Word — see — He Never Said a Mumbling Word

He Never Said a Mumbling Word Murmering Word Crucifixion — see — He Never Said a Mumbling Word

He's Jus' de Same Today — see — He's Just the Same Today

Heab'n — see — Going to Shout All Over God's Heaven

Heab'n — see — Heaven

Healin' Waters — see — Healing Waters

Hear de Angels Singin' — see — Hear the Angels Singing

Hear de Lambs A-Cryin' — see — Hear the Lamb's Crying

Hear Gabriel Blow in Dat Morn — see — Hear Gabriel Blow in That Morn

Hear Me Prayin' — see — Hear Me Praying

Hear the Lambs A-Crying — see — Hear the Lamb's Crying

Heav'n Bells A-Ringin' in Mah Soul — see — Heaven Bells Ringing in My Soul

Heav'n Heav'n — see — Going to Shout All Over God's Heaven

Heav'n-Boun' Soldier — see — Heaven-Bound Soldier

Heaven Bell A-Ring — see — Heaven Bell Ring

Heaven Bells Ringin' and I'm A-Goin' Home — see — Heaven Bells Ringing and I'm Going Home

Hebben Is A-Shinin' — see — Heaven Is Shining

Heben Goin' to Be Muh Home — see — Heaven Is Going to Be My Home

Heben Is a Beautiful Place — see — Heaven Is a Beautiful Place

Hide-a-Me — see — Hide Me

-I-

-J-

-K-

Keep Me f'om Sinking Down — see — Keep Me from Sinking Down
Keep Uh Runnin' — see — Keep Running
Keep Your Lamps Trimmed and A-Burning — see — Keep Your Lamps
    Trimmed
King Jedus Is Muh Only Fr'en' — see — King Jesus Is My Only Friend
King Jesus Is A-Listenin' — see — King Jesus Is Listening
King Jesus Sittin' on de Water Side — see — King Jesus Sitting on the
    Water Side

-L-

Lam' Done Been Down Here an' Died — see — Sinner Won't Die No More
Lamb Blood Dun Wash Me Clean — see — Lamb's Blood Done Washed
    Me Clean
Lawd Ah Wants to Be a Christian — see — Lord I Want to Be a Christian
Lawd How Long — see — Before This Time Another Year
Lawd I Want Two Wings — see — Two Wings
Lawd W'a Haa'm I Done — see — Lord What Harm I Done
Lawd's Laid His Han's on Me — see — I Know the Lord Laid His Hands
    on Me
Lawdy Lawdy Lawdy — see — Lordy Lordy Lordy
Lay Dis Body Down — see — Lay This Body Down
Leanin' on Dat Lamb — see — Leaning on That Lamb
Leanin' on de Lord — see — Leaning on the Lord
Lebe Yuh een duh Han' ob duh Kin' Sabeyuh — see — Leave You in the
    Hand of a Kind Savior
Leddown Dan'ul Tek Yo' Res' — see — Lay Down Daniel Take Your Rest
Let de Church Roll On — see — Let the Church Roll On
Let de Heb'n-Light Shine on Me — see — Let the Heaven Light Shine
    on Me
Let Me Shine Shine like de Mornin' Star — see — Let Me Shine
Let Us Break Bread Togeder on Our Knees — see — Let Us Break Bread
    Together
Li'l Boy Name David — see — Little Boy Named David
Li'l David Play on Yo' Hawp — see — Little David
Ligion So Sweet — see — Religion So Sweet
Lil' David Play Yo Harp — see — Little David
Lily ob de Valley — see — He's the Lily of the Valley

-M-

-N-

-O-

O'er the Crossing — see — Over the Crossing
Ol' Ark's A-Moverin' — see — Old Ark Is Moving Along
Ol' Man Devil Gotta Go Some — see — Old Man Devil Gotta Go Some
Ol' Time Religion — see — Old Time Religion
Ole Egyp' — see — Old Egypt
Ole Sheep Done Know the Road — see — Old Sheep Done Know the Road
Ole Ship Maria — see — Old Ship Maria
Ole Ship o' Zion — see — Old Ship of Zion
Ole-Time Religion — see — Old Time Religion
On Ma Journey — see — On My Journey
On the Other Side of Jordan — see — Going to Roll in My Jesus' Arms
One-a These Days — see — One of These Days
Onnuh duh Lamb — see — On the Lamb
Opon de Rock — see — Upon the Rock
Our Lord Heal' de Sick — see — Our Lord Healed the Sick

-P-

Peter Go Ring-a Dem Bells — see — Peter Go Ring Them Bells
Peter on De Sea Sea Sea Sea — see — Peter on the Sea
Play on Yuh Haa'p uh Lee'l Dabid Play — see — Little David
Plunged in a gulf of dark despair — see — Shine on Me (2)
Po' Heathens Are Dyin' — see — Poor Heathens Are Dying
Po' Li'l Jesus — see — Poor Little Jesus
Po' Little Jesus — see — Poor Little Jesus
Po' Me — see — Poor Me
Po' Mo'ner Got a Home At Las' — see — Poor Mourner's Got a Home
  At Last
Po' Mona You Shall Be Free — see — Poor Moaner You Shall Be Free
Po' Pilgrim — see — Poor Pilgrim
Po' Sinner Fare You Well — see — Poor Sinner Fare You Well
Po' Sinner Man — see — Poor Sinner Man
Praise de Lamb — see — Praise the Lamb
Prancin' Horses — see — Prancing Horses
Pray Is de Key to de Kingdom — see — Praying Is the Key to the Kingdom
Prayer Is de Key of Heaven — see — Prayer Is the Key of Heaven

-S-

Samson's Wife Sot on His Knees — see — Samson's Wife Sat on His Knees

Samuel' Sistuh — see — Samuel's Sister

Samyul Sistuh — see — Samuel's Sister

Saomebawdy een Yuh It Mus' be Jedus — see — Somebody's in You It Must Be Jesus

Satan's Camp A-Fire — see — Satan's Camp Fire

Save Me Jedus Save Me Now — see — Save Me Jesus Save Me Now

Save Me Lord Save Me — see — I Want God's Heaven to Be Mine

Sea Gwine Deliver Up Dry Bones — see — Sea Is Going to Deliver Up Dry Bones

Seddown Saa'bent — see — Sit Down Servant

Sen' Dem Angels Down — see — Send Them Angels Down

Sen'er One Angel Down — see — Send One Angel Down

Settin' Down by de Side of de Lamb — see — Sitting Down Beside the Lamb

Shoot Dat Buffey — see — Trip to Raleigh

Shout Jubalee — see — Shout Jubilee

Show Me de Way — see — Show Me the Way

Silbuh Spade — see — You Can Dig My Grave

Sim-me Yuh Muh Leaduh — see — See Me Here My Leader

Sing-a Ho That I Had the Wings of a Dove — see — Sing Ho That I Had the Wings of a Dove

Singin' wid a Sword in Ma Han' — see — Singing with a Sword in My Hand

Singin' with A Sward in My Hand — see — Singing with a Sword in My Hand

Singing on de Ol' Church Groun' — see — Singing on the Old Church Ground

Sinner Please Don't Let Dis Harves' Pass — see — Sinner Please Don't Let This Harvest Pass

Sinnuh W'ah Yuh Doin' Down Deh — see — Sinner What Are You Doing Down There?

Sinnuh W'y W'i Yuh Die on Da' Day — see — Sinner Why Would You Die on That Day

Siporatin' Line — see — Separating Line

Sister Git Yo' Ticket Right — see — Sister Get Your Ticket Right

Sister Mary Had-a but One Child — see — Sister Mary Had but One Child

Sitting Down Side ob My Jesus — see — Sitting Down Side of My Jesus

Slav'ry Chain — see — Slavery's Chain

So Glad I Done Done — see — I Done What You Told Me to Do

So Soon in the Mornin' — see — Soon in the Morning

Some Come Cripple — see — Hail the Crown

Some o' Dese Mornin's — see — Some of These Mornings

Some o' These Days — see — Some of These Days

Some o' These Days — see — I'm Going to Sit at the Welcome Table

Some Will Lub Yo' and Some Will Hate Yo' — see — Some Will Love You and Some Will Hate You

Somebawdy Knockin' at duh Do' — see — Somebody's Knocking at Your Door

Somebody een Yuh It Mus' Be Jedus — see — Somebody's in You It Must Be Jesus

Somebody Got Lost in de Storm — see — Somebody Got Lost in the Storm

Somebody Knocking at Yo' Do' — see — Somebody's Knocking at Your Door

Sometimes I Feel Like a Motherless Chile — see — Sometimes I Feel Like a Motherless Child

Soon in de Morning — see — Soon in the Morning

Soon One Mawnin' Death Come Creepin' In Yo' Room — see — Soon One Morning

Soon One Morn — see — Soon One Morning

Soon-A Will Be Done — see — Soon I Will Be Done

Spirit o' the Lord Done Fell on Me — see — Spirit of the Lord Done Fell on Me

Stan' by Me — see — Stand by Me

Stan' Steady — see — Stand Steady

Stan' Still Jordan — see — Stand Still Jordan

Standin' in de Need of Prayer — see — Standing in the Need of Prayer

Standin' in the Need of Prayer — see — I Couldn't Hear Nobody Pray

Standin' on de Sea ob Glass — see — Standing on the Sea of Glass

Stannin' een duh Need ob Prayuh — see — Standing in the Need of Prayer

Stay in de Field — see — Stay in the Field

Steady Jesus Listenin' — see — Steady Jesus Is Listening

Steal Away to Jesust — see — Steal Away

Steal Away to Mah Father's Kingdom — see — Steal Away to My Father's Kingdom

Sun Don't Set in de Mornin' — see — Sun Don't Set in the Morning

Sund'y Mornin' Ban' — see — Sunday Morning Band

Sweet Hebben — see — Sweet Heaven
Sweet Water Rollin' — see — Sweet Water Rolling
Sweet Watuh Rollin' — see — Sweet Water Rolling
Swing Low Sweet Cha'iot — see — Swing Low Sweet Chariot

-T-

T'ree Long Nights and T'ree Long Days — see — Three Long Nights and
    Three Long Days
Takes a Little Bit ob Man to Rock Dan — see — Takes a Little Bit of
    Man to Rock Dan
Takin' Names — see — There's a Man Going Around Taking Names
Tall Angel at De Bar — see — Tall Angel at the Bar
Tell 'Em I'm Gone — see — Tell Them I'm Gone
Tell Bruddah Lijah — see — Tell Brother Elijah
Tell Jawn Don' Call duh Roll — see — Don't Call the Roll
Tell Jesus I Done Done All I Can — see — Tell Jesus
Tell John Don' Call duh Roll — see — Tell John Don't Call the Roll
Tell Me Brudder — see — Tell Me Brother
Tell Me How Yuh Feel — see — Come Out the Wilderness
Thank God I'm in de Field — see — Thank God I'm in the Field
There Are Angels Hov'rin' 'Roun' — see — There Are Angels Hovering
    Around
There's a Little Wheel A-Turnin' — see — Little Wheel Turning in My Heart
These All of My Father's Children — see — These Are All My Father's
    Children
This Is de Healin' Water — see — This Is the Healing Water
This Lit'l Light of Mine — see — This Little Light of Mine
This May Be My Las' Time — see — This May Be My Last Time
This Ole Worl's A-Rollin' — see — This Old World's Rolling
This Ole World's a Hell to Me — see — This Old World's a Hell to Me
Time Is Drawin' Nigh — see — Time Is Drawing Nigh
'Tis the Ol' Ship of Zion — see — Get On Board Old Ship of Zion
To See Gawd's Bleedin' Lam' — see — Want to Go to Heaven When I Die
Toll de Bell Angel I Jus' Got Over — see — Toll the Bell Angel
Tone de Bell — see — Toll the Bell
Towe the Bell — see — Toll the Bell
Tone de Bell Easy — see — Tone the Bell Easy

Trampin' — see — Tramping
Trimble trimble trimble — see — Were You There
Trouble's Gwine ter Weigh Me Down — see — Trouble's Going to Weigh
  Me Down
Trubble Dun Bore Me Down — see — Trouble Done Bore Me Down
Tryin' to Get Home — see — Trying to Get Home

-U-

Udder Worl' Is Not Lak Dis — see — Other World Is Not Like This
Uh Leetle W'eel uh Tu'nnin' een Yuh Ha'at — see — Little Wheel Turning
  in My Heart
Uh Look Down duh Road — see — I Looked Down the Road
Until I Reach-a Ma Home — see — Until I Reach My Home

-V-

View de Land — see — View the Land
View de Road — see — View the Land

-W-

W'at Harm Has Jesus Dun — see — What Harm Has Jesus Done
W'en I'm Gone — see — When I'm Gone
W'en I'm Gone Gone Gone — see — When I Am Gone Gone Gone
W'en Israel Was in Egypt's Lan' — see — Go Down Moses
W'en the Saints Go Maa'chin Home — see — When the Saints Go
  Marching In
W'en Yuh Go tuh Pray — see — You'd Better Mind
Wade in de Water — see — Wade in the Water
Wade in nuh Watuh Childun — see — Wade in the Water
Wait 'til I Put on My Crown — see — Oh Yes
Walk een Jerusalem Jes' luk Jawn — see — Walk in Jerusalem Just like John
Walk Gawd's Hebbenly Road — see — Walk God's Heavenly Road
Walk in Jerusalem Jis like John — see — Walk in Jerusalem Just like John
Walk Mary Down de Lane — see — Walk Mary Down the Lane

-Y-

Ya duh Key Gone Home — see — Carry the Key Gone Home
Yes Yes Wait 'til I Git on My Robe — see — Oh Yes
Yo' Better Run Run Run — see — You'd Better Run
Yo' Better Run to de City of Refuge — see — You Better Run to the City of Refuge
Yo' Cyan' Find a New Hidin' Place — see — You Can't Find a New Hiding Place
Yo' Go I Go wid Yo' — see — You Go I'll Go with You
Yo' Mus' Hab Dat True Religion — see — You Must Have That True Religion
Yo' Publican Yo' Pharisee — see — You Publican You Pharisee
Yo' Sins Are Gonna Find You Out — see — Your Sins Are Going to Find You Out
You Better Git Religion Sinner Man — see — You Better Get Religion Sinner Man
You Better Git Yo' Ticket — see — You Better Get Your Ticket
You Cya(n)' Hide — see — You Can't Hide
You Goin' to Reap Jus' What You Sow — see — You Going to Reap Just What You Sow
You Hear the Lambs A-Cryin' — see — Hear the Lamb's Crying
You Mus' Come in By an' Thro' de Lamb — see — My God Is So High
You Must Come In at de Door — see — You Must Come In at the Door
You'd Better Min' — see — You'd Better Mind
You're Tired Chile — see — You're Tired Child
Young Lamb Mus' Fin' de Way — see — Old Sheep Done Know the Road

-Z-

Zekiel Saw de Wheel — see — Ezekiel Saw the Wheel
Zion Weep A-Low — see — Zion Weep Low

First Line Index

-A-

-B-

-C-

-D-

Death went out to the sinner's house come and go — see — Traveling Shoes
Deep river my home is over Jordan deep river Lord I want to cross over
    into campground — see — Deep River
Delilah was a woman fine and fair — see — Samson
Dem bones dem bones dem bones — see — Them Bones
Dem bones dem dry bones I hear the word of the Lord — see — Dry
    Bones (3)
Dere's a balm in Gilead — see — Balm in Gilead
Dere's one little two little three little angels — see — Band of Angels
Dese ole bones o' mine (these old bones of mine) — see — Dry bones (2)
Det' ain't yuh got no shame — see — Death Ain't You Got No Shame
Devil was a busy ole man — see — Roll Him Out Again
Dey turn 'way Mary an'a Joseph — see — Round the Glory Manger
Dey's a light een duh walley fuh me — see — There's a Light in the Valley
Did you hear how they crucified my Lord — see — Did You Hear How
    They Crucified My Lord
Didn't it rain children rain the whole night long? — see — Didn't It Rain (3)
Didn't it rain oh didn't it rain — see — Didn't It Rain (2)
Didn't it rain some forty days and nights — see — Didn't It Rain (1)
Didn't my Lord deliver Daniel and why not every man — see — Didn't
    My Lord Deliver Daniel
Didn't old Pharaoh get lost — see — Trying to Cross the Red Sea
Didn't you hear my Lord when He called — see — Didn't You Hear
Didn't you know pilgrim — see — Hear Gabriel Blow in That Morn
Dig deep children — see — Dig Deep Children
Dis union oh dis union band — see — Big Camp Meeting in the Prom-
    ised Land
Dis union sing dis union — see — Stand on a Sea of Glass
Divers never gave nothing to the poor — see — Divers Never Gave
    Nothing to the Poor
Do don't a my garment good Lord good Lord — see — Do Don't Touch
    My Garment Good Lord
Do don't you weep for the baby — see — Do Don't You Weep for the Baby
Do Lord come show me de way — see — King Jesus Sitting on the Water
    Side
Do Lord do Lord do remember me — see — Do Lord Remember Me
Do Lord remember me — see — Remember Me
Do tell de worl' I love ma Jesus — see — Who Love My Lord
Do you think I'll make a sojer sojer — see — Jacob's Ladder (1)

Down in de valley de sperret spoke — see — Dry Bones (1)

Down in Hell — see — Down in Hell

Down on me down on me — see — Down on Me

Downward road is crowded crowded the wind blows east — see — Downward Road Is Crowded (2)

Downward road is crowded with unbelievin' souls — see — Downward Road Is Crowded (1)

Draw lebble de ainjul am a comin' down — see — Draw Level

Duh fau(l)t een me eh Lawd en' duh fau(l)t een me eh Lawd — see — In the Fault in Me

Duh preachuh gawt 'uh moob — see — Move the Camping Ground

Dus' dus' en' ashish 'e rose f'um duh dead — see — He Rose from the Dead

Dust dust and ashes fly over on my grave — see — Dust and Ashes

-E-

E dat belieb' 'e dat belieb' — see — He Does Believe

Early in de mornin' honey I'm goin' rise — see — Early in the Morning

Eb'rybawdy who is libbin' gawt'uh die gawt'uh die — see — Everybody Who Is Living (Has) Got to Die (1)

Een muh time ob dyin' uh don' wa(n)' nobody fuh moan — see — In My Time of Dying

Ef de Lord calls you — see — If the Lord Calls You

Ef uh can only hol' out ef uh can only hol' out — see — If I Can Only Hold Out

Elder you say you love King Jesus — see — Elder You Say You Love King Jesus

Elder you say you love King Jesus — see — Love King Jesus

Elijah rock shout shout — see — Elijah Rock

En uh wonduh wey mosey en 'e mus' be dead — see — Children of the Wilderness Moan for Bread

En't muh Mammy en't muh Pappy — see — Standing in the Need of Prayer

Ev'ry little step goes higher higher higher — see — Every Little Step Goes Higher

Ev'ry time I feel the spirit movin' in my heart I will pray — see — Every Time I Feel the Spirit

Ev'rybody bids you welcome welcome welcome — see — Welcome to the Undying Lamb

Eve where is Adam — see — Adam in the Garden Pinning Leaves
Every time I feel the spirit — see — I Will Pray
Every time I think about Jesus — see — Calvary (2)
Everybody wants to know just how I die — see — Everybody Wants to Know Just How I Die
Everybody who am living everybody got to die — see — Everybody Got to Die
Everybody who is living got to die the rich and the poor the great and the small — see — Everybody Who Is Living Got to Die (2)
Everywhere I go everywhere I go my Lord — see — Everywhere I Go My Lord
Ezekiel connected them dry bones — see — Dry Bones (1)
Ezekiel saw the wheel turnin' way up in the middle of the air — see — Ezekiel Saw the Wheel (2)
Ezekiel's wheel oh my soul — see — Ezekiel's Wheel

-F-

Fadduh len' me yuh walkin' shoe — see — Father Lend Me Your Walking Shoe
Fairest Lord Jesus ruler of all nature — see — Fairest Lord Jesus
Faith of our fathers — see — Faith of Our Fathers
Farewell farewell to my only child — see — Like a Rough and a Rolling Sea
Farewell farewell to my only child — see — Rough and Rolling Sea
Farewell my brother farewell forever — see — Farewell My Brother
Farewell my dear mother — see — Farewell My Dear Mother
Father Abraham sittin' down-side of the Holy Lamb — see — Father Abraham
Father Abraham sitting down side-a the Holy Lamb — see — Tell It
Feasting on milk and honey and wine — see — Brothers Don't Get Weary
Fi-yer Lord fi-yer gonna burna ma soul — see — Fire
Fields are all white the harvest is near — see — End of the World
Fighting on hallelujah we are almost down to shore — see — Fighting On
Fire my Savior fire — see — Satan's Camp Fire
Firs' time Gawd called Adam Adam 'fused to answer — see — Adam in the Garden Pinning Leaves
Fisherman Peter on the sea — see — Fisherman Peter

-G-

Gospel train is coming through the sun is getting out of view — see —
   Gospel Train
Gospel train is passing through — see — Last Call
Gospel train's a comin' — see — Get On Board Little Children
Gospel train's a-comin' — see — The Gospel Train
Got a crown up in de Kingdom ain't dat good news — see — Ain't That
   Good News (2)
Got glory an' honor praise Jesus — see — Glory and Honor (1)
Got glory an' honor praise Jesus — see — Got Glory and Honor
Got glory an' honor praise Jesus — see — Praise the Lamb
Got my letter got my letter — see — Got My Letter
Got to go to judgmemt stand your trial — see — Got to Go to Judgment
Got to go to judgment by myself — see — So Sad
Got two wings to veil your face — see — Two Wings
Graveyard I'm walking through the graveyard — see — Lay This Body Down
Great big stars 'way up yonder — see — Great Big Stars
Great day for me great day for me I am so happy — see — Great Day
   for Me
Great day great day de righteous marchin' — see — Great Day
Great God He rules all around the mountain — see — Jesus Rolling in
   His Arms
Green trees a-bowin' — see — Steal Away
Green trees rocky road — see — Green Trees
Guide me oh Thou great Jehovah — see — I Found Jesus Over in Zion
Guide my feet Lord while I run this race — see — Guide My Feet
Guide my head while I run this race — see — Guide My Head
Gwine to git on de evening train — see — Get on the Evening Train
Gwine to hold out to de end gwine to hold out to de end — see — Going
   to Hold Out to the End
Gwine to lay down my burden down by the riverside — see — Down
   by the Riverside
Gwine to lay down my burden down by the riverside — see — I Ain't
   Going to Study War No More (2)

-H-

Hab' Ile een duh wessel 'en duh bride groom come — see — Have You
   Seen the Vessel
Hail de King of Babylon — see — Hail the King of Babylon

-I-

I just come from the fountain — see — His Name So Sweet

I ain' got long to stay here — see — Steal Away

I ain't going to grief my Lord no mo' — see — I Ain't Going to Grieve My Lord No More

I ain't going to trust nobody — see — I Ain't Going to Trust Nobody

I ain't got time to tarry — see — Poor Sinner Fare You Well

I ain't got weary yet I've been in the wilderness a mighty long time and I ain't got weary yet — see — I Ain't Got Weary Yet

I am a Baptist preacher and scorned on every hand — see — Missionary Baptist Song

I am a poor pilgrim of sorrow I'm in this wide world alone — see — Poor Pilgrim (2)

I am a poor pilgrim of sorrow I'm tossed in dis wide worl' alone — see — City Called Heaven

I am a poor wayfaring stranger — see — Poor Pilgrim (1)

I am a poor wayfaring stranger while journeying thru this world of woe — see — Pilgrim's Song

I am a-troubled in the mind I ask my Lord what shall I do — see — I'm Troubled in Mind (1)

I am bound for the Kingdom — see — I Am Bound for the Kingdom

I am bound for the promised land — see — I Am Bound for the Promised Land

I am free ma Lord — see — I Am Free

I am goin' obuh dere in muh Father's house — see — I Am Going Over There

I am goin' over there — see — I Am Going Over There

I am goin' to walk with Jesus by myself — see — I'm Going to Walk with Jesus by Myself

I am going to join in this army of my Lord — see — I Am Going to Join in This Army

I am huntin' for a city for to stay a while — see — I Am Hunting for a City

I am hunting for a city — see — Hunting for a City

I am just a weary pilgrim — see — When the Saints Go Marching In

I am leaning on the Lord I am leaning on the Lord — see — Come Out the Wilderness (1)

I am not afraid to die I am not afraid to die — see — I Am Not Afraid to Die

I know that the bell done rung — see — Bell Done Ring (1)
I know the Lord I know the Lord — see — I Know the Lord
I know uh bin change — see — I Know I've Been Changed
I knows I's a witness for my Lord — see — Samson's Wife Sat on His Knees
I look away yonder what do I see — see — John's Gone Down on the Island
I look down duh road en duh road so lawnsome — see — I Look Down the Road
I love everybody I love everybody in my heart — see — I Love Everybody
I love my blessed Savior — see — I Love My Blessed Savior
I love the Lord — see — I Love the Lord
I love to hear my bass-o — see — Band of Music
I mean to lift up a standard for my King — see — I Mean to Lift Up the Standard for My King
I meet little Rosa early in the morning — see — Early in the Morning
I met my mother the other day — see — Scandalize My Name
I met my sister the other day I give her my right hand — see — Scandalize My Name
I must walk this lonesome valley I must walk it for myself — see — Lonesome Valley (1)
I never felt such love in my soul before — see — I Never Felt Such Love in My Soul Before
I pitch my tent on dis camping groun(g) — see — King Oh King
I promised my Lord I would deny Him not — see — Pray on the Way
I saw de light — see — I Saw the Light
I saw the beam in my sister's eye — see — I Saw the Beam in My Sister's Eye
I see the signs of the judgment — see — See the Signs of Judgment
I shall not be moved like a tree planted by the water — see — I Shall Not Be Moved
I sought my Lord in the wilderness — see — I'm Going Home
I stood on the river of Jordan to see that ship come sailin' over — see — I Stood on the River of Jordan
I stood outside the gate — see — I Stood Outside the Gate
I t'ank Gawd fer I got religion — see — I Got My Religion on the Way
I take my text in Matthew — see — There's a Meeting Here Tonight (1)
I thank God and I thank you too — see — I've Got a Mother in the Heaven (2)
I thank God for I got religion — see — I Got My Sword in My Hand
I think I hear my brother say — see — Stars Begin to Fall
I think I heard a rumbling in the sky — see — There's No One like Jesus

I woke up dis mornin' wid mah min' an' it was stayed — see — Woke Up This Morning

I woke up this morning with my mind — see — My Mind Stayed on Freedom

I wonder where is my sister she is gone away — see — Israelites Shouting

I'll be singing up there — see — I'll Be Singing Up There

I'll be there I'll be there — see — General Roll

I'll be there in the morning — see — When the General Roll Is Called

I'll be there in the morning when he gen'ral roll is called — see — I'll Be There in the Morning

I'll meet you way up yonder in a few day — see — I'll Meet You Way Up Yonder

I'm a child of grace — see — I'm a Child of Grace

I'm a going to travel — see — L'Envoi

I'm a gonna walk on the streets of glory — see — Some of These Days (3)

I'm a poor li'l orphan in this worl' good Lord can't stay here by myself — see — I'm a Poor Little Orphan

I'm a rolling I'm a rolling I'm a rolling thro' an unfriendly world — see — I'm Rolling (2)

I'm a soldier for Jesus — see — Soldier for Jesus

I'm a soldier in the army of the Lord I'm a soldier in the army — see — I'm a Soldier in the Army of the Lord

I'm a soldier let me ride — see — Let Me Ride

I'm a soldier of de cross in de ahmy o' my Lawd — see — I'm a Soldier of the Cross

I'm a travelin' to the land — see — I'm Going Down to the River of Jordan

I'm a travelin' to the land — see — I'm Traveling to the Land

I'm a witness faw mah Lord — see — I'm an Everyday Witness (2)

I'm a witness for my Lord — see — I'm an Everyday Witness (1)

I'm a-going to eat at the welcome table — see — I'm Going to Eat at the Welcome Table

I'm a-rollin' I'm a-rollin' I'm a-rollin' — see — I'm Rolling (1)

I'm a-rolling in Jesus' arms — see — Rolling in Jesus' Arms

I'm a-tellin' yo' mah bredren a mortal fac' — see — Oh Yes (3)

I'm a-trav'ling to the grave I'm a-trav'ling to the grave — see — I'm Traveling to the Grave

I'm all wore out a-toiling for the Lord — see — I'm All Wore Out Toiling for the Lord

I'm alone so unbearably alone — see — I Want Jesus to Walk with Me

I'm born of God I know I am — see — View the Land (2)

I'm jes' a-goin' over on de other side of Jordan — see — Going Over on the Other Side of Jordan

I'm just a poor wayfarin' stranger a travelin' through this world of woe — see — Pilgrim's Song

I'm just a-goin' over Jordan — see — I'm Just Going Over Jordan

I'm just going over Jordan — see — I'm Just Going Over There

I'm no ways weary I'm no way tired — see — Old Ship of Zion (2)

I'm not weary yet — see — Not Weary Yet

I'm on my way up there — see — In My Father's House

I'm runnin' on I'm runnin' on — see — I'm Running On

I'm running for my life — see — I'm Running for My Life

I'm running for my life — see — Running for My Life

I'm so glad — see — Glad I Got Religion

I'm so glad dere aint no devil in our lan' — see — No Devil in Our Land

I'm so glad done just got out of that Egypt land — see — I'm So Glad (2)

I'm so glad I got my religion in time — see — I'm So Glad I Got My Religion in Time

I'm so glad I'm so glad — see — I'm So Glad (3)

I'm so glad Jesus lifted me — see — I'm So Glad Jesus Lifted Me

I'm so glad the angels brough the tidings down — see — I'm So Glad (1)

I'm so glad trouble don't last always — see — What Shall I Do

I'm so glad troubles don't last always — see — I'm So Glad Troubles Don't Last Always

I'm sometimes up I'm sometimes down — see — Trouble Will Bury Me Down

I'm trampin' trampin' try'n' to make Heaven ma home — see — Tramping

I'm troubled about my soul when I get up in the Kingdom won't be troubled no more — see — I'm Troubled Lord

I'm troubled in mind if Jesus won't help me I surely will die — see — I'm Troubled in Mind (2)

I'm walking on borrowed land poor sinner aint got no home — see — I'm Walking on Borrowed Land

I'm working on the building for my Lord — see — I'm Working on the Building

I'se a gwine tuhleab yuh en' it won' be long — see — Ain't Gonna Worry My Lord No More

I'se gwine to bear Lord — see — Bear Your Burden (2)

I'se mighty tired — see — I'm Mighty Tired

I'se uh gwine 'uh lebe yuh een duh han' — see — Leave You in the Hand of a Kind Savior

If you wanna know where I'm going — see — Going Up (2)

If you want to get to Heaven come along come along — see — Did You Hear My Jesus

If you want to get to Hebben come along come along — see — Did You Hear My Jesus

If you want to go to Heaven — see — Blood—Strained Banders

If you want to go to Heaven you must be new-born again — see — New Born Again

If you want to see Jesus — see — Leaning on the Lord (1)

If you want to see Jesus go in the wilderness — see — If You Want to See Jesus

If you want your souls converted you'd better be a—praying — see — Pharaoh's Army

In bright mansions above Lord I want to live up yonder in bright mansions above — see — In Bright Mansions Above

In de Lord in de Lord my soul's been anchored — see — My Soul's Been Anchored in the Lord (2)

In de mornin' by de bright light — see — In the Morning

In God we trust with all our heart and soul — see — In God We Trust

In that great getting-up morning — see — In That Great Getting Up Morning (1)

In the morning — see — I Going Put On My Golden Shoes

In the morning oh in the morning I want to see Jesus — see — I Want to See Jesus in the Morning

In the morning when I rise — see — Good Old Chariot (1)

In the morning when I rise — see — Tell My Jesus Morning

In the morning when I rise give me Jesus — see — Give Me Jesus (3)

In the River of Jordan John baptized — see — In the River of Jordan

In the River uv Jurdun — see — Sabbath Has No End (2)

In the time of change I'm-a pressin' on — see — A Change Has Got to Come

In the wilderness (een duh wilduhness) — see — Blood Done Sign My Name

In this band we have sweet music — see — Jesus Is Risen from the Dead

Is there anybody here that loves my Jesus anybody here that loves my Lord — see — Is There Anybody Here

Isaac a-ransom while he lay upon an altar bound — see — Didn't Old Pharaoh Get Lost

Isra'lites down yondah in de Egypt lan' — see — March On (2)

Israel was in Egypt's land let my people go — see — Go Down Moses (2)

It ben sad w'en duh grabe sinkin' down — see — Grave Sinking Down

It breaks my heart to see my baby part — see — It's Moving Day

It makes no difference what church you may belong to — see — You're My Brother So Give Me Your Hand

It may be the last time — see — It May Be the Last Time

It was all ober dis worl' — see — All Over This World (2)

It was po' little Jesus — see — Poor Little Jesus

It'll be Lawd Lawd Lawd when I'm gone — see — When I'm Gone (2)

It's a mighty rocky road an' I'm mos' done trabbelin' — see — Mighty Rocky Road

It's alright my Jesus said He'll fix it — see — It's Alright

It's always midnight way down in Hell — see — Way Down in Hell

It's cool down there on the banks of Jordan — see — On the Banks of Jordan

It's down into the water — see — Baptism

It's going to be a mighty day — see — It's Going to Be a Mighty Day

It's me oh Lord standin in de need of prayer — see — Standing in the Need of Prayer

It's the old ship of Zion — see — Get On Board Old Ship of Zion

-J-

Jacob rassled with the angels all night long — see — Who Shall Deliver Poor Me (2)

Jacob's ladder long an' tall — see — Jacob's Ladder Long and Tall

Jay Gooze said-a befo' he died — see — Jay Gooze

Jehova hallelujah — see — Jehovah Hallelujah

Jerusalem Lawd — see — Walk in Jerusalem Just like John (4)

Jerusalem my happy home — see — Ring Jerusalem

Jes you git on de boat little chillun — see — Get on the Boat Little Children

Jes' wait a little while I'm gwine to tell ye — see — Old Ark Is Moving Along (2)

Jesus done just what He said — see — Jesus Done Just What He Said

Jesus He wore the starry crown — see — Jesus Wore the Crown

Jesus heal' de sick give sight to de blin' — see — Jesus Healed the Sick

Jesus is a rock in a weary land — see — Jesus Is a Rock in a Weary Land

Joshua fought the battle 'round Jericho's wall — see — I'm Going Where There Ain't No More Dying
Joys are flowing like a river — see — Blessed Quietness
Jubilee what is the matter with the mourners — see — Jubilee
Judgment judgment oh how I long to go — see — Judgment
Judgment judgment judgment day is rolling around — see — Judgment Day Is Rolling Around
Juniors ride all around God's altar — see — No Liar Can Stand
Just above my head — see — Just Above My Head
Just as I am without one plea — see — Just as I Am
Just as you live just as you die — see — Judgment Will Find You So
Just behold how many dangers — see — Apollyon and the Pilgrim
Just behold that number — see — From Every Graveyard
Just behold that number — see — Just Behold That Number
Just let me get up in the house of God — see — Let Me Get Up

-K-

Keep a-inchin' along Massa Jesus comin' by an' by — see — Keep Inching Along
Keep a-moving keep a-moving — see — Keep Moving
Keep in the middle of the road — see — Keep in the Middle of the Road
Keep uh runnin' — see — Old Egypt (1)
Keep un runnin' keep uh runnin' — see — Keep Running
Keep your hand on-a that plow hold on — see — Hold On (1)
Keep your lamps trimmed and burning — see — Keep Your Lamps Trimmed
King cried — see — Daniel Daniel Servant of the Lord
King David was good — see — King David
King Jesus built me a house above — see — King Jesus Built Me a House Above
King Jesus is a-listenin' all day long — see — King Jesus Is Listening
King Jesus is my only friend — see — King Jesus Is My Only Friend
King Jesus lit the candle by de water side — see — Honor Honor
King Jesus will be mine I'm mom' done working with crosses — see — I'll Reach to Heaven
King of Heav'n His table spreads — see — Ho Every One That Thirsts
Kumbayah my Lord kumbayah — see — Kum ba Yah

-L-

Lamb beautiful lamb — see — Lamb Beautiful Lamb
Lamb done been down here and died — see — Sinner Won't Die No More
Lamb of God just as I am oh Lamb of God I come — see — Just as I Am
Lamb sitting down side ob my Jesus — see — Sitting Down Side of My Jesus
Land I am bound for — see — Sweet Canaan
Land I am bound for sweet Canaan's happy land — see — Land I Am Bound For
Last Sunday morning last Sunday morning — see — Walk in Jerusalem Just like John (1)
Lawd He thought He'd make a man — see — These Bones Going to Rise Again
Lawd I cyan' help from cryin' sometime — see — Can't Help from Crying Sometimes
Lawd I jes come from de fountain — see — His Name So Sweet
Lawd if I got my ticket can I ride — see — If I Got My Ticket Lord
Lazareth is dead oh bless God — see — I Am the Truth and the Light
Lead me lead me my Lord — see — Lead Me to the Rock
Lead me to the Rock lead me to the Rock — see — King Jesus Is the Rock
Lead on o King Eternal — see — Lead On O King Eternal
Leaduh don' let yo' elduh condemn yuh — see — Old Egypt (2)
Leaduh leaduuh do(n)' let yuh elduh condemn yuh — see — Don't Let Your Elder Condemn You
Led-down Daniel tek yo' res' (lay down Daniel take your rest) — see — Lay Down Daniel Take Your Rest
Leddown Dan'ul tek yo res' — see — Lay Down Daniel Take Your Rest
Lemme shine — see — This Little Light of Mine
Let de church roll on Lord — see — Let the Church Roll On
Let me ride oh let me ride — see — Let Me Ride
Let me shine — see — Let Me Shine
Let me tell you 'bout Lord Lord Lord — see — Lamb's Blood Done Washed Me Clean
Let me tell you what is naturally the fact — see — Who Is on the Lord's Side
Let the heaven light shine on me — see — Let the Heaven Light Shine on Me
Let the words of my mouth — see — Let the Words
Let us break bread together — see — Communion

Live humble humble humble your soul — see — Bell Done Ring
Live humble humble humble yourselves — see — Live Humble (1)
Live humble humble Lord — see — Humble Yourself
Live humble yourselves de bell done ring — see — Glory and Honor (2)
Long time mo'ner — see — Leaning on That Lamb
Look away in—a—Heaven — see — Look Away in the Heaven (1)
Look down duh road en duh road look foggy (I looked down the road
    and the road looked foggy) — see — I Looked Down the Road
Look how they done my Lord — see — Look at How They Done My Lord
Look what a wonder Jedus done — see — Look What a Wonder Jesus Done
Look-a death look-a death — see — Never a Man Speak like This Man
Lord bless Thee and keep Thee — see — Benediction
Lord called David an He called three times — see — Little David (1)
Lord Daniel's in de lion's den — see — Daniel's in the Lion's Den
Lord don't move this mountain but give me strength — see — Lord Don't
    Move This Mountain
Lord giv' me mer trumpet an' tole me ter blow — see — Going Lay Down
    My Life for My Lord
Lord have mercy have mercy when I come to die Lord — see — Lord
    Have Mercy
Lord help me to hold out — see — Lord Help Me to Hold Out
Lord help the poor and needy — see — In This Land
Lord how come me here — see — Lord How Come Me Here
Lord I can not stay here by mase'f — see — Lord I Can Not Stay Here
    by Myself
Lord I can't stay away — see — I Can't Stay Away
Lord I can't stay here by myself — see — Lord I Can't Stay Here by Myself
Lord I can't turn back Lord I can't turn back Lord I can't turn just because
    I been born again — see — Lord I Can't Turn Back
Lord I cannot stay here by myself — see — Lord I Cannot Stay Here by
    Myself
Lord I cried I cried — see — Until I Found the Lord
Lord I done done o Lord I done done — see — Lord I Done Done
Lord I hear show'rs of blessing — see — Even Me
Lord I just can't keep from cryin' sometime — see — Lord I Just Can't
    Keep from Crying
Lord I just can't keep from crying' some time — see — Lord I Can't Keep
    from Crying

Lord the big fish swallow ole Jonah whole — see — Big Fish
Lord the Lord the Lord is my shepherd — see — Lord Is My Shepherd
Lord these bones of mine — see — Lord These Bones of Mine
Lord until I reach my home — see — Lord Until I Reach My Home
Lord w'at shall I do trubble dun bore me down — see — Trouble Done Bore Me Down
Lord when I go and tell them what You say — see — You Go I'll Go with You (2)
Lord will preserve him if he will only pray — see — Lord Heal Him
Lord write my name — see — Lord Write My Name
Lord you must have dat pure religion — see — Pure Religion
Lord's been here and blessed my soul — see — Lord's Been Here
Lordy jes' give me a lone white robe — see — Choose You a Seat and Set Down
Lordy won't You he'p me — see — In This Field
Love come twinkling down — see — Love Come Twinkling Down

-M-

Make a me holy I do love — see — Make a Me Holy
Mammy's baby go ter sleep — see — Negro Lullaby
March along march along I will see Him again — see — March Along
March along oh Canaan land — see — Walk God's Heavenly Road
March on and we shall gain the victory — see — March On (1)
Marching up the heavenly road — see — Marching Up the Heavenly Road
Mary and Martha's just gone along — see — Mary and Martha
Mary don't you weep don't you mourn — see — Mary Don't You Weep
Mary had a baby my Lord Mary had a baby my Lord — see — Mary Had a Baby (1)
Mary had a baby O Lord — see — Mary Had a Baby (2)
Mary set her table in spite of all her foes — see — Did You Hear When Jesus Rose
Mary wat yuh weepin' about — see — Mary What You Weeping About
Mary wept an'-a Marthy moaned — see — Mary Wept and Martha Moaned
Mary what you goin' to name the pretty little baby — see — What You Going to Name That Pretty Little Baby
Mary wo' three links of chain every link was Jesus' name — see — Mary Wore Three Links of Chain

My soul is a witness for my Lord my soul is a witness for my Lord
— see — Witness (1)

My soul wants something that's new — see — My Soul Wants Something That's New

My soul's been anchored in the Lord — see — My Soul's Been Anchored in the Lord (1)

My time is come o my time is come — see — My Time Is Come

-N-

Never leave me alone — see — Never Leave Me Alone

Never saw such a man before — see — Never Saw Such a Man

New Jerusalem new Jerusalem — see — Sitting Down Beside the Lamb

Newborn oh my good Lord there in the manger lies the Savior — see — New Born

No harm have I done you on my knees — see — Come Here Jesus If You Please

No harm no harm no harm tell brudder 'Lijah — see — Poor Mourner's Got a Home At Last

No hidin' place — see — No Hiding Place

No I ain't ashamed — see — No I Ain't Ashamed

No mo' my dear brother — see — No More My Dear Brother

No more auction block for me — see — Many Thousand Gone

No more peck of corn for me — see — Many Thousand Go

No more rain fall for wet you — see — No More Rain Fall to Wet You

Noah let me come in — see — Hold On (2)

Noah Noah who built this ark — see — Noah Noah

Nobody knows de trouble I've had — see — Nobody Knows the Trouble I've Had

Nobody knows the trouble I feel — see — Nobody Knows the Trouble I Feel

Nobody knows the trouble I see Lord brothers will you pray for me — see — Nobody Knows the Trouble I See (2)

Nobody knows the trouble I see nobody knows but Jesus — see — Nobody Knows the Trouble I See (1)

Nobody knows the trouble I see nobody knows my sorrow — see — Nobody Knows the Trouble I See (1)

Nobody knows the trouble I've seen — see — Steal Away to Heaven

-O-

Oh duh fault een me eh Lawd — see — Fault in Me

Oh fare ye well my brother fare ye well by the grace of God — see — Fare Ye Well

Oh freedom oh freedom after a while — see — Oh Freedom

Oh freedom over me and before I'd be a slave I'd be buried in my grave — see — Oh Freedom

Oh glory there's room enough in Paradise — see — Oh Glory

Oh graveyard oh graveyard — see — Oh Graveyard

Oh Heaven's a beautiful place I believe — see — Heaven Is a Beautiful Place (1)

Oh Holy Lord done with the sin and sorrow — see — Oh Holy Lord

Oh Holy Savior — see — Oh Holy Savior

Oh Jerusalem oh my Lord — see — Oh Jerusalem

Oh Lawd trouble een duh lan' — see — Got to Take the Children out of Pharaoh's Hand

Oh Lord I'm in your care — see — I'm in Your Care

Oh Lord what manner of man is this — see — Witness (2)

Oh Mary o Martha o Mary ring dem bells — see — Rocking Jerusalem

Oh Mary oh Martha go tell my disciples — see — Oh Mary Oh Martha

Oh Mary what you gonna name that pretty little baby — see — Oh Mary

Oh my golden slippers am a—laid away — see — Golden Slippers

Oh oh ah ah oh ah — see — Dark Was the Night

Oh oh fix me oh oh fix me — see — Oh Fix Me

Oh pray right on jes' pray right on — see — Separating Line

Oh rally aw(l) roun'(g) duh founting Lawd — see — Rally All Around the Fountain Lord

Oh rise and shine and give God the glory — see — Rise and Shine (3)

Oh shout oh shout — see — Oh Shout Away

Oh sinner man you had better pray — see — Sinner You Better Get Ready

Oh sinner yo' bed's too short — see — Oh Sinner

Oh the sunshine — see — Oh the Sunshine

Oh turkle dub 'e flewd away — see — Noah Hoist the Window

Oh Uh gawt uh manshum up on high w'ut en'(t) mek wid han' — see — Promise Land

Oh watch the sun see how it runs the sun goes down and another day is done — see — Watching the Sky

Oh wey yuh gwine muh bredduh wey yuh gwine uh say — see — You Can't Cross Here

Only a look at Jesus oh so bowed down with care — see — Only a Look
Onnuh yuh mudduh fuh duh good 'e hab done — see — On the Lamb
Onward Christian soldiers — see — Onward Christian Soldiers
Open the window Noah — see — Open the Window Noah
Our Father which art in Heaven hallowed a-be Thy name — see — The
  Lord's Prayer
Our Lord heal' de sick gave sight to de blin' — see — Our Lord Healed
  the Sick
Over my head I hear music in the air — see — Over My Head
Over my head there's trouble in the air — see — Over My Head

-P-

Paul an' Silas laid in jail all night long — see — Who Shall Deliver Poor
  Me (1)
Paul and Silas bound in jail — see — All Night Long
Peter and John stood on the shore — see — Send Them Angels Down
Peter go ring dem bells I heard f'om Heav'n today — see — Peter Go
  Ring Them Bells
Peter on the sea — see — Peter on the Sea
Phar'oh why don't you let Gawd's people go — see — Why Don't You
  Let God's People Go
Plenty good room in my Father's Kingdom plenty good room my Lord's
  done just what He said — see — Plenty Good Room (2)
Po' heathens are dyin' — see — Poor Heathens Are Dying
Po' li'l Jesus hail Lawd! Child o' Mary hail Lawd! — see — Poor Little Jesus
Poor Daniel he lean on the Lord's side — see — Lean on the Lord's Side
Poor mourner's got a home at last — see — Poor Mourner's Got a Home
  At Last
Poor Rosy poor gal — see — Poor Rosy
Poor sinner now is your time — see — Poor Sinner
Poor sinner now is your time — see — What You Going to Do When
  the Lamp Burns Down
Praise member praise God — see — Praise Member
Pray all the members — see — Pray All the Members
Pray is the key to the Kingdom — see — Praying Is the Key to the Kingdom
Pray on brothers — see — Pray On
Pray on brothers pray all night — see — Pray All Night

Pray on my brudder don't you get tired — see — Enlisted in the Field
of Battle
Prayer is the key of Heaven — see — Prayer Is the Key of Heaven
Praying in de lan' — see — Praying in the Land
Preacher you oughta been there — see — Roll Jordan Roll (1)
Prepare me one body — see — Prepare Me One Body
Prepare me when death shall shake this frame — see — Prepare Us
Prettiest singing ever I heard — see — Singing with a Sword in My Hand
Pure city Babylon's falling to rise no more — see — Babylon's Falling

-R-

Rain fall and wet Becca Lawton — see — Rain Fall and Wet Becca Lawton
Read 'bout Samson from his birth he was de stronges' man on earth
— see — You Better Run to the City of Refuge (1)
Read in de gospel o' Mathayew — see — Mary Where Is Your Baby
Read in Genesis you understand— see — Witness (3)
Rebawn again ef yuh wn'tuh git tuh Heben got tuh rebawn again — see —
Reborn Again
Redeem redeem been washed in the blood of the Lamb — see — Oh
Redeemed Redeemed
Redeemed redeemed been washed in the blood — see — Been Washed
in the Blood
Reign my Saviour reign Master Jesus — see — Reign My Savior
Reign oh reign oh reign my Savior — see — Reign Oh Reign
Reign oh reign oh reign Saviour — see — Reign Master Jesus
Religion is a fortune I really do believe — see — Religion Is a Fortune
Religion that my Lord gave me — see — Religion That My Lord Gave Me
Repent sinner hammer ring — see — Christians Hymn of the Crucifixion
Restitution it's a great great doctrine — see — Restitution
Rich folks worries' 'bout trouble — see — Satisfied
Ride on King Jesus no man can-a hinder me — see — Ride On King
Jesus (1)
Ride on King Jesus ride conquering King I want to go to Heaven in the
morning — see — Ride On King Jesus (2)
Ride on ride on — see — Ride On
Ride on Ride on ride on Jesus ride on conquering King — see — Ride
On Jesus

Ride the chariot in the morning Lord — see — Ride the Chariot

Ride up in the chariot — see — I Hope I'll Join the Band

Ring the bells all God's children — see — Ring the Bells

Rise mourner rise mourner o can't you rise and tell — see — Rise Mourners Rise

Rise shine for Thy light is a-coming — see — Rise Shine for Thy Light Is Coming

Rise up shepherd rise up shepherd — see — Rise Up Shepherd and Follow

Road is rugged but I must go — see — Road Is Rugged but I Must Go

Rock chariot I told you to rock judgment goin' — see — Rock Chariot

Rock Mount Sinai in de mawnin — see — Rock Mount Sinai

Rock oh my soul in the bosom of Abraham — see — Rock My Soul (1)

Rock of jubilee poor fallen soul — see — Rock of Jubilee

Rocka my soul — see — Rock My Soul (2)

Rocks and the mountains shall all flee away — see — New Hiding Place

Rocks and the mountains shall flee away — see — Rocks and the Mountains

Rocks don't fall on me — see — Rocks Don't Fall on Me

Roll an' rock can't you come along — see — Roll and Rock

Roll away that stone brother and let Lord Jesus out — see — Roll Away That Stone

Roll de ol' chariot along yes roll de ol' chariot — see — Roll the Old Chariot Along

Roll Jordan roll roll Jordan roll I want to go to Heaven when I die to hear old Jordan roll — see — Roll Jordan Roll (1)

Roll on roll on sweet moments roll on — see — Roll On

Round about de mountain 'round about de mountain my God's a-rulin' — see — Round About the Mountain

Run here Jeremiah — see — Run Here Jeremiah

Run here mama run here mama — see — Pick and Shovel Song

Run Mary run hallelu hallelu — see — Resurrection Morn

Run Mary run I know de udder worl' is not like dis' — see — Run Mary Run

Run mo'ner run Heaven is a shinin' — see — Run Moaner Run

Run mo'ner run Hebben is a shinin' — see — Heaven Is Shining

Run Mona run Heaven is ashouting — see — Run Mona Run

Run sinner run — see — Run Sinner Run

Run to Jesus shun de danger — see — Run to Jesus

Run here Jeremiah ho ma Lord — see — Run Here Jeremiah

-S-

Sinnah ain you tired of sinnin' — see — Tell Brother Elijah

Sinner die sinner die — see — Sinner Die

Sinner going to sing around — see — Hope I Join the Band

Sinner man how can it be — see — Wheel in the Middle of the Wheel

Sinner man where you gonna run to — see — Sinner Man

Sinner now is de time for to pray — see — Sinner Now Is the Time for to Pray

Sinner please don't let this harvest pass — see — Sinner Please Don't Let This Harvest Pass

Sinner sinner you better pray — see — Cold Icy Hand

Sinner sinner you better pray — see — Death's Going to Lay His Cold Icy Hands on Me (1)

Sinner today you better repent — see — Tomorrow You May Die

Sinner what you goin' to do — see — What You Going to Do

Sinner you know you're bound to die — see — Sinner You Know

Sinner you'd better get ready ready my Lord — see — Sinner You Better Get Ready

Sinnuh w'ah yuh doin' down dere — see — Sinner What Are You Doing Down There?

Sister Cath'rine hold your light sister Cath'rine hold your light — see — On Canaan Shore

Sister Dolly light the lamp — see — White Marble Stone

Sister get your ticket right — see — Sister Get Your Ticket Right

Sister Mary 'ought to been there — see — Roll Jordan

Sister Mary Aunt Jane — see — Workmen's Jingles

Sister Mary had-a but one child — see — Sister Mary Had but One Child

Sister Rosy you get to Heaven before I go — see — Travel On

Sister when you pray you must pray to the Lord — see — I'm on My Journey Home

Sister you can't stay away — see — You Can't Stay Away

Sit down servant I can't sit down — see — Sit Down Servant

Sit down sister sit down I know you're tired — see — You're Tired Child

Slavery's chain done broke at last — see — Slavery's Chain

Sleep my love and peace attend thee all through the night — see — All Through the Night

So glad I'm here Lord so glad I'm here in Jesus' name — see — So Glad I'm Here

So soon in the mornin' when the clouds roll away I'll never go astray — see — Soon in the Morning (2)

Sorry to tell you — see — Sorry to Tell

Sounds like Jesus o hark — see — Somebody's Knocking at Your Door

Sperrit say I want yuh fo' to go down death — see — Go Down Death

Stan' steady bretheren — see — Stand Steady

Stan' still Jordan Lord I can't stand still — see — Stand Still Jordan (1)

Stand the storm — see — We'll Stand the Storm

Stand up stand up for Jesus — see — Stand Up Stand Up for Jesus

Standin' on de sea ob glass wit' de gospel — see — Standing on the Sea of Glass

Stars in the elements are falling — see — Stars in the Elements

Stay in de field 'til de war is ended — see — Stay in the Field

Stay in the field childeren ah stay in the field — see — Stay in the Field

Steady Jesus is listening — see — Steady Jesus Is Listening

Steal away and pray — see — Steal Away and Pray

Steal away in prayer I'm looking for my Jesus — see — I'm Looking for My Jesus (Can't Stay Away)

Steal away steal away — see — Steal Away to My Father's Kingdom

Steal away to Jesus steal away steal away home I ain't got long to stay here — see — Steal Away

Sun don't set in the morning — see — Sun Don't Set in the Mornin'

Sun gives a light in the Heaven all around — see — Give Up the World (1)

Sun shine sun shine sun shine into my soul — see — Sun Shine into My Soul

Sun will never go down go down — see — Sun Will Never Go Down

Surely surely He's able to carry you thro' — see — Surely God Is Able

Sweep it clean ain't goin er tarry here — see — Ain't Going to Tarry Here

Sweet Heaven is a handsome place — see — Sweet Heaven Is a Handsome Place

Sweet home sweet home — see — Sweet Home

Sweet Jesus sweet Jesus — see — Sweet Jesus

Sweet turtle dove she sing-a so sweet — see — Sweet Turtle Dove

Sweet watuh rollin' sweet watuh rollin' — see — Sweet Water Rolling

Sweetest sound I ever heard — see — Sweetest Sound I Ever Heard

Swing down chariot and let me ride — see — Swing Down Chariot

Swing low oh swing low — see — Swing Low Sweet Chariot (3)

Swing low chariot low in the eas' let God's people — see — Swing Low Chariot

Swing low sweet chariot comin for to carry me home — see — Swing Low Sweet Chariot (1)

Tell yuh 'bout a man wat live befo' Chris' — see — Troubles Was Hard

Tell-a me who dat had a rod — see — Moan Member Moan

Thank You Lord I just want to thank You Lord — see — Thank You Lord

That same train's going to be back tomorrow — see — That Same Train

That sun going down — see — That Sun Going Down

That was a mighty day — see — Wasn't That a Mighty Day

The Book of Revelation God to us revealed — see — Going to Heaven

Them bones them bones them dry bones — see — Dry Bones (2)

Then let us go down to Jordan — see — Let Us Go Down to Jordan

There are angels hov'rin' 'roun' there are angels hov'rin' 'roun' — see — There Are Angels Hovering Around

There are four and twenty elders on their knees — see — Four and Twenty Elders

There are some things I may not know — see — Yes God Is Real

There is a balm in Gilead to make the wounded whole — see — Balm in Gilead

There is a light shining in the heavens for us — see — There Is a Light Shining

There is rest for the weary traveler — see — There Is Rest for the Weary Traveler

There were ten virgins when the bridegroom came — see — There Were Ten Virgins

There's a handwriting on the wall — see — There's a Handwriting on the Wall

There's a heavenly home up yonder — see — There's a Heavenly Home Up Yonder

There's a heavenly home up yonder — see — When Shall I Get There

There's a little wheel turning in my heart — see — Little Wheel Turning in My Heart

There's a love feast in Heaven — see — Love Feast in Heaven

There's a love-feast in the Heavens by an' by — see — Love Feast in Heaven

There's a man going around taking names — see — There's a Man Going Around Taking Names

There's a mighty war in Heaven — see — There's a Mighty War in Heaven

There's a sick man at the pool — see — Lord Heal Him

There's a star in the east on Christmas morn rise up shepherd and follow — see — Rise Up Shepherd and Follow

Thou art great and Thou art good — see — Grace Before Meat

Three long nights and three long days — see — Three Long Nights and
  Three Long Days

Three long nights and three long days — see — Walk Mary Down the Lane

Throw me any way — see — In That Old Field

Time ain't long there's a star in the east — see — Time Ain't Long

Time for praying won't be long — see — Time for Praying

'Tis de ole ship Maria don't yo' want to go — see — Old Ship Maria

'Tis Jordan's river and I must go 'cross — see — 'Tis Jordan's River

'Tis the old Ship of Zion — see — Old Ship of Zion (2)

Titty Mary you know I am going to follow — see — Going to Follow

Tol' Jesus it would be all right if He changed — see — Changed My Name

Tone the bell done got over — see — Toll the Bell

Too late too late sinner — see — Too Late

Traveling traveling we are traveling — see — We Are Traveling to the Grave

Trees don't want to be mountains they just praise — see — Trees

Trials dark on ev'ry hand and we cannot understand — see — When
  Morning Comes

Trouble trouble all Ah see — see — Trouble

Trouble's going to weigh me down — see — Trouble's Going to Weigh
  Me Down

Trumpet sounds it in my soul — see — Moaning

Truth that frees is from above — see — Half Has Never Been Told

Tuckle dub come flawp dis way — see — Noah Hoist the Window

Turn sinner turn today — see — Turn Sinner Turn

Turn sinner while your maker asks you to turn — see — Turn Sinner

'Twas dahk as midnight wen Jesus brought the light — see — When Jesus
  Brought the Light to Me

'Twas on one Sunday morning — see — 'Twas on One Sunday Morning

-U-

Under the rail under the tie — see — Under the Rail

Until I reach-a ma home I nevah inten' to — see — Until I Reach My Home

Virgin Mary had a little baby — see — Pretty Little Baby

Virgin Mary had one son the cruel Jews they had Him hung — see —
  Jesus Ain't Coming Here to Die No More (2)

-W-

Way down yonder in the middle of the field — see — Let Me Fly

Way down yonder on Jordan's stream I hear them crying — see — Sitting Down by the Side of the Lamb

Way down yonduh een duh haa'bes fiel' — see — Walk in Jerusalem Just like John (2)

Way in the Heaven by and by — see — Way in the Heaven By and By

Way out yondah in de ocean — see — My Lord God Rocking in the Weary Land

Way over in the Egypt land — see — March On (2)

Way over in the Egypt land you shall gain the victory — see — Way Over in the Egypt Land

Way over Jordan — see — Way Over Jordan

Way over Jordan view de land view de land — see — View the Land (1)

Way up on the mountain Lord — see — Up on the Mountain

Way up on the mountain Lord — see — Way Up on the Mountain

We are almost home to ring those charming bells — see — We Are Almost Home (1)

We are building on a rock on high — see — We Are Building on a Rock

We are climbing Jacob's ladder soldiers of the cross — see — Jacob's Ladder (1)

We are climbing the hills of Zion — see — We Are Climbing the Hills of Zion

We are going to wear a crown — see — Wear a Starry Crown

We are our heavenly Father's children — see — He Knows Just How Much We Can Bear

We are sailin' over yonder on de udder side de sho — see — Sailing Over Yonder

We are walkin' down the valley our Savior so low — see — We Are Walking Down the Valley

We are walking in de light of God — see — Walking in the Light

We going to do what the spirit say — see — Do What the Spirit Say Do

We got deacons in the church — see — God's Going to Straighten Them

We need more reapers in the harvest field — see — Work's Being Done

We shall walk thro the valley in peace — see — We Shall Walk Through the Valley

We shall walk through the valley and the shadow of death — see — Walk Through the Valley

We shall walk through the valley and the shadow of death — see — We Shall Walk Through the Valley

Winter oh the winter — see — Winter
Winter'll soon be ober children — see — Winter Will Soon Be Over
Wo' his purple an' linen too — see — Dives and Lazarus
Woe be unto you — see — Woe Be unto You
Won't you come won't you come — see — Come Sinner Come
Won't you sit down Lord I can't sit down — see — Won't You Sit Down
Wonder where is good ole Daniel — see — Wonder Where Is Good Old Daniel
Wonder where is my brother gone — see — Wonder Where Is My Brother Gone
World is full of forms and changes — see — After a While
World of form and changes is just now so confusing — see — Is It True
Wrastlin' Jacob Jacob day is breaking — see — Wrestling Jacob (3)
Wrestling Jacob let me go — see — Wrestling Jacob (2)
Wretched man that I am — see — Wretched Man That I Am
Write my name de angels in de Heab'n — see — Angels in Heaven Going to Write My Name

-Y-

Yes I know you goin' talk 'bout me — see — Talk About Me
Yes I want God's Heab'n to be mine — see — I Want God's Heaven to Be Mine
Yes I'm boun' to carry ma soul to ma Jesus — see — I'm Almost Done Traveling
Yes I'm goin' up — see — Yes I'm Going Up
Yes I'm going up — see — Going Up (1)
Yes I'm gwine tu march down — see — March Down to Jordan
Yes I'm gwine up gwine all the way — see — Going Up (3)
Yes the Book of Revolution's to be bro't forth — see — Mighty Day
Yes we'll all fall on our knees — see — Lord Have Mercy
Yes we'll gain this world — see — Down by the River (3)
Yes yonder comes my Lord — see — Yes Yonder Comes My Lord
Yo' save muh brudduh save me now — see — Save Me Now Save Me
Yonder come er sister all dressed in black — see — Cross Me Over
Yonder come sister Mary — see — Yonder Comes Sister Mary
You are not higher than your lowest thought — see — Hymn to Parnassus
You better git religion sinner man — see — You Better Get Religion Sinner Man

-Z-

Zekus wheel oh my soul — see — Ezekiel's Wheel
Zion halleluiah — see — Zion Hallelujah
Zion weep-a low Zion weep-a low — see — Zion Weep Low
Zion's children comin along — see — Zion's Children

Song Classification Index

Admonition/Judgment

Don't Let the Wind Blow Here No More
Don't You Weep After Me
Down in Hell
Downward Road
Downward Road Is Crowded (1)
Downward Road Is Crowded (2)
End of That Morning
End of the World
Every Day
Face the Rising Sun
Fault in Me
Flood Comes Creeping
Gabriel's Trumpet Going to Blow
Gambler Get Up Off of Your Knees
Get in the Union
Get Your Ticket
God Don't Like It
God Knows It's Time
God's Going to Straighten Them
Going Home in the Chariot
Good Lord Done Been Here
Got to Go to Judgment
Gotta Meet the Judgment
Great Judgment Day
Hail Sinners Hail-lo
Hammering Judgment
He Is Waiting
He's Got His Eyes on Me
He's Got His Eyes on You
Hear Gabriel Blow in That Morn
Heaven Bell Ring
Hide Me
Hymn to Parnassus
I Ain't Going to Trust Nobody
I Got My Sword in My Hand
I Got to Lie Down
I Heard the Preaching of the Elder
I'll Be There
If I Have My Ticket Lord

Rock Chariot
Rocks Don't Fall on Me
Run Here Jeremiah
Run Sinner Run
Run to Jesus
Satan's Camp Fire
Sea Is Going to Deliver Up Dry Bones
See the Signs of Judgment
Sin Sick Soul
Sinner Die
Sinner Man
Sinner Now Is the Time for to Pray
Sinner Please Don't Let This Harvest Pass
Sinner What Are You Doing Down There?
Sinner You Better Get Ready
Sinner You Know
Sitting Down Beside the Lamb
Sitting Down by the Side of the Lamb
So Sad
Some of These Days (1)
Somebody's Knocking at Your Door
Stand Up like Soldiers
Stars Begin to Fall
Stars in the Elements
Stay in the Field
Sweet Turtle Dove
Talk About Me
Tall Angel at the Bar
That Sabbath Has No End
That Sun Going Down
There's a Handwriting on the Wall
There's a Mighty War in Heaven
There's No Hiding Place Down There
These Bones Going to Rise Again
They Shall Receive a Blessing
This Old World's Rolling
Time Is Drawing Nigh
Tomorrow You May Die
Too Late

True Religion
Wake Up Children
What You Going to Do
What You Going to Do When the Lamp Burns Down
Where Shall I Be (1)
Where Shall I Be (2)
Woe Be unto You
Working on the Building
Yes Yonder Comes My Lord
You Better Get Religion Sinner Man
You Better Run
You Better Run to the City of Refuge
You Can't Find a New Hiding Place
You Can't Stay Away
You Going to Reap Just What You Sow
You Shall Reap
You'd Better Mind (1)
You'd Better Mind (2)
You'd Better Run
Your Low-Down Ways
Your Sins Are Going to Find You Out

Aspiration

According to My Lord's Command
Am I a Soldier
Animals a Coming
Band of Music
Built a House in Paradise
Coming Down the Line
Dig Deep Children
Divers Never Gave Nothing to the Poor
Dives and Lazarus
Do Lord Remember Me
Do What the Spirit Say Do
Don't Leave Me Lord
Even Me
Free Free My Lord

When the Saints Go Marching In
White Marble Stone

Christmas

Behold That Star
Children Go Where I Send Thee
Glory Hallelujah to the New-Born King
Go Tell It on the Mountain (1)
Go Tell It on the Mountain (2)
Mary Had a Baby (1)
Mary Had a Baby (2)
Mary Where Is Your Baby
Meet Oh Lord
New Born
New Born Baby
Oh Mary
Rise Up Shepherd and Follow
There Are Angels Hovering Around
What Month Was Jesus Born In

Church

Church Bell Tolling Ding Dong
Church of God
It Just Suits Me
John Done Saw That Number
John the Revelator
John Was Writing
Join Them
Let the Church Roll On
Move Members Move
Old Time Religion
The Church Is Moving On
There's a Meeting Here Tonight (1)
There's a Meeting Here Tonight (2)

Everybody Who Is Living Got to Die (2)
Farewell My Brother
Farewell My Dear Mother
Fold My Hands and Tie My Feet
For I Ain't Going to Die No More
From Every Graveyard
Getting Ready to Die
Go Mary and Toll the Bell (1)
Go Mary and Toll the Bell (2)
God's Going Wake Up the Dead
Going to Pull My War Clothes
Gone Along
Good Bye Mother
Grave Sinking Down
Graveyard
Hammer Keeps Ringing
How Long
Hush Somebody's Calling My Name
I Am Not Afraid to Die
I Feel Like My Time Ain't Long (1)
I Feel Like My Time Ain't Long (2)
I Got to Lay in Yonder Graveyard
I Know My Time Ain't Long
I Stood on the River of Jordan
I Want to Die Easy When I Die
I Want to Die like Lazarus
I Want to Die Shouting
I Will Sleep Away
I'm Almost Done Traveling
I'm Going to Lay Down My Heavy Load
I'm Going to Rest from All My Labor
I'm Mighty Tired
I'm Traveling to the Grave
In My Time of Dying
In Some Lonesome Graveyard
In That Old Field
It's Getting Late in the Evening
Jesus Going to Make Up My Dying Bed
Job

Deliverance

I Went to the Hillside
I'll Be Sleeping in My Grave
I'm Going Back with Jesus
I'm Walking on Borrowed Land
In Bright Mansions Above
In My Father's House
In That Great Getting Up Morning (1)
In That Great Getting Up Morning (2)
In the Mansions Above
Israelites Shouting
Keep Me from Sinking Down
Kind Savior
Kum Ba Yah
Lamb's Blood Done Washed Me Clean
Lead Me to the Rock
Lean on the Lord's Side
Leave You in the Hand of a Kind Savior
Let Me Ride
Lord I Just Got Over
Lord Make Us More Holy
Many Thousand Go
March Along
March On
Moaning
Moses Smote the Water
My Army's Crossing Over
My Lord Delivered Daniel
My Name's Been Written Down
My Ship Is on the Ocean
My Sin's Been Taken Away
Now Is the Needy Time
Oh Freedom
Oh Holy Savior
Old Churchyard
Old Ship Maria
Old Ship of Zion (1)
Old Ship of Zion (2)
Old Ship of Zion (3)

Old Ship of Zion (4)
Pharaoh's Army
Pilgrim's Song
Poor Moaner You Shall Be Free
Praise Chant
Ride On Moses
Roll Jordan
Same Train
Samson
Save Me Jesus Save Me Now
Save Me Now Save Me
Send Them Angels Down
Slavery's Chain
Soon and Very Soon
Spirit of the Lord Done Fell on Me
Steal Away to My Father's Kingdom
Swing Down Chariot
Swing Low Sweet Chariot (1)
Swing Low Sweet Chariot (2)
Swing Low Sweet Chariot (3)
Tell Brother Elijah
Tell Them I'm Gone
The Gospel Train
Them Bones
This Train
Turn Back Pharaoh's Army
Walk in Jerusalem Just like John (1)
Way Up on the Mountain
Wear a Starry Crown
When Morning Comes
When Moses Smote the Water
Where Shall I Go
Who Locks the Lion's Jaw
Who Shall Deliver Poor Me
Who Will Join the Union
Who's That Coming Over Yonder
Why Don't You Deliver Me
Why Don't You Let God's People Go

You Better Get Your Ticket
You Can't Cross Here
Zion

Easter

All the Way to Calvary
Angel Roll the Stone Away
Calvary
Calvary's Mountain
Christians Hymn of the Crucifixion
Did You Hear How They Crucified My Lord
Did You Hear When Jesus Rose
Go and Tell Mary and Martha
He Arose
He Never Said a Mumbling Word (1)
He Never Said a Mumbling Word (2)
He Rose from the Dead
Jews Killed Poor Jesus
Jews They Took Our Savior
Last Supper
Look at How They Done My Lord
Sinking Down
They Led My Lord Away
'Twas on One Sunday Morning
Were You There

Faith/Assurance

A Change Has Got to Come
A Little More Faith in Jesus
A Little Talk with Jesus Makes It Right
Ain't Going to Tarry Here
Ain't Gonna Let Nobody Turn Me Round
Ain't Gonna Worry My Lord No More
Ain't You Glad You Got Good Religion
All Through the Night

Amen
Anchor in the Lord
Angels Are Watching Over Me
Angels Watching Over Me
Apollyon and the Pilgrim
Archangel
Balm in Gilead
Be with Me
Believer I Know
Bell Done Ring
Bell Done Rung
Big Fish
Black Sheep Where You Left Your Lamb
Blessed Hope
Blessed Quietness
Calinda
Certainly Lord
Children Do Linger
Children We All Shall Be Free
Children You'll Be Called On
Come All of God's Children
Come Here Lord
Come On In My Room
Come to Me
Come Trembling Down
Didn't You Hear
Do You Think I'll Make a Soldier
Don't Get Weary
Don't Let Your Elder Condemn You
Don't You Let Nobody Turn You Around
Done Found My Lost Sheep
Done Found the Way At Last
Faith of Our Fathers
Father Lend Me Your Walking Shoe
Fighting On
Fire Song
Fisherman Peter
For My Lord
Galman Day

Wheel in the Middle of the Wheel
When I Rise Crying Holy
When My Lord Calls Me I Must Go
When the Bridegroom Comes
When We Do Meet Again
White Horse Pawing in the Valley
Who Is on the Lord's Side
Who Is This Coming
Who's Been Here
Winter Will Soon Be Over
Woke Up This Morning
Wrestle On Jacob
Wrestling Jacob (1)
Wrestling Jacob (2)
Wrestling Jacob (3)
Yes God Is Real
You Go I'll Go with You (2)
You Got a Right
You May Bury Me in the East

Heaven

Ain't That Good News (1)
Ain't That Good News (2)
Ain't You Glad
Angels in Heaven Going to Write My Name
Archangel Open the Door
Away in the Kingdom
Away in the Middle of the Air
Band of Angels
Bright Sparkles in the Churchyard
Brother Guide Me Home
Brother Moses Gone
Brothers Don't Stay Away
Chatter with the Angels
Choose You a Seat and Set Down
City Called Heaven
Climb Up Ye Little Children

I Ain't Going to Die No More
I Am Bound for the Kingdom
I Am Going Over There
I Can't Stay Behind (1)
I Can't Stay Behind (2)
I Don't Care for Riches
I Going Put On My Golden Shoes
I Going Try the Air
I Got a Home
I Got a Key to the Kingdom
I Got a Mother in the Bright Shining World
I Got Shoes
I Have Another Building
I Heard from Heaven Today
I Heard of a City Called Heaven
I Hope I'll Join the Band
I Hope My Mother Will Be There
I Know I Have Another Building
I Saw the Light
I Want Jesus to Walk with Me
I Want to Go Where Jesus Is
I Won't Die No More
I'll Be Singing Up There
I'll Be There in the Morning
I'll Fly Away
I'll Meet You Way Up Yonder
I'll Reach to Heaven
I'm Crossing Jordan River
I'm Going to Join the Great Association
I'm Going to Live with Jesus
I'm Going to See My Loving Father When I Get Home
I'm Going Up to Heaven Anyhow
I'm on My Journey Home
I'm So Glad (1)
I'm So Glad (2)
I'm So Glad (3)
I'm So Glad (4)
I've Got a Mother in the Heaven

Jesus

Pretty Little Baby
Ride On Jesus
Ride On King Jesus
Roll Away That Stone
Round the Glory Manger
Sinner Won't Die No More
Somebody's in You It Must Be Jesus
Sweet Jesus
Take My Mother Home
Talk About a Child
Tell My Jesus Morning
There's No One like Jesus
These Are All My Father's Children
They Nail Him to the Cross
This Is the Man
Wasn't That a Mighty Day
What You Going to Name That Pretty Little Baby
When Christ the Lord Was Here
When Jesus Brought the Light to Me
When Jesus Comes
Who Do You Call the King Emanuel
Who's That Yonder
Yes He did
You Won't Find a Man Like Jesus

Praise

Ain't Got Time to Die
All God's Children Got a Song
Amen
Around About the Mountain
Benediction
Brothers Are You Getting Ready
Christians Hold Up Your Heads
Communion
Glory and Honor (1)
Glory Glory Hallelujah
God Has Smiled on Me

Rise and Shine
Rocking Jerusalem
Serving My God
Shine like a Star in the Morning
Shout Away
Shout for Joy
Shout Jerusalem
Shout on Children
Singing with a Sword in My Hand
So Glad I'm Here
Sun Will Never Go Down
Sunday Morning Band (1)
Sunday Morning Band (2)
Tell Me Brother
Thank You Lord
This Little Light of Mine
Trees
Who Love My Lord
Wonderful Counselor
Wondrous Love
You Can Tell the World
You Publican You Pharisee
Zion Hallelujah
Zion Weep Low

Prayer

Bow Low Elder
Brother You'd Better Be a Praying
Daniel's in the Lion's Den
Down in the Valley on My Praying Knees
Down in the Valley to Pray
Every Hour in the Day
Four and Twenty Elders
Guide My Head
Hear Me Praying
Holy Holy You Promised to Answer Prayer
How Can I Pray
I Couldn't Hear Nobody Pray

I Fold Up My Arms and I Wonder
I Will Pray
I Won't Stop Praying
If I Keep Praying On
In That Low Land
Jesus Is Listening
Lord Abide with Me
Lord Answer My Prayer
Pray All Night
Pray All the Members
Pray On
Pray on the Way
Prayer Is the Key of Heaven
Praying in the Land
Praying Is the Key to the Kingdom
See Me Here My Leader
Sometimes I Feel Like I Wanna Go Home
Standing in the Need of Prayer
Steal Away and Pray
Sun Don't Set in the Morning
Tell All the World John
The Lord's Prayer
There's Something on My Mind
This Is the Way I Pray
Time for Praying
Two Wings
We're Some of the Praying People

Rituals of Preparation for Renewal/Regeneration

Angels Done Changed My Name
Baptism
Baptizing
Baptizing Hymn
Be Still and Listen
Been Washed in the Blood
Book of Life
Carry the Key Gone Home
Chilly Water

Don't Be Weary Traveler
Drive Satan Away
Dry Bones (2)
Dry Bones Going to Rise
Ezekiel Saw the Wheel (1)
Ezekiel Saw the Wheel (2)
Ezekiel's Wheel
Fare Ye Well
Fix Me Jesus
Gift of God Is Eternal Life
Give Up the World (1)
Give Up the World (2)
Going to Heaven
Going to Roll in My Jesus' Arms
Good Old Way
Got My Letter
Healing Waters
Holy Is My God
I Believe I'll Go Back Home
I Want to See Jesus in the Morning
I'm Going to Wait Until the Holy Ghost Comes
I've Been Redeemed
I've Just Come from the Fountain
If You Want to See Jesus
In the River of Jordan
Just Now
Lamb Beautiful Lamb
Let Us Break Bread Together
Lord I Can't Turn Back
Lord These Bones of Mine
Lord's Been Here
My Good Lord's Been Here
My Head Wet with the Midnight Dew
New Born Again
No Condemnation in My Soul
No I Ain't Ashamed
Oh Fix Me
Oh Redeemed Redeemed
Old Sheep Done Know the Road
Poor Heathens Are Dying

Reborn Again
Ring Jerusalem
Run Mona Run
Run Mourner Run
Send One Angel Down
Separating Line
Steady Jesus Is Listening
Sweet Water Rolling
Take Me to the Water
The Golden Street
This Is the Healing Water
Wade in the Water
Walking in God's Commandments
Wasn't That a Witness for My Lord
Welcome to the Undying Lamb
Where Do You Think I Found My Soul
Why Don't You Come Along
Wide Deep Troubled Water
Witness
You Go I'll Go with You (1)
You Must Be Pure and Holy

Satan

Hard to Rise Again
Hell and Heaven
I and Satan Had a Race
Old Man Devil Gotta Go Some
Old Satan
Roll Him Out Again
Toll the Bell
Wait Mr Mackright

Songs of Spiritual Journey

Ain't Got Long to Stay Here
Almost Done Traveling
Aye Lord Don't Leave Me

Suffering

Sometimes I Feel Like a Moanin' Dove
Sometimes I Feel Like a Motherless Child
Sometimes I Feel Like I Wanna Go Home
Sorry to Tell
That Lonesome Stream
These Dry Bones of Mine
This Is a Sin Trying World
This Old World's a Hell to Me
Trouble Done Bore Me Down
Trouble of the World
Trouble Will Bury Me Down
Trouble's Going to Weigh Me Down
Troubled in Mind
Troubles Was Hard
Trying to Get Home
Until I Found the Lord
Wasn't That Hard Trials
Way Down in Hell
What a Trying Time
What Harm Has Jesus Done
When You Feel Like Moaning
Winter
Wonder Where Is My Brother Gone
Wretched Man That I Am
You Can't Hide

Women

Mary and Martha
Mary Don't You Weep
Mary Wept and Martha Moaned
Mary What You Weeping About
Run Mary Run
Sister Hannah
Sister Mary Had but One Child
Weeping Mary (1)
Weeping Mary (2)
Where Is Mary Gone

Woman at the Well
Yonder Comes Sister Mary

Work Songs

Baby Mine
Baby's in Memphis
Cotton Needs Picking
Day I Left My Home
Draw Level
Dry Bones (3)
Enlisted in the Field of Battle
Enlisted Soldiers
Glow Within
Grade Song
Green Trees
Grey Goose
Heave Away
Heave-A-Hora
Hint to the Wise
Ho-Ho
Hold On (1)
Hold On (2)
I Thought I Had a Friend
If You Don't Like the Way I Work
It's Moving Day
Jay Gooze
Keep the Ark Moving
Lordy Lordy Lordy
Noah Hoist the Window
Noah Noah
Noah's Ark
Old Ark Is Moving Along (1)
Old Ark Is Moving Along (2)
Open the Window Noah
Pick and Shovel Song
Raise the Iron
Satisfied

Scriptural References Index

1 Chronicles	
1 Chronicles 29:13	So Glad I'm Here
2 Chronicles	
2 Chronicles 6:21	Kum Ba Yah
1 Corinthians	
1 Corinthians 10:17	Let Us Break Bread Together
1 Corinthians 15:22	'Tis Jordan's River
1 Corinthians 15:55	Now We Take This Feeble Body
1 Corinthians 15:55	I'm Traveling to the Grave
2 Corinthians	
2 Corinthians 4:8–11, 12:8–9	I'm Troubled in Mind (1)
2 Corinthians 4:8–11, 12:8–9	I'm Troubled in Mind (2)
2 Corinthians 4:17	I Went to the Hillside
2 Corinthians 5:10	Sinner You Better Get Ready
2 Corinthians 5:10	Judgment Day Is Rolling Around
2 Corinthians 12:20	Does You Call That Religion
Daniel	
Daniel 2:34, 45, 6:10, 22	Daniel Saw the Stone (1)
Daniel 2:34, 45, 6:10, 22	Daniel Saw the Stone (2)
Daniel 3:23, 6:16	Wonder Where Is Good Old Daniel
Daniel 3:23, 6:16	Daniel's in the Lion's Den
Daniel 3:28, 6:1–24	My Lord Delivered Daniel
Daniel 5:5, 12, 24–28	There's a Handwriting on the Wall
Daniel 6:1–24	Didn't My Lord Deliver Daniel
Daniel 6:16	Peter on the Sea

Daniel 6:16, 22	He's Just the Same Today
Daniel 6:18–22	Daniel, Daniel, Servant of the Lord
Daniel 6:20–21	Oh Daniel
Deuteronomy	
Deuteronomy 9:1	'Tis Jordan's River
Deuteronomy 9:1	Wasn't That a Wide River
Deuteronomy 11:31	Deep River
Deuteronomy 26:7	Going to Write to Master Jesus
Deuteronomy 34:1–5	Brother Moses Gone
Ephesians	
Ephesians 1:11–23	Peter Go Ring Them Bells
Ephesians 4:29–31	Does You Call That Religion
Ephesians 6:4	Walk You in the Light
Ephesians 6:6	Lord I Want to Be a Christian
Ephesians 6:10–13	We'll Overtake the Army
Ephesians 6:15	He's the Lily of the Valley
Exodus	
Exodus 1:8–11, 3:7–10, 14	Let God's Saints Come In
Exodus 2:23, 14:21–22, 27–28	Turn Back Pharaoh's Army
Exodus 3:4	When the Lord Called
Exodus 3:4–5, 5:1	Why Don't You Let God's People Go
Exodus 3:10	Little David (1)
Exodus 3:10	Little David (2)
Exodus 3:15	Go Down Moses (1)
Exodus 3:15	Go Down Moses (2)
Exodus 4:21, 5:1–2, 16:4	Didn't Old Pharaoh Get Lost
Exodus 12:51, 14:10, 21–22	He's Just the Same Today
Exodus 14:10	Going to Write to Master Jesus
Exodus 14:16	Come Along Moses
Exodus 14:19–31	Wade in the Water
Exodus 15:3	We'll Overtake the Army
Exodus 15:20	Walk You in the Light
Exodus 16:3	I Don't Intend to Die in Egypt Land
Exodus 16:3	I Wish I Had Died in Egypt Land

Exodus 33:22	Steal Away
Exodus 33:22	Steal Away and Pray
Ezekiel	
Ezekiel 1:15–21, 10:10	Ezekiel Saw the Wheel (1)
Ezekiel 1:15–21, 10:10	Ezekiel Saw the Wheel (2)
Ezekiel 1:15–21, 10:10	Ezekiel's Wheel
Ezekiel 1:15–21, 10:10	Wheel in a Wheel
Ezekiel 2:10, 9:4	Wheel in the Middle of the Wheel
Galatians	
Galatians 4:26	Oh Freedom
Genesis	
Genesis 1:1	He's Got the Whole World in His Hands
Genesis 1:1–27, 2:7	I'll Make Me a Man
Genesis 2:2, 22, 3:2–3, 16	Wasn't That a Witness for My Lord
Genesis 2:7	Poor Sinner
Genesis 2:7–9, 16–25, 3:1–24	These Bones Going to Rise Again
Genesis 3:6	Good Lord Done Been Here
Genesis, 3:6, 16–19	Troubles Was Hard
Genesis 3:7–10	Adam in the Garden Pinning Leaves
Genesis 5:25	Samson's Wife Sat on His Knees
Genesis 5:27	Witness
Genesis 6:14–22	Noah Noah
Genesis 6:14–22	Open the Window Noah
Genesis 6:14–22	Noah Hoist the Window
Genesis 6:14–22	Noah's Ark
Genesis 6:14–22	Who Built the Ark
Genesis 6:14, 7:8–9	Story of Noah
Genesis 6:14–22, 7:12, 9:13–14	How Long Watchman
Genesis 7:2–3, 8–9	Animals a Coming
Genesis 7:14	I Heard the Preaching of the Elder
Genesis 7:7, 12	Forty Days and Nights
Genesis 22:9, 37:28	Didn't Old Pharaoh Get Lost
Genesis 28:10–12	Climb Up Ye Little Children
Genesis 28:10–17	Jacob's Ladder (1)

Genesis 28:10–17	Jacob's Ladder (2)
Genesis 28:12–17	Jacob's Ladder Long and Tall
Genesis 32:22–32	Wrestling Jacob (1)
Genesis 32:22–32	Wrestling Jacob (2)
Genesis 32:22–32	Wrestling Jacob (3)
Genesis 32:24–29	Wake Up Jacob
Genesis 32:26	He's the Lord of Lords
Habakkuk	
Habakkuk 3:8	He's the Lily of the Valley
Hebrews	
Hebrews 6:19	Anchor in the Lord
Hebrews 6:19	My Soul's Been Anchored in the Lord (1)
Hebrews 6:19	My Soul's Been Anchored in the Lord (2)
Hebrews 10:19–21	Steal Away
Hebrews 10:19–21	Steal Away and Pray
Hebrews 11:16	I Am Seeking for a City
Hebrews 12:25	Lord I Wish I Had Come
Isaiah	
Isaiah 6:3, 7	Oh Holy Lord
Isaiah 6:7	All My Sins Been Taken Away
Isaiah 9:6	Wonderful Counselor
Isaiah 35:10	Getting Ready to Die
Isaiah 35:10	Soon I Will Be Done
Isaiah 40:31	Steal Away
Isaiah 40:11	Listen to the Lambs
Isaiah 40:31	Steal Away and Pray
Isaiah 43:1, 7	Hush Somebody's Calling My Name
Isaiah 50:4, 58:1	Let Us Cheer the Weary Traveler
Isaiah 60:1	Rise and Shine
James	
James 2:21	Didn't Old Pharaoh Get Lost
James 5:13	Standing in the Need of Prayer
James 5:15–16	Prayer Is the Key of Heaven
Jeremiah	
Jeremiah 8:22	Balm in Gilead

Job	
Job 1:18–21	Job
Job 12:10	He's Got the Whole World in His Hands
Job 16:20	I've Been Rebuked
Job 31:32	Let Us Cheer the Weary Traveler
John	
John 1:14	He Is King of Kings
John 1:28	In the River of Jordan
John 1:29	I've Been Listening All Night Long
John 1:51	I'm on My Journey Home
John 1:51	On My Journey
John 3:3	New Born Again
John 4:24	Every Time I Feel the Spirit
John 4:34–38	Work's Being Done
John 4:35	Come All of God's Children
John 5:4	Wade in the Water
John 5:4, 7	Come Down Angels
John 5:8, 9:7, 14:3	Anchor in the Lord
John 5:14	Reign My Savior
John 6:50–51	I Fold Up My Arms and I Wonder
John 8:36	Oh Freedom
John 11:23–40	Go and Tell Mary and Martha
John 11:42–43	He Raised Poor Lazarus
John 12:35	I Want Jesus to Walk with Me
John 12:35	Walk You in the Light
John 14:2	In Bright Mansions Above
John 14:2	Plenty Good Room (1)
John 14:2	Plenty Good Room (2)
John 14:3, 16:33	Keep Inching Along
John 14:13	Keep Moving
John 15:11	Little Wheel Turning in My Heart
John 15:18–19	I Come This Night
John 15:18–19	I'm Rolling (1)
John 15:18–19	I'm Rolling (2)
John 19:23–34	He Never Said a Mumbling Word (1)

John 19:23–34	He Never Said a Mumbling Word (2)
John 20:1, 11	He Arose
John 20:1, 11	Jews Killed Poor Jesus
John 20:2	Jacob's Ladder Long and Tall
John 20:27–28	Wonder Where Is Good Old Daniel
John 21:15	Listen to the Lambs
John 21:15–17	Hear the Lamb's Crying
1 John	
1 John 1:9	Fix Me Jesus
1 John 3:13	I'm Rolling (1)
1 John 3:13	I'm Rolling (2)
1 John 3:13	I Come This Night
I John 3:18	Lord I Want to Be a Christian
3 John	
3 John 4	Walk Together Children
Jonah	
Jonah 1:1–17	According to My Lord's Command
Jonah 1:5–6	Wake Up Jonah
Jonah 1:15–2:10	Didn't My Lord Deliver Daniel
Jonah 1:17	Peter on the Sea
Jonah 1:17	How Long Watchman
Jonah 1:17	I Heard the Preaching of the Elder
Jonah 2:1–2	Daniel's in the Lion's Den
Jonah 2:10	Daniel Daniel Servant of the Lord
Joshua	
Joshua 3:1–17	I Couldn't Hear Nobody Pray
Joshua 3:15	Roll Jordan Roll (1)
Joshua 3:15	Roll Jordan Roll (2)
Joshua 6:1–20	I'm Going Where There Ain't No More Dying
Joshua 6:1–27	Joshua Fought the Battle of Jericho
Jude	
Jude 14–15	When the Saints Go Marching In
Judges	
Judges 7:5	Four and Twenty Elders

Judges 7:7, 16	Band of Gideon
Judges 13:24, 14:15–17, 16:17–18	Wasn't That a Witness for My Lord
Judges 16:6, 17	Samson's Wife Sat on His Knees
Judges 16:17–19, 28–30	Witness
2 Kings	
2 Kings 2:1–12	Swing Low Sweet Chariot (1)
2 Kings 2:1–12	Swing Low Sweet Chariot (2)
2 Kings 2:11–12	Going to Ride Up in the Chariot
2 Kings 2:11–12	Good News the Chariot's Coming
2 Kings 6:2	Let Us Go Down to Jordan
Leviticus	
Leviticus 25:8–13	My Way's Cloudy
Leviticus 25:8–13	Rise and Shine
Luke	
Luke 1:19	Who Is This Coming
Luke 1:26–38	Mary Had a Baby
Luke 1:26–38	Mary Had a Baby (2)
Luke 1:78–79	Guide My Feet
Luke 2:6–20	Go Tell It on the Mountain (1)
Luke 2:6–20	Go Tell It on the Mountain (2)
Luke 2:8–14	Good News Angels Bring the Tidings
Luke 2:8–14	I'm So Glad (1)
Luke 2:8–14	I'm So Glad (2)
Luke 2:8–14	I'm So Glad (3)
Luke 2:8–14	I'm So Glad (4)
Luke 2:8–20	Rise Up Shepherd and Follow
Luke 3:3	Come Out the Wilderness (1)
Luke 3:3	Come Out the Wilderness (2)
Luke 4:40	I Know the Lord Laid His Hands on Me
Luke 6:12	How Can I Pray
Luke 7:48–50	Come Down Angels
Luke 9:27–36	Peter Go Ring Them Bells
Luke 10:1–2	Work's Being Done
Luke 10:38–42	Mary and Martha

Luke 11:1	Down in the Valley to Pray
Luke 13:24	Let the Heaven Light Shine on Me
Luke 14:17, 22, 23	Brothers Don't Stay Away
Luke 14:18	Oh Freedom
Luke 15:3–10	Where Do You Think I Found My Soul
Luke 16:1–6, 24:2–4, 12	'Twas on One Sunday Morning
Luke 16:19–25	Dives and Lazarus
Luke 16:20–26	Sinner Man So Hard to Believe
Luke 16:20–31	Divers Never Gave Nothing to the Poor
Luke 18:37	My Good Lord's Been Here
Luke 23:1–49	Calvary (1)
Luke 23:1–49	Calvary (2)
Luke 23:40–43	Do Lord Remember Me
Luke 23:40–43	Lord Remember Me
Luke 23:40–43	Remember Me
Luke 24:1–6	Dust and Ashes
Luke 24:5–12	Go and Tell Mary and Martha
Luke 24:29	Come On in My Room
Mark	
Mark 1:4–5	Come Out the Wilderness
Mark 1:10	I'm on My Journey Home
Mark 1:10	On My Journey
Mark 1:15	You Must Have That True Religion
Mark 1:15, 16:8	He Rose from the Dead
Mark 1:16–18	Way Over in the Egypt Land
Mark 6:12	Work's Being Done
Mark 6:46	I Went to the Hillside
Mark 7:37	By and By (1)
Mark 7:37	By and By (2)
Mark 9:1–13	Peter Go Ring Them Bells
Mark 9:24, 11:23	A Little More Faith in Jesus
Mark 12:30	Elder You Say You Love King Jesus
Mark 14:38	Keep Inching Along
Mark 15:45, 16:1–6	Dust and Ashes

Mark 16:6–7	Go and Tell Mary and Martha
Mark 16:16	Certainly Lord (1)
Mark 16:16	Certainly Lord (2)
Matthew	
Matthew 1:18–25	Mary Had a Baby (1)
Matthew 1:18–25	Mary Had a Baby (2)
Matthew 2:1–12	Rise Up Shepherd and Follow
Matthew 2:10–11	Behold That Star
Matthew 4:18–20	Way Over in the Egypt Land
Matthew 5:8	Lord I Want to Be a Christian
Matthew 5:14–16	This Little Light of Mine
Matthew 7:14	Let the Heaven Light Shine on Me
Matthew 9:35	He Raised Poor Lazarus
Matthew 9:37–38	Work's Being Done
Matthew 11:5	Daniel Saw the Stone (1)
Matthew 11:5	Daniel Saw the Stone (2)
Matthew 11:5	I Know the Lord Laid His Hands on Me
Matthew 11: 28–30	By and By (1)
Matthew 11: 28–30	By and By (2)
Matthew 14:12	Tell Jesus
Matthew 14:29–30, 24:31	Peter on the Sea
Matthew 14:30	Keep Me from Sinking Down
Matthew 16:26	Give Me Jesus
Matthew 21:28–32	Done Made My Vow to the Lord
Matthew 24:27, 31	My Way's Cloudy
Matthew 24:29–31	My Lord What a Morning
Matthew 25:1–10	Zion
Matthew 25:1–13	There Were Ten Virgins
Matthew 26:41	Brother Have You Come
Matthew 27:24	When Christ the Lord Was Here
Matthew 27:35	He Never Said a Mumbling Word (1)
Matthew 27:35	He Never Said a Mumbling Word (2)
Matthew 27:35, 57–60, 28:1–6	Dust and Ashes
Matthew 27:59, 28:2	He Arose

Matthew 27:59, 28:2	Jews Killed Poor Jesus
Matthew 28:2	Angel Roll the Stone Away
Matthew 28:2	'Twas on One Sunday Morning
Matthew 28:5–7	Go and Tell Mary and Martha
Matthew 28:13	Jacob's Ladder Long and Tall
Numbers	
Numbers 14:1–2, 21:5	I Don't Intend to Die in Egypt Land
Numbers 14:1–2, 21:5	I Wish I Had Died in Egypt Land
Numbers 34:2	Land I Am Bound For
2 Peter	
2 Peter 1:16–21	Peter Go Ring Them Bells
Philippians	
Philippians 3:8–10	When I Come to Die
Philippians 3:20–21	Now We Take This Feeble Body
Proverbs	
Proverbs 7:5	Good Lord Done Been Here
Proverbs 14:25	Witness
Proverbs 25:25	Ain't That Good News (1)
Proverbs 25:25	Ain't That Good News (2)
Psalms	
Psalm 5:2	Standing in the Need of Prayer
Psalm 22:4	Old Time Religion
Psalm 23:2	Down in the Valley to Pray
Psalm 23:2	I Fold Up My Arms and I Wonder
Psalm 23:4	I Couldn't Hear Nobody Pray
Psalm 24:3	We Are Climbing the Hills of Zion
Psalm 27:5	My Soul's Been Anchored in the Lord (1)
Psalm 27:5	My Soul's Been Anchored in the Lord (2)
Psalm 31:16	Shine on Me
Psalms 38:4, 42:5	How Can I Pray
Psalms 43:1, 35:1	Come Along Moses
Psalms 99:1–9, 149:1–9	Peter Go Ring Them Bells
Psalm 107:2	Certainly Lord (1)
Psalm 107:2	Certainly Lord (2)
Psalm 149:2	Zion's Children

Revelation	
Revelation 1:1–2	John Was Writing
Revelation 1:5	All My Sins Been Taken Away
Revelation 1:9, 21:21	John's Gone Down on the Island
Revelation 1:17	I Know the Lord Laid His Hands on Me
Revelation 2:2, 9	Nobody Knows the Trouble I See (1)
Revelation 2:2, 9	Nobody Knows the Trouble I See (2)
Revelation 2:2, 9	Nobody Knows the Trouble I've Seen
Revelation 2:17, 3:12	I Went to the Hillside
Revelation 3:20	Somebody's Knocking at Your Door
Revelation 4:10, 5:8, 5:14, 19:14	Four and Twenty Elders
Revelation 5:8, 9–11, 7:14, 14:3	John Done Saw That Number
Revelation 5:9–11, 14:3	John Saw the Number No Man Could Number
Revelation 6:11, 7:9–14	Fix Me Jesus
Revelation 6:14–17	Rocks and the Mountains
Revelation 7:9	I'm Going to Join the Great Association
Revelation 7:9, 14	Just Behold That Number
Revelation 7:9, 15:2	Good News the Chariot's Coming
Revelation 7:9–10	Going to Shout All Over God's Heaven
Revelation 7:14	Oh, Redeemed, Redeemed
Revelation 7:17	I Fold Up My Arms and I Wonder
Revelation 7:17	I've Just Come from the Fountain
Revelation 11:15	Reign My Savior
Revelation 12:7–11	What Do You Say
Revelation 12:14	Two Wings
Revelation 14:13	Wake Up Jacob
Revelation 15:2–3	Good Lord Done Been Here
Revelation 19:6	We'll Wait 'til Jesus Comes
Revelation 19:11–16	He's the Lily of the Valley
Revelation 19:11–16	Ride On
Revelation 19:11–16	Ride On Jesus
Revelation 19:16, 1:8	He's the Lord of Lords
Revelation 20:12, 19:11–16	Come Down My Lord
Revelation 21:1–14	Getting Ready to Die
Revelation 21:2	I Want to Be Ready

Revelations 21:4	Ain't I Glad I've Got Out the Wilderness
Revelations 21:4	I Ain't Going to Die No More
Revelation 21:4	Soon I Will Be Done
Revelation 21:12–21	What a Beautiful City
Romans	
Romans 3:24, 5:15	I've Just Come from the Fountain
Romans 5:8	Walk You in the Light
Romans 8:34	It's Alright
Romans 10:15	He's the Lily of the Valley
1 Samuel	
1 Samuel 3:1–10	Hush Somebody's Calling My Name
1 Samuel 16:19, 17:15, 34, 49–51	Little Boy Named David
1 Samuel 16:19, 17:15, 34, 49–51	Rock Mount Sinai
1 Samuel 16:23	Little David (1)
1 Samuel 16:23	Little David (2)
1 Samuel 16:23	Little David (3)
1 Samuel 17:34, 49–50, 16:11, 19	King David
1 Samuel 17:49–50, 19:10–12	Troubles Was Hard
1 Thessalonians	
1 Thessalonians 4:1, 6	Two Wings
1 Thessalonians 4:13–18	Free At Last
1 Thessalonians 4:16	In That Great Getting Up Morning (1)
1 Thessalonians 4:16	In That Great Getting Up Morning (2)
1 Thessalonians 4:16	Keep Moving
1 Thessalonians 4:16	Who Is This Coming
1 Thessalonians 5:25	Nobody Knows the Trouble I See (1)
1 Thessalonians 5:25	Nobody Knows the Trouble I See (2)
1 Thessalonians 5:25	Nobody Knows the Trouble I've Seen
Zechariah	
Zechariah 1:3	Steal Away
Zechariah 1:3	Steal Away and Pray
Zechariah 13:1	I've Just Come from the Fountain

Bibliography

Abbreviations used throughout the index precede the bibliography entry in **bold** type.

ABBE Abbot, Francis H., and Alfred J. Swan. *Eight Negro Songs* (from Bedford Co. Virginia). Enoch, 1923.

AAH *African American Heritage Hymnal.* GIA Publications. 2001.

AFR *Afro-America Sings.* Board of Education of the City of Detroit, 1971.

ALBGH Albritton, Andy M. *Great Spirituals: An Anthology or Program for Solo Voice and Piano for Concert and Worship (high voice).* Alfred Publ., 2007.

ALBGL Albritton, Andy M. *Great Spirituals: An Anthology or Program for Solo Voice and Piano for Concert and Worship (low voice).* Alfred Publ., 2007.

ALLS Allen, William Francis, Charles Pickard Ware, and Lucy McKim Garrison. *Slave Songs of the United States.* New York: A. Simpson, 1867. Reprints, New York: John Ross, 1871; Peter Smith, 1929, 1951, 1965; Oak Publications, 1965; Books for Libraries, 1971; Clearfield, 1992, 1997; Ayer, 1992; Applewood Books, 1995; Dover, 1995; Genealogical Pub., 1997, 2004; Pelican, 1998; Hal Leonard, 2005, 2007; MT Kessinger, 2008, 2010; Lightning Source, 2009.

ALTAH Althouse, Jay. *American Folk Songs for Solo Singers: Medium High Voice.* Arranged by Jay Althouse. Alfred Publishing Company, 2011.

ALTAL Althouse, Jay. *American Folk Songs for Solo Singers: Medium Low Voice.* Alfred Publishing Company, 2011.

ALTRH Althouse, Jay. *Ready to Sing–Spirituals: Eleven Spirituals Simply Arranged for Voice and Piano, for Solo or Unison Singing, Medium High Voice.* Alfred Publishing, 2000.

ALTRL Althouse, Jay. *Ready to Sing–Spirituals: Eleven Spirituals Simply Arranged for Voice and Piano, for Solo or Unison Singing, Medium Low Voice.* Alfred Publishing, 2000.

ALTSH Althouse, Jay, comp., ed., arr. *Spirituals for Solo Singers: 11 Spirituals Arranged for Solo Voice and Piano: for Recitals, Concerts, and Contests, Medium High Voice.* Alfred Publishing, 1994.

ALTSL Althouse, Jay, comp., ed., arr. *Spirituals for Solo Singers: 11 Spirituals Arranged for Solo Voice and Piano: for Recitals, Concerts, and Contests, Medium Low Voice.* Alfred Publishing, 1994.

AASB *American Art Songs for the Progressing Baritone/Bass.* G. Schirmer, 2017.

AASM *American Art Songs for the Progressing Mezzo-Soprano.* G. Schirmer, 2017.

AASS *American Art Songs for the Progressing Soprano.* G. Schirmer, 2017.

AAST *American Art Songs for the Progressing Tenor.* G. Schirmer, 2017.

ANDM Anderson, Marian, and Franz Rupp. *Marian Anderson Album of Songs and Spirituals.* G. Schirmer, 1948.

ANDW Anderson, Walter F. *Look Away: 50 Negro Folk Songs.* Cooperative Recreation Service, 1950.

APPA Appleby, Amy. *America's All-Time Favorite Songs for God and Country: Over 175 Best-Loved Songs in One Volume.* Amsco Publications: Exclusive distributors, Music Sales Corp., 2006.

ARMH Armstrong, Mary Frances Morgan, Helen W. Ludlow, and Thomas P. Fenner. *Hampton and Its Students.* New York: G. P. Putnam's Sons, 1874. Reprints, Afro-Am Press, 1969; Books for Libraries Press, 1971; AMS Press, 1972.

BALF Balentine, James Scott. *Five Spirituals for Baritone Voice and Cello.* American Concert Editions: American Composers Alliance, 1997.

BALS Ballanta-Taylor, Nicholas George Julius. *Saint Helena Island Spirituals.* G. Schirmer, 1925.

BAP *Baptist Hymnal.* Convention Press, 1975.

BAP1 *Baptist Hymnal.* Convention Press, 1991.

BARO Barton, William Eleazar. *Old Plantation Hymns: A Collection of Hitherto Unpublished Melodies of the Slave and the Freedman, with Historical and Descriptive Notes.* Boston: Lamson, Wolffe, 1899. Reprint, AMS Press, 1972.

BARN Barnwell, Ysaye M., and Sweet Honey in the Rock, eds. *Continuum: The First Songbook of Sweet Honey in the Rock.* Transcribed by J. David Moore and Roma Catherine. Contemporary A Cappella Pub., 1999.

BAYF Baynes, Sidney. *Francis & Day's Album of Famous Negro Spirituals.* Francis, Day & Hunter, 1932.

BECK Beck, Andy. *Spirituals for Solo Singers. Volume 2: 10 spirituals Arranged for Solo Voice and Piano for Recitals, Concerts, and Contests.* Alfred, 2006.

BELS Belafonte, Harry. *Songs Belafonte Sings.* Duell, Sloan, and Pearce, 1962.

BELT Bell, Craig. *Ten Negro Spirituals.* Pitman Hart, 1956.

BENF Bennett, Richard Rodney. *Four American Carols: For Unison High Voices and Piano.* Novello, 2010.

BLA5 Blacher, Boris. *5 Negro Spirituals: Für Singstimme und Instrumentalsolisten bearb.* Bote & Bock, 1963.

BLOR Blood, Peter, and Annie Peterson. *Rise Up Singing: The Group Singing Songbook.* Sing Out Corp., 1988, 1992, 2004.

BOAS Boatner, Edward. *Spirituals Triumphant Old and New: Printed in Both Round and Shaped Notes.* Sunday School Pub. Board, Edition: Rev. and enl., 1927.

BOAT Boatner, Edward. *The Story of the Spirituals: 30 Spirituals and Their Origins* (voice and piano/guitar). McAfee Music Corp., 1973.

BOCH Bock, Fred. *Hymns for the Family of God.* Paragon Associates, 1976.

BONF Bonds, Margaret. *Five Spiritual Songs in High and Low Keys.* Edited by John Michael Cooper and Louise Toppin. Classical Vocal Reprints, 2024.

BONI Bonds, Margaret. *In His Hand: Seven Spirituals for Voice and Piano.* King of Prussia: Theodore Presser, 2010.

BONR Bonds, Margaret. *Rediscovering Margaret Bonds: Art Songs, Spirituals, Musical Theater and Popular Songs.* Edited by Louise Toppin. Classical Vocal Reprints, sole distributor, 2021.

BOY3M Boytim, Joan Frey, ed. *36 More Solos for Young Singers.* Hal Leonard, 2012.

BOY3S Boytim, Joan Frey, ed. *36 Solos for Young Singers.* Hal Leonard, 2001.

BOYE Boytim, Joan Frey, ed. *Easy Songs for the Beginning Baritone/Bass.* G. Schirmer, 2000.

BOYFB Boytim, Joan Frey, ed. *The First Book of Baritone/Bass Solos.* G. Schirmer, 2008.

BOYFB2 Boytim, Joan Frey, ed. *The First Book of Baritone/Bass Solos, Part II.* G. Schirmer, 1993.

BOYFM Boytim, Joan Frey, ed. *The First Book of Mezzo-Soprano/Alto Solos.* G. Schirmer, 1991.

BOYFT Boytim, Joan Frey, ed. *The First Book of Tenor Solos Part II.* G. Schirmer, 1991.

BOYFT2 Boytim, Joan Frey, ed. *The First Book of Tenor Solos Part II.* G. Schirmer, 1993.

BRON Brown, Lawrence. *Negro Folk Songs.* Associated Music Publishers, 1930.

BROS Brown, Lawrence. *Spirituals: Five Negro Songs.* Classical Vocal Reprints, 2019.

BRUO Brown, Uzee, Jr. *O Redeemed!: A Set of African–American Spirituals, for Medium–High Voice and Piano.* R. Dean Publishing, 1994.

BRUS Brown, Uzee, Jr. *Spirituals and Inspirational Songs.* GIA Publications, 2023.

BRUT Brown, Uzee, Jr. *Tryin' to Make Heaven My Home.* R. Dean Publishing, 2002.

BRYA Bryan, Ashley. *All Night All Day: A Child's First Book of African-American Spirituals.* Atheneum, 1991, reprint 2004.

BRYI Bryan, Ashley. *I'm Going to Sing: Black American Spirituals*, volume two. Atheneum, 1982.

BRYW Bryan, Ashley. *Walk Together Children: Black American Spirituals.* Atheneum, 1974.

BUCS Buckland, Graham, arranger. *Spirituals: 12 Arrangements for Variable Instruments.* Barenreiter, 2013.

BULA Bullock, Kathy W., and Donna M. Cox. *Art Songs and Spirituals by Contemporary African American Composers.* PBM Press, 2012.

BURA Burleigh, Harry Thacker. *Album of Negro Spirituals.* Belwin Mills, 1969; G. Ricordi, 1917; Franco Colombo Publications, c/o CPP/Belwin: Warner

Bros. Publications, 2000; CPP/Belwin: Warner Bros. Publications, 2000, 1917; Alfred, 2007.

BURC1 Burleigh, Harry Thacker. *The Celebrated Negro Spirituals, vol. 1.* G. Ricordi, 1917.

BURC2 Burleigh, Harry Thacker. *The Celebrated Negro Spirituals, vol. 2.* G. Ricordi, 1919.

BUR2H Burleigh, Harry Thacker. *25 Spirituals (high voice).* Hal Leonard, 2012.

BUR2L Burleigh, Harry Thacker. *25 Spirituals (low voice).* Hal Leonard, 2012.

BUR4H Burleigh, Harry Thacker. *47 Art Songs: For High Voice.* Edited by Louise Toppin, Ann Sears, and Jean Snyder. Classical Vocal Reprints, 2023.

BUR4L Burleigh, Harry Thacker. *47 Art Songs: For Low Voice.* Edited by Louise Toppin, Ann Sears, and Jean Snyder. Classical Vocal Reprints, 2023.

BURP Burleigh, Harry T. *Plantation Melodies Old and New.* G. Schirmer, 1901.

BURS Burleigh, Harry T. *The Spirituals of Harry T. Burleigh.* Belwin-Mills Corp., 1999.

CALA Caldwell, Hansonia L. *African American Music, Spirituals: The Fundamental Communal Music of Black Americans.* 3rd ed. Ikoro Communications, 2003.

CARS Carter, Roland Marvin. *Sweetest Sound I Ever Heard: Spiritual Art Songs for High Voice and Piano.* Classical Vocal Reprints, 2020.

CHAT Chambers, Herbert Arthur. *The Treasury of Negro Spirituals.* Foreword by Marian Anderson. Emerson Books, 1963, 1970, 1982; Blandford Press 1953, 1959; Blandford Press, 1964, 1970, 1982.

CHEA Cheatham, Wallace. *Wallace Cheatham: A Collection of Songs.* 2nd edition, American Composers Alliance, 2019.

CHET Chenu, Bruno. *The Trouble I've Seen: The Big Book of Negro Spirituals.* Translated from the French by Eugene V. LaPlante. Judson, Press, 2003.

CHIA Children's Music Workshop. *African-American Spirituals: A Collection of Great American Music (Music, Chord Changes, and Lyrics).* Children's Music Workshop, 2020.

CLAC Clark, Edgar Rogie. *Copper Sun: A Collection of Negro Folk Songs.* Theodore Presser, 1957.

CLAN Clark, Edgar Rogie. *Negro Art Songs: Album by Contemporary Composers for Voice and Piano.* Edward B. Marks Music, 1946.

CLASB *Classical Contest Solos* (baritone/bass ed). Hal Leonard, 1997.

CLASM *Classical Contest Solos* (mezzo-soprano/alto ed). Hal Leonard, 1997.

CLASS *Classical Contest Solos* (soprano ed). Hal Leonard, 1997.

CLAST *Classical Contest Solos* (tenor ed). Hal Leonard, 1997.

CLES Cleveland, J. Jefferson, and Verolga Nix. *Songs of Zion.* Abingdon Press, 1981.

COLS Coleman, Satis N., and Alanson Hewes. *Songs of American Folks.* The John Day Company, 1942.

COUN Courlander, Harold. *Negro Folk Music, U.S.A.* Columbia Press, 1963; Columbia University Press, 1970.

COUNS Courlander, Harold, and John Benson Brooks. *Negro Songs from Alabama.* New York: Published with the assistance of the Wenner-Gren Foundation for Anthropological Research, 1960.

CREO Credit, Roosevelt André. *Ol' Time Religion: A Collection of Spirituals and Original Songs.* Laurendale Associates, 2006.

DANF Dann, Hollis. *Fifty-Eight Spirituals for Choral Use.* C. C. Birchard, 1924.

DEF *The Definitive Hymn Collection: 218 Multi-Denominational Hymns* (Piano, Vocal, Guitar). Hal Leonard, 2002; Hal Leonard, 2005.

DETD1 Dett, R. Nathaniel. *The Dett Collection of Negro Spirituals: First Group: Originals, Settings, Anthems, and Motets.* Hall & McCreary, 1936.

DETD2 Dett, R. Nathaniel. *The Dett Collection of Negro Spirituals: Second Group: Originals, Settings, Anthems, and Motets.* Hall & McCreary, 1936.

DETD3 Dett, R. Nathaniel. *The Dett Collection of Negro Spirituals. Third Group: Originals, Settings, Anthems and Motets with Essay "The Authenticity of the Spiritual."* Hall & McCreary, 1936.

DETD4 Dett, R. Nathaniel. *The Dett Collection of Negro Spirituals: Fourth Group: Originals, Settings, Anthems, and Motets.* Hall & McCreary, 1936.

DETR Dett, R. Nathaniel. *Religious Folk-Songs of the Negro as Sung at Hampton Institute.* Hampton Institute Press, 1927, 1984. Reprints, AMS Press, 1972.

DETS Dett, R. Nathaniel. *Spirituals.* Mills Music, 1946; Mills Music, 1943.

DITT Diton, Carl. *Thirty-Six South Carolina Spirituals.* G. Schirmer, 1928; G. Schirmer, 1930.

FENC Fenner, Thomas P., and Frederic G. Rathbun. *Cabin and Plantation Songs as Sung by the Students.* New York: G. P. Putnam's Sons, 1874. Reprints, New York: G. P. Putnam's Sons, 1875, 1878, 1879, 1890, 1892, 1893, 1901; Hampton Institute Press, 1908; AMS Press, 1977, 1901.

FENR Fenner, Thomas P. *Religious Folk Songs of the Negro as Sung on the Plantations.* Arr. by the musical directors of The Hampton Normal and Agricultural Institute. Institute Press, 1909.

FISS Fisher, William Arms. *Seventy Negro Spirituals.* Oliver Ditson, 1926.

FIST Fisher, William Arms. *Ten Negro Spirituals.* Oliver Ditson, 1925.

FOUS Fountain, Clarence. *Soul! The Gospel of Clarence Fountain and The Blind Boys of Alabama.* Flomar Music, 1967.

FRAS Frank, Bernd. *Spirituals & Gospels for Aspiring Singers: 33 Songs for Medium or Low Voice and Piano.* Schott, 2015.

FREC Frey, Hugo. *Collection of 25 Selected Famous Negro Spirituals.* Robbins-Engel, 1924.

GAIF Gainer, Patrick W. *Folk Songs from the West Virginia Hills.* West Virginia University Press, 2017.

GLAS Glass, Paul. *Songs and Stories of Afro-Americans.* Grosset & Dunlap, 1971.

GREF Grey, Gerald. *Fifty Negro Spirituals.* J. A. Parks, 1930.

GRIN Grissom, Mary Allen. *The Negro Sings a New Heaven.* University of North Carolina Press, 1930; Dover Publications, 1969; AMS Press, 1973.

GUIU Guillen, Jeff. *The Ultimate Gospel Song Book: Thirty Great Gospels and Spirituals.* Zebe, 1995

GUL *Gullah Lyrics to Carolina Low Country Spirituals.* Society for the Preservation of Spirituals, 2007.

HAG3 Hagen, Daron. *38 Songs & Arias.* Burning Sled Music, 2016.

HAIS Hairston, Jacqueline B. *Songs and Spirituals, Volume 1.* Classical Vocal Reprints, 2019.

HALC Hallowell, Emily. *Calhoun Plantation Songs.* C.W. Thompson, 1901, 1907, 1923. AMS Press, 1976.

HALU Hall, Frederick. *Unusual Negro Spirituals.* Rodeheaver, HallMack, 1964.

HAWD Hawkins, John Dewey. *Daily Food in Negro Spirituals.* J. D. Hawkins, 1943.

HAY1H Hayes, Mark. *10 Spirituals for Solo Voice: For Concerts, Contests, Recitals, and Worship, (high voice).* Alfred Publ., 1998.

HAY1L Hayes, Mark. *10 Spirituals for Solo Voice: For Concerts, Contests, Recitals, and Worship (low voice).* Alfred Pub., 1998.

HAYMF Hayes, Roland. *My Favorite Spirituals: 30 Songs for Voice and Piano.* Dover Publications, 2001. M1670.H4 M9 2001.

HAYMS Hayes, Roland. *My Songs: Aframerican Religious Folk Songs.* Little, Brown (An Atlantic Monthly Press Book), 1948.

HELC Helvey, Howard. *Classic Spirituals for Solo Voice: Eleven Spirituals Arranged for Medium to Medium-High Voice and Piano.* Beckenhorst, 2009.

HERB Herder, Nicole Beaulieu, and Ronald Herder. *Best-loved Negro Spirituals: Complete Lyrics to 178 Songs of Faith.* Dover Publications, 2001.

HOGDH Hogan, Moses. *The Deep River Collection (high voice).* H. Leonard Pub., 2000.

HOGDL Hogan, Moses. *The Deep River Collection (low voice).* H. Leonard Pub., 2000.

HUTS Hutson, Katharine, Josephine Pinckney, Caroline Pinckney Rutledge, and Society for the Preservation of Spirituals. *Spirituals of the Carolina Low Country.* The Society, 2004.

JACL Jackson, Irene V., ed. *Lift Every Voice and Sing: A Collection of Afro-American Spirituals and Other Songs.* Church Hymnal, 1981.

JESM Jessye, Eva A. *My Spirituals.* Robbins-Engel, 1927.

JOHDT Johnson, David N. *Twelve Folksongs and Spirituals.* Augsburg Publishing House, 1968.

JOHHG Johnson, Hall. *The Green Pastures Spirituals.* Carl Fischer, 1930.

JOHHH Johnson, Hall. *The Hall Johnson Collection: Over 50 Classic Favorites for Voice and Piano.* Carl Fischer, 2003.

JOHHT Johnson, Hall. *Thirty Spirituals Arranged for Voice and Piano.* G. Schirmer, 1949.

JOHJB Johnson, James Weldon. *The Books of American Negro Spirituals*. Includes *The Book of American Negro Spirituals* (Viking, 1925) and *The Second Book of Negro Spirituals* (Viking Press, 1926.). Musical arrangements by J. Rosamond Johnson with additional numbers by Lawrence Brown. DaCapo, 2003.

JOHRA Johnson, John Rosamond. *Album of Negro Spirituals*. Edward B. Marks Music, 2000.

JOHRR Johnson, John Rosamond. *Rolling Along in Song*. Viking Press, 1937.

JOHRS Johnson, John Rosamond. *Sixteen New Negro Spirituals*. Handy Bros. Music, 1939.

JONF Johnston, Richard. *Folk Songs North America Sings*. Caveat Music Publishers, 1984.

JORS Jordan, Ronald C. *Soul Praise: Amazing Stories Behind the Great African American Hymns and Negro Spirituals*. Honor Books, 2005.

KENM Kennedy, Robert Emmet. *Mellows: A Chronicle of Unknown Singers*. A. & C. Boni, 1925. Reprint, Greenwood, 1979.

KENMM Kennedy, Robert Emmett. *More Mellows*. Dodd, Mead, 1931.

KINC King, Betty Jackson. *Climbing High Mountains*. Jacksonian Press, 1990.

KINS Kinscella, Hazel Gertrude. *Folk Songs and Fiddle Tunes of the U.S.A.* C. Fischer, 1959.

KREA Krehbiel, Henry Edward. *Afro-American Folksongs: A Study in Racial and National Music*. Frederick Ungar Publishing Company, 1967.

LABC Labenske, Victor. *Concert Hall Spirituals: Settings for Piano and Voice*. Woodland Music Press, 1999.

LANC Lanstaff, John. *Climbing Jacob's Ladder: Heroes of the Bible in African-American Spirituals*. Maxwell Macmillan International, 1991.

LIES Liebergen, Patrick. *Spirituals for Young Voices*. Shawnee Press, 2013.

LIF *Lift Every Voice and Sing II: An African American Hymnal*. Church Pub., 1993.

LLOA Lloyd, Ruth, and Norman Lloyd. *The American Heritage Songbook*. American Heritage Pub., 1969.

LOGR Logan, William Augustus. *Road to Heaven: Twenty-Eight Negro Spirituals*. University of Alabama Press, 1955.

LOMAF Lomax, Alan. *The Folk Songs of North America, in the English Language*. Doubleday, 1960.

LOMJA Lomax, John A., and Alan Lomax. *American Ballads and Folk Songs*. Macmillan Company, 1934.

LOMJF Lomax, John A., and Alan Lomax. *Folk Song U.S.A.: The 111 Best American Ballads*. Duell, Sloan, and Pearce, 1947. Reprint, New American Library, 1975.

LOMJO Lomax, John A., and Alan Lomax. *Our Singing Country: Folk Songs and Ballads*. Edited by Ruth Crawford Seeger; introduction to the Dover edition by Judith Tick. Dover Publications, 2000.

LOMJO2 Lomax, John A., and Alan Lomax. *Our Singing Country: A Second Volume of American Ballads and Folk Songs*. Macmillan Company, 1941.

LOYS Loyd, Charles, Jr. *The Spiritual Art Song Collection*. Warner Bros. Publications, 2000.

LUEB Luedeman, H. *Best of Spirituals & Gospels: 59 Great Songs*. Schott, 2001.

MACS MacLean, Douglas. *Song Session: A Community Song Book*. Remick Music, 1953.

MARS Marsh, James Brainerd Taylor. *The Story of the Jubilee Singers: With Their Songs*. Boston: Houghton, Mifflin, 1880, 1881; revised edition, Negro Universities Press, 1969. Reprint, AMS Press, 1971.

MAR3 Marsh, James Brainerd Taylor, and F. J. Loudin. *The Jubilee Singers and Their Songs*. Cleveland Printing and Publishing, 1892. Reprint, Dover, 2003.

MCIB McIlhenny, E. A. *Befo' de War Spirituals*. AMS Press, 1973.

MCIS McIntyre, Phillip. *Spirituals for Church and Concert*. H. T. Fitz Simons, 1990.

MCKF McKay, Neil. *Four Spiritual Songs*. Leyerle Publications, 1992.

MCLS McLin, Lena J. *Songs for Voice & Piano* (Med. High Voice ed.). Kjos Music, 2003.

MIL3 Milkey, E. T. *34 Spirituals*. E. H. Morris: C. Hansen, 1961.

MILF Mills, Marvin. *Four Spirituals for Denyce Graves*. DC Press, 1998.

NAA *NAACP Song Book: Lift Ev'ry Voice*. National Association for the Advancement of Colored People, 1972.

NEW *New National Baptist Hymnal: A Hymnal for the 21st Century*. Triad Publications [National Baptist Publishing Board], 2001.

NILS Niles, John J., and Marion Kerby. *Seven Negro Exaltations: As Sung by Marion Kerby and John J. Niles*. G. Schirmer, 1929.

NORS Nordoff, Paul. *Spirituals: For Children to Sing and Play*. Theodore Presser, 1972.

ODUN Odum, Howard, and Guy B. Johnson. *The Negro and His Song: A Study of Typical Negro Songs in the South*. The University of North Carolina Press, 1925; Negro Universities Press, 1968.

OKS1 Okpebholo, Shawn E. *The Shawn E. Okpebholo Collection of Spirituals*, volume 1. Yellow Einstein Press, 2013.

OKS2 Okpebholo, Shawn E. *The Shawn E. Okpebholo Collection of Spirituals and Folk Hymns*. Yellow Einstein Press, 2018.

OWEN Owens, Robert. *Negro Spirituals für Bass und Klavier (Negro Spirituals for Bass [Baritone] and Piano)*. Ostinato–Musikverlag, 2005.

PARS Parrish, Lydia. *Slave Songs of the Georgia Sea Islands*. Creative Age Press, 1942; Folklore Associates, 1965; University of Georgia Press, 1992.

PATN Patterson, Willis C. *The New Negro Spiritual Collection*. Willis C. Patterson, 2002.

PAYN Payne, John. *Negro Spirituals: For Low Voice with Piano Accompaniment*. G. Schirmer, 1942.

PETL Peters, Erskine. *Lyrics of the Afro-American Spiritual*. Greenwood Press, 1993.

PIKJ Pike, Gustavus. *The Jubilee Singers, and Their Campaign for Twenty Thousand Dollars.* Lee and Shepard, 1873.

PITG Pitts, Lilla Belle. *The Girls' Book.* Ginn, 1959.

PRI4 Price, Florence. *44 Art Songs and Spirituals.* Edited by Richard Earl Heard. ClarNan Editions, 2015.

PRIF Price, Florence. *Four Songs.* Southern Music, 2000.

RAGS Ragland, Dave. *Spirituals & Art Songs.* Vol. 1. Dave Ragland, 2017.

RAIJ Raim, Walter. *The Josh White Song Book.* Quadrangle Books, 1963.

RUPM Rupp, Franz, ed. *Marian Anderson Album of Songs and Spirituals.* Schirmer, 1948.

RUTF Rutter, John. *Feel the Spirit: A Cycle of Spirituals for Mezzo-Soprano Solo, Mixed Choir, and Orchestra or Chamber Ensemble.* Oxford University Press, 2016.

SAAT Saar, R. W. and Bernard Russell. *Twelve Negro Spirituals: For Solo Voice and Optional Harmonized or Unison Chorus.* W. Paxton, 1927.

SAAT2 Saar, R. A., and Alvin D Keech. *Twelve Negro Spirituals: For Solo Voice and Optional Harmonized or Unison Chorus, Book 2.* W. Paxton, 1934.

SANH Sandilands, Alexander. *A Hundred and Twenty Negro Spirituals*, 2nd ed. Morija Basutoland, 1964.

SCHG Schubert, Tomas. *Great day!: 5 Negro Spirituals.* Laurentius-Musikverlag, 2011.

SEV *The Seventh-Day Adventist Hymnal.* Review and Herald Pub. Association, 1985.

SEWJ Seward, Theodore Frelinghuysen, and American Missionary Association. *Jubilee Songs as Sung by the Jubilee Singers, of Fisk University, (Nashville, Tenn.) Under the Auspices of the American Missionary Association.* New York; Chicago: Biglow & Main, 1872.

SEWJC Seward, Theodore Frelinghuysen. *Jubilee Songs: Complete.* Chicago: Biglow & Main, 1872.

SHEH Sheridan, Dick. *Hallelujah Ukulele: 19 of the Best and Most Beloved Hymns & Spirituals: A Diverse Sampling of Religious Traditions Arranged for Ukuleles in Standard C Tuning, Adaptable to Other Chord and Fretted Instruments.* Centerstream, 2013.

SILS Silverman, Jerry. *Songs of Protest and Civil Rights.* Chelsea House, 1992.

SILSP Silverman, Jerry. *Spirituals.* Chelsea House, 1995.

SIMA Simpson-Curenton, Evelyn. *African American Music for the Classical Singer: Spirituals and Hymns.* E. C. Curenton Publishers, 2018.

SIX *Sixty-Two Southland Spirituals.* Rodeheaver Hall-Mack, 1946.

SKEG Skellern, Peter. *The Gospel Train: 20 Gospels & Spirituals.* Chester Music, 2001.

SLA *Slave Songs, Jubilee Hymns, and Spirituals, as They Appeared in Early Published Sources, 1867–1918.* Taurus Moon Editions, 1998.

SNES Sneed, Damien. *Spiritual Sketches.* Lechateau Arts Publishing, 2013.

SNYS Snyder, Jack. *Jack Snyder's Collection of Favorite American Negro Spirituals.* Jack Snyder Pub., 1926.

SPAG *Spirituals and Gospels.* Hal Leonard, 1975.

STIA Still, William Grant. *An Art Song Collection.* Compiled and with an introduction by Celeste Anne Headlee. William Grant Still Music: Published by arrangement with The Master-Player Library, 2000.

STIT Still, William Grant. *Twelve Negro Spirituals.* W. G. Still Music, 2008.

TAYA Taylor, Vivian. *Art Songs and Spirituals by African-American Women Composers.* Hildegard Pub., 1995.

TOBB Tobit, Janet E. *A Book of Negro Songs.* J. E. Tobitt, 1950.

TRAH Traum, Happy, and Homespun Tapes. *The Homespun Songbook: 100 Timeless Songs to Learn and Play.* Hal Leonard, 2023.

UNI The *United Methodist Hymnal: Book of United Methodist Worship.* United Methodist Pub. House, 1989.

WAL14H Walters, Richard, ed. *14 Sacred Solos (high voice).* Hal Leonard, 2018.

WAL14L Walters, Richard, ed. *14 Sacred Solos (low voice).* Hal Leonard, 2004.

WAL15H Walters, Richard, ed. *15 Easy Spiritual Arrangements for the Progressing Singer (high voice).* Hal Leonard, 2005.

WAL15L Walters, Richard, ed. *15 Easy Spiritual Arrangements for the Progressing Singer (low voice).* Hal Leonard, 2005.

WAL25H Walters, Richard, ed. *The Student Singer: 25 Songs in English for Classical Voice (high voice).* Hal Leonard, 2005.

WAL25L Walters, Richard, ed. *The Student Singer: 25 Songs in English for Classical Voice (low voice).* Hal Leonard, 2005.

WALA Walters, Richard, and Bryan Stanley. *American Folksongs: 35 Arrangements for Voice and Piano.* Hal Leonard, 2002.

WALB Walters, Richard. *The Boy's Changing Voice: 20 Vocal Solos.* Hal Leonard, 2013.

WALCH Walters, Richard, ed. *The Christmas Collection: 53 Songs for Classical Singers (high voice).* Hal Leonard, 2002.

WALCL Walters, Richard, ed. *The Christmas Collection: 53 Songs for Classical Singers (low voice).* Hal Leonard, 2002.

WALSH Walters, Richard. *The Sacred Collection (high voice).* Hal Leonard, 2001.

WALSL Walters, Richard. *The Sacred Collection (low voice).* Hal Leonard, 2001.

WAR1 Ward, Laura. *12 Sacred Songs.* G. Schirmer, 1993.

WARE Warren, Gwendolin Sims. *Ev'ry Time I Feel the Spirit: 101 Best-Loved Psalms, Gospel Hymns, and Spiritual Songs of the African-American Church.* H. Holt, 1997.

WHAG Whalum, Wendell, Betty Jackson King, and Roland Carter. *God Is a God!* Mar-Vel. Jacksonian Press, 1983.

WHIF White, Clarence Cameron. *Forty Negro Spirituals.* Theodore Presser, 1927.

WHII White, Clayton. *I Hear Music in the Air: Spirituals for Solo Voice and Piano.* Augsburg Fortress, 2021.

WIES Wier, A. E. *The Scribner Radio Music Library, volume seven.* C. Scribner's Sons 1931.

WORF Work, Frederick J. *New Jubilee Songs as Sung by the Fisk Jubilee Singers.* Fisk University, 1902.

WORJA Work, John W. *American Negro Songs and Spirituals.* Bonanza Books, 1940.

WORJF Work, John W. *Folk Songs of the American Negro.* Negro Universities Press, 1969.

WORJT Work, John W. *Ten Spirituals.* Ethel Smith Music, 1952.

About the Author

Kathleen A. Abromeit (she/her) is the head of the Oberlin Conservatory Library. Kathy has an MLIS from the University of Wisconsin Milwaukee and an MMus from the University of Colorado. She completed a mindful leadership course at the Weatherhead School of Management at Case Western Reserve University. Her areas of scholarly interest include music information literacy, faculty/librarian collaboration, African American spirituals, library inclusion and advocacy, and outreach. Her publications include the monographs *An Index to African American Spirituals for the Solo Voice* (Greenwood Press, 1999), *Spirituals: A Multidisciplinary Bibliography for Research and Performance* (Music Library Association and A-R Editions, 2015), *Ideas, Strategies, and Scenarios in Music Information Literacy* (Music Library Association and A-R Editions, 2018), and *Music Information Literacy: Inclusion and Advocacy* (Library Juice Press, 2024). She is active in the Music Library Association. She oversees the "Quarterly Scores List," a regular column in *Notes: The Quarterly Journal of the Music Library Association* to assist librarians build scores collections of underrepresented composers.